ISCHIA

ISLAND IN THE SUN

A bend in the road revealed a charming white house

p. 18

ISLAND IN THE SUN

BY
GEOFFREY & KIT BRET HARTE

Illustrated by Robert Merman

BOSTON
LITTLE, BROWN AND COMPANY
1937

CONTENTS

ILLUSTRATIONS

ILLUSTRATIONS

PREFACE

THIS IS THE STORY of a supremely happy year.

Two events of the greatest importance to us contributed to make it so. We were married, and we discovered our 'Island in the Sun.' The latter was the natural outcome of the former, for it was through our egotistical desire for solitude in which to enjoy our happiness that we came to live in Ischia.

How one of the most beautiful and least known islands in the Mediterranean should for so long have escaped the devastating contact with so-called modern civilisation, retaining unspoilt throughout the centuries all its natural charm and loveliness, is a mystery, for it lies in the very heart of a tourist-ridden world, the Bay of Naples, and within sight of that Mecca of pleasure-seekers, Capri.

With a history that dates back to Grecian and Phœnician days, the island, which in Roman times became the private property of Augustus, and later the domain of the most brilliant woman of the Renaissance, Vittoria Colonna, lies almost forgotten. Few, even of those who know its name, have visited its shores or experienced the kindness, the simple-hearted generosity, of its inhabitants. We owe to Ischia more than a revelation of beauty and charm ; we owe the island a debt of gratitude for the happiness it has given us.

This is not a novel, neither is it in any sense a guide-book. It guides nobody anywhere. The owner of the village emporium which stocked most of the ninety-odd varieties of macaroni, hearing that we intended to write about his beloved island, begged us not to forget to mention that the port was round, the hills green, and the air salubrious. Well, there it is; but, apart from this meagre fulfilment of his request, we have failed him miserably.

Taking the reader with us across the sparkling, deep blue sea to Ischia, we leave him to his leisure. He can roam through the vineyards, where the peasants at work will soon discover that he is a *forestiere* and, with their mixture of curiosity and friendliness, will take him off to sample the new wine in one of those great cellars hewn out of the rock where it is kept cool. The wine is strong, and he will take leave of his hosts a trifle hilarious, perhaps, carrying somewhat unsteadily the basket of peaches, grapes, and other fruit that they have given him as a final offering.

He can laze on the great golden beaches, in the shade of the tall pine-trees that come down to meet the water, or lend a hand when the fishermen haul in their nets for the evening catch. He can stroll through the narrow, busy streets of the old town, bordered with little pink and white and blue houses, or drive like mad over the rough cobblestones in one of those swaying, rollicking *carrozze* drawn by a *cavallo da corsa*, as these beasts are proudly called by their owners.

If he feels lonely, he can come with us and sip his vermouth in the company of friends, in the shade of a deep, cool loggia, watching the changing scene at his feet: the goats being driven from house to house for their afternoon milking; the barefooted, bronze-faced youths running swiftly beside their mules saddled with barrels of wine; the peasant girls carrying on their heads baskets of oranges, or, with equal grace, a load of bricks for the building of somebody's new *casetta*. Or he can ignore these busy scenes and, directing his gaze to where the old castle, red in the setting sun, rises from the sea on its jagged, lonely rock, and beyond

PREFACE

toward the smoking Vesuvius and the wide sweep of the Gulf of Naples, feast his eyes upon such beauty as he has never seen before.

The memory of our Ischian life, once a vivid reality, is fast assuming the nebulous quality of a dream. Did we really lead such a care-free, happy-go-lucky existence, indulge in such amazing whims, keep goats, giant rabbits, dogs, and ourselves under the same roof? Did we really consume those gargantuan meals with our friend Cesare Giusto at Barano, to the accompaniment of innumerable and remarkable vintages, and shamelessly sleep them off in his orchard? Did we spend our days in the sun and our nights amid festas and fireworks? Did we explore strange smoking caverns, bathe in volcanic waters, and sleep through an earthquake?

Under our practical and, alas, too often grey skies it does not seem possible, but now and then our thoughts take flight, and, bridging time and space, carry us back to our beloved island, where we live our memories again.

This book is the reflection of the life we lived together, and it is written in the same close collaboration. 'From Kit's Diary' have come the chapters so necessary to complete it. To say that we enjoyed writing this book is to put it mildly; we enjoyed ourselves immensely. If, after reading it, you find you are tempted to follow in our footsteps, above all if you go to Ischia and find there some of the happiness which was ours, we shall be repaid for having written it and you for having read it.

CASTELLO
d'ISCHIA
R.M.

CHAPTER I

I

WE ASKED THE CONCIERGE of our Capri hotel about Ischia.
What sort of place was it? How did one get there?

Suddenly our feeble Italian seemed incomprehensible to
him. Up till then he had indulged our whim for massacring
his native tongue by a ready understanding and a suave
smile. Now his face was a blank.

'That beautiful island just across the bay,' we said. 'The
one you see from the piazza, rising to a high mountain
peak.'

The blank face drooped. 'Oh, you mean Ischia,' he
repeated, correcting our pronunciation. 'You don't want
to go *there*. Nobody goes to Ischia. No hotels, no foreigners,
no amusements.' He spoke with earnest conviction. 'Now,
here in Capri, for instance . . .'

Kit and I did not listen. We exchanged knowing glances.
We had met the obstacle everywhere since our marriage in
Naples two weeks before. Even the Italian judge who

13

performed the civil ceremony had seemed quite alarmed at our suggestion of going there for our honeymoon. Capri, he said quite emphatically, was *the only place* for honeymoons, especially where foreigners were concerned. It had a wide reputation abroad as well as in Italy for meeting all the requirements of the newly wed. With the national colours still encircling his generous waist in a wide silk band, he entreated us quite paternally to abandon any such dangerous ideas. If we began our new life by doing the wrong thing, heaven only knew where we might end. These last reflections, although clearly understood, were not expressed in words.

So to Capri we had come, and we had done everything that was expected of us. We had stayed at the biggest hotel, in the best matrimonial suite; we had seen the sights, visited the Blue Grotto and all the other grottoes, and now we felt entitled to do as we pleased. No doubt the island was beautiful in spite of everything which man, in conjunction with tourist agencies, had done to turn it into a self-conscious resort, but it held no charm for us.

The longer we stayed, the more enticing appeared that wonderful island across the water so notoriously lacking in the amenities of civilisation. Rising from the blue sea, veiled in a light summer haze, it seemed to call us.

'No hotels, no foreigners, no amusements,' the concierge had said. 'No paintings of the Blue Grotto in all colours and sizes,' we added to ourselves. 'No coral vendors, no persecution of the newly wed by boatmen, cab-drivers, shopkeepers, guides, and hotel porters. Nothing but solitude.'

'Now, for instance,' the concierge continued, in ignorance of our mental processes, 'why not go to Sorrento, and from there take the beautiful Amalfi drive – four hundred lire return – or go all the way up Vesuvius by car – six hun . . .'

'No,' we interrupted in unison. 'No. We are going to

14

Ischia, and, if there is no ordinary service between the islands, we will take a motor-boat.'

That was a fortunate touch. The concierge's face lit up.

'We have two excellent motor-boats,' he said. 'One large one, suitable for the trip, at . . .'

'Yes,' we said, sensing the inevitable, 'that one. The biggest, the fastest, the most expensive you have, at once.'

II

At last we were off. Hands had been shaken, others more numerous had been tipped. In the centre of an admiring group of idlers the boat was waiting. Snow-white, her motor softly purring, she strained at her moorings, as eager to be off as an impatient greyhound. Standing aboard her was the crew, consisting of two *marinai* busily engaged in posing for the gaping crowd, with boat-hooks erect and important expressions, as though we were setting off on some daring adventure.

A great splashing, a lot of noise both human and mechanical, blue water churned into white foam, and Capri was behind us. The two men had disappeared into the cabin, leaving us to ourselves. It was indeed the first time since our marriage that we had really felt alone. Our boat was paid for in advance, the contract being to take us to the island and leave us there, and the sailors were determined to get it over as soon as possible.

We were supremely happy, thrilled by our new adventure, completely undisturbed at the thought of where we should sleep that night.

Kit said, 'Let us make plans. When we reach Ischia we must find lodgings somewhere, and then, after a few days, perhaps a little house by the sea. We shall bathe and be lazy on the beaches, take lovely drives and walks, and soon have all the fun of keeping house. And all the time we shall have each other for company.'

The sailors had asked us what part of the island we wanted to go to; there were several towns on the coast – Porto d'Ischia, Casamicciola, Lacco Ameno, Forio. We chose the first because it was presumably the nearest and because it sounded nice. We could always move the next day if we found another place we liked better. Were we not free? Did we not share the same likes and dislikes? Was there anybody in the world more happy than we were? Well, then!

Two hours had passed since we had left Capri, and our boat had almost devoured the distance that separated us from our destination. Ischia lay spread out before us, villages and houses now plainly visible. A great isolated rock, rising sheer and precipitous from the blue sea, loomed up like an advance guard at our approach. Crowning its unscalable summit were ruins of an ancient castle, of churches, of apparently an entire village. Both ruins and rock were mellow gold, fused into one in the late afternoon sunlight, their reflections mirrored in the smooth water below. As we rounded the rock, our boat a speck of white in its shadow, we saw that it was joined to the island by a long narrow causeway.

'Il Castello d'Ischia,' one of the boatmen emerged from the cabin to tell us.

Fishing-boats at anchor danced in our wake; in them men were standing, hauling in their long brown nets. Green undulating hills covered with vineyards rose softly, one behind the other, higher and higher towards the one lofty, solitary peak. By the water's edge, a long white village stretched itself along a sandy beach. Further on, pine-trees, those

Around the Port all was asleep

graceful umbrella pines of which Italy is justly proud, swept down to meet the sea, and in their shade nestled other houses.

Our boat gave no sign of approaching the shore, nor of slackening its speed. In another moment we would round a bend and leave all this charm behind. We were just about to order our men to turn back and deposit us with our luggage on the beach, when our boat made a wide semicircle and, slowing down, approached a narrow opening in the rocks.

Gently we slipped through into the little port of Ischia. Completely encircled by hills and bordered by multi-coloured houses, it was a round inland lake of unbelievable beauty. Mirrored in this great unruffled pool were sailing-ships at anchor, their decks and the little wharf teeming with activity. Barrels of wine and olive-oil were being loaded, and sacks of flour were being unloaded. Little donkeys saddled with casks, and led by barefooted bronzed youths, clattered over the cobblestones, while women with baskets of vividly coloured fruit neatly balanced on their heads stepped aside to let them pass.

At the sight of our launch a group of onlookers, men, women, and children, had concentrated on the wharf, arrested in their various occupations by this event of major interest. All of them were speculating as to who we were, where we came from, and where we would land, thereby affording the best 'close-up.' The latter thought did not perhaps trouble them, for they must have known that, in true Italian fashion, the boatmen would make straight for the centre of attraction.

Amid shouting of orders the launch turned and backed. There was a discreet bump, and a moment later we had stepped ashore.

However great its amazement, no Italian crowd can long remain speechless. A bunch of little boys assumed possession of our luggage, each one carrying a separate piece, and stood by waiting, not apparently for instructions, but for us to follow them. Meanwhile the motor-boat, its duty done, had fled with disdain from such a scene.

From the first, there did not seem to be the slightest doubt among our youthful porters about our destination. They knew, if we didn't, just where we were going to stay, and as they set out ahead of us there was much turning round to make sure that we were following.

A bend in the road revealed a charming white house, with wide arches below and a loggia above, smothered by a giant wistaria in bloom. Above the door, painted in large letters, were the words 'Albergo del Porto.' A moment later we had crossed a large, cool hall, one end of which was occupied by a wide counter littered with bottles and coffee-cups. The room was deserted except for the presence of a lady behind the counter, who was placidly combing out her shining black hair and singing lustily.

At the sight of us she stopped, speechless with amazement. Then, with a most hospitable smile and a resonant '*Buona sera*,' she bade us wait while she deftly clutched her abundant tresses and, with the aid of hairpins strewn over the counter, wound them into a neat and becoming head-dress.

Meanwhile she summoned the family. 'Mama, Maria, Rosina! Come quickly. Foreigners have arrived.'

They came; first Mama, wiping her hands on her apron – a wizened old lady who must once have been as pretty as the bevy of daughters who followed her. With outstretched hands they all advanced to welcome Kit. With me they were more shy, but they hid their embarrassment under peals of laughter. If we had fondly imagined that we looked like

18

an old married couple, as we had tried so hard to do, the illusion was shattered; they knew all about it at a glance.

'*Bella! Bella!*' they exclaimed, looking at Kit. '*Nuovi sposi?*' they asked, looking at me. 'Come to stay at Ischia? *Ischia é molto bella; anche la signora é molto bella!* Newly wed, indeed? Bravo, bravo!' This volley of self-answered questions was shot at us by all the family at once.

'A room with matrimonial bed, of course?' Angelina asked as she led us away from the others. She considered that, having been the first to discover us, we were her protégées. We followed her up the stairs to the loggia covered with wistaria, and from there into a closed verandah. Off this were four gigantic rooms with vaulted ceilings, each room big enough for a family of five, each furnished with the traditional *letto matrimoniale* and two single beds as well.

'Take your choice,' said Angelina, adjusting a strand of shining black hair that had gone astray. '*Tutto a loro.* You are the only guests.' She pointed to the spacious verandah and laughed. 'This will be your private *salotto.*'

Pensione, she told us, consisted of breakfast with coffee, bread, and cheese; *colazione* at midday, three courses; *pranzo* in the evening, three courses; red or white wine, one litre per person per meal. Price, twenty lire a day each. Would that be all right? We asked her how much extra it would be if we had milk with our morning coffee and butter with our bread, and black coffee after our other meals. She reflected in silence, counting on her fingers, then laughed. It would be twenty lire just the same.

Angelina turned to leave us. When we were hungry, she said, we could come downstairs and Mama would show us what there was to eat. We could hear her singing on her way down, her wooden sandals tapping out an accompaniment on the stone floor.

We stood quite still and looked at each other. I think we were afraid to move or talk for fear we might suddenly wake up and find it was only a dream. These two hours across the bay had certainly brought us to a different world, and what a picturesque one!

Since it was evident to Ischian eyes that we were newly wed, there was no longer any need to try to disguise the fact. Arm in arm we went out on to the loggia and looked down on to the little street below. Dusk was falling; the lights were lit. The day's activities were over; people strolled leisurely past, stopping to talk on the middle of the road, making way for an occasional *carrozza* as it went clattering noisily by over the cobblestones to the cracking of whips, or sat in the little cafés that sprawled out lazily on to the sidewalk.

The concierge in Capri had been right. Here were no foreigners and no palace hotels. Beyond, the port lay now in stillness and in darkness, felt rather than seen, and the air was heavily laden with wistaria, for we were standing among the branches.

Even this fragrance could not exclude the more material odours that were wafted up from the kitchen, and which reminded us that dinner was probably waiting. Whetted by the mixture of sea air, excitement, and happiness, our appetites needed no cajoling.

The dining-room was empty, but, judging from the commotion, there seemed to be an important social gathering in the kitchen. We pushed open the door, to be greeted with a chorus of welcome, mingled with protests that the kitchen was no place for *signori*. The old mother and her three daughters were there, and a great many other people as well. These turned out to be more daughters, some sons, and a sprinkling of 'in-laws' and cousins.

Introduced by Angelina, we shook hands all round. The room was vast, with a low ceiling and smoke-stained walls. A faint odour of wood smoke mingled pleasantly with others from innumerable pots that covered a gigantic range. This range interested us very much. It looked like a long bench, and was tiled in blue and white, and ran the entire length of the room. In it were sunk eight little grates, each about a foot square, and in each of them a fire was burning. It was our first introduction to the Ischian way of cooking. Charcoal was used instead of coal, and as there was no smoke there was no chimney. Beneath each grate was a square opening for the draught. This type of fire, we later discovered, is common to all parts of southern Italy, which have not suffered from the invasion of modern ideas.

Fascinated, we watched old Mama standing before her pots and pans, armed with a large straw-plaited fan, furiously fanning the fire through the air-hole to speed up the cooking. Occasionally she would hand her fan to one of her daughters or cousins while she attended to more pressing needs. Kit and I got hold of some extra fans and set to work on the other fires, but with very little success. It was easy enough to scatter ashes all over the place, but quite another to make the charcoal glow.

From some of the pots came powerful odours, especially when Kit lifted some of the covers to sniff with relish the subtle concoctions they contained. Whenever she did this, Mama hurriedly explained that it was only *baccalà*; a dish for the family, not for the *signori*. Judging from the number of pots filled with it, there was going to be a generous helping for everybody. The *baccalà* was dried cod from Norway, which had to be chopped up with a hatchet and soaked in water for two days before it was supple enough to be cooked. And Ischia was an island where fishing was an industry!

As to the reason for the number of fires, we had only to look back into the room. Across the middle of it was an enormous table bare of cloth but covered with soup-plates and glasses. When we had been served, Angelina explained, the family would sit down to dine, joined by whatever relatives might happen to drift in. Hospitality was evidently on a grand scale.

'*Pronto a tavola*,' announced Mama, and Angelina led us to a corner of the dining-room where a spacious table was laid for two. On it were red and white wines thoughtfully decanted into old champagne bottles, their necks enveloped in tattered gold foil – more decorative, no doubt, than the ordinary bottles. Kit's eye appraised the linen, which was hand made and of the sort we must certainly have, she said, for the new house.

Some people acquire the art of cooking; others are born to it. Old Mama was born to it without a doubt. What subtle mixture of herbs, spices, and wines; of tomatoes, red peppers, and garlic! Certain sophisticated people will probably recoil in horror as they read this. Let them do so by all means. As for us, we fell upon the meal with undisguised zest.

While we ate, Angelina kept up an uninterrupted flow of conversation; a conversation that was all on her side. We did nothing but lend our ears. The white wine was delicious, and tasted, strangely enough, like the best Capri vintage. Angelina informed us that her father, Alessandro Bonifacio, was the chief wine merchant of the Port. Wine was the principal product of the island, and Naples the principal market for it. As, however, Ischia was so little known, it was not a good trade name, so that when the wine reached Naples it was bottled and labelled 'Capri' or 'Vesuvio,' and commanded, in this way, a much higher price. Angelina said that Ischia did a roaring trade in Capri wines, for the latter's vineyards were meagre and what they produced was *molto acido*. The resemblance was fully explained!

While she talked, the door on to the street frequently opened to admit youths, who, after a rapid glance in our direction, disappeared into another room. That room, we suspected, had a more direct entrance, and the little detour was merely a means of satisfying general curiosity in the new arrivals. Once out of sight, their timidity vanished, and we could hear their animated conversations, interrupted occasionally by loud guffaws, no doubt at our expense. Angelina explained that the adjoining room was the billiard and bathroom combined, and was much frequented in the evenings in its former capacity by the youths of the village.

As we puzzled over this curious combination of uses, an ear-splitting, thunderous noise broke loose. It was produced in part by what must originally have been a piano, and partly by a person of exceptional physique. The result defied description. The instrument had travelled far beyond the help of tuners, but if many of its notes were mercifully for ever silenced, the loud pedal had become permanently jammed in the downward direction, giving the notes which remained a particularly piercing resonance. In addition to physical force, the player, if he or she could be called by such a musical name, displayed a grim determination to drown all opposition on the part of the audience. Discordant and cataclysmic, a veritable crescendo of pandemonium, there was a barbaric splendour about it like the fury of the elements let loose.

Taking our dismay for flattering astonishment, Angelina bent down, and in a shrill whisper which tried to overcome the crashing roar announced that it was *un po' di musica* especially for us ! Her sister, she said, was *molto brava* with the piano, but a little *timida*. A compliment from us would give her great encouragement.

We were spared from perjury by a dramatic incident. When Angelina had shown us our table, we had noticed with surprise the presence of another one facing our own. It was laid for one person, and it intrigued us, for we had been told that we were the only guests in the *albergo*. As this room was, however, also a *ristorante*, we thought that it might have been set for the sake of appearance, either to impress us with the possible arrival of a fellow guest or to tempt an outsider. Neither was right.

A cry of *'Ecco Papa!'* rang out from somewhere, the music was abruptly broken off, and dead silence reigned. Angelina scurried from the room, and at the same moment the front door opened to admit an imposing figure. Square-shouldered, powerfully built, with a weather-beaten face and the air of a Roman emperor, Alessandro Bonifacio strode into the room. He wore a brown corduroy suit, carried a gun, and was evidently returning home from a day's hunting.

This unquestionably was the master. The fact was written all over him, yet without a trace of arrogance. His manner was simple, but his carriage and his expression denoted a forcible personality; more than that, a life-long habit of commanding and of being obeyed. He bowed affably to us, and, having stood his gun in the corner, seated himself at the immaculately laid table.

He clapped his hands, and immediately from the kitchen came pouring in the family's entire female contingent – Angelina, Rosina, Maria, Serafina, and, trailing in the background, old Mama. Each of them carried a dish, which was presented to him in turn. At some of these dishes he hardly glanced before waving them away; at others he sniffed with more appreciation, and finally from two or three he helped himself copiously. Meanwhile those whose dishes had not met with approval returned from the kitchen with more. No wonder that, with such a master, eight fires going at once were necessary.

During this time no greetings were wasted on the members of the family; in fact, no notice was taken of them at all; and, after the dishes he had selected were arranged in a circle around him, they withdrew in silence.

Before starting his dinner, Signor Bonifacio addressed us. '*Volete favorire?*' he asked courteously, and, as politely as we could, we declined. This gesture we knew to be an old Italian custom still widely in use wherever modern education has not instilled disdain for the ancient forms of politeness. By these words, 'Will you favour?' the last arrival asks you to share his meal, a courtesy which, needless to say, is always politely refused.

Spellbound, we watched an enormous plate of spaghetti dripping with tomato sauce dwindle before our eyes. This was a spectacular feat, for, once the contact had been established between the dish and the consumer with the aid of a spoon and a fork, the spaghetti seemed to rise by itself in a long spiral column like a waterspout, to disappear into the grey cloud of his beard.

As the meal progressed the master mellowed. It was a beautiful demonstration of Montaigne's famous epigram: 'The shortest way to a man's heart is through his stomach.' Although the Bonifacio family had probably never heard of Montaigne, they must have frequently observed the phenomenon in Papa, because from where we sat we could see various members of the clan collecting behind the door, waiting for the moment when their presence would be agreeable.

In this they were forestalled by the appearance of an extremely dirty little girl, about four years old, with a piercing nasal voice, who fought and squeezed her way through the solid female rampart that blocked the kitchen exit and ran brazenly up to the sacred table, now piled high with the remnants of the feast. She was barefooted, and clad in an old cotton frock whose original colour had long been replaced by a roseate hue of innumerable food stains, mostly tomato sauce.

We held our breath, waiting for an explosion of wrath which did not come. On the contrary, the stern muscles of the tyrant's face relaxed into a broad smile. Taking her into his arms and seating her upon his knee, he proudly announced to us that she was his granddaughter. Her face was remarkable. As dirty as the rest of her, it sparkled with intelligence unhampered by restraint. It was set off by a close crop of jet-black curls and eyes to match, and flashing teeth worthy of a savage.

The pleasure of their meeting was mutual. In dialect, and in a voice already hoarse from the long effort of making herself audible above her elders, she poured forth a torrent of feminine loquacity. Jumping up and down like a jack-in-the-box, tugging at the august beard with the right amount of cunning, she finally climbed on to the table and proceeded to devour pell-mell what remained on the dishes, beginning with what happened to be nearest.

Cheese, fish, an orange, bits of cold spaghetti, and a quantity of bread were thus consumed, much to the old man's amusement, although, as he informed us, she had already had her supper in the kitchen. Only when she had firmly seized between her two hands the special bottle of wine was a restraining hand applied. She was only allowed by her grandfather half a large glass of the rich golden contents, and, from the way she smacked her lips afterwards, we could see that she fully appreciated the difference in quality from that which was served in the kitchen.

Seeing that everything was progressing satisfactorily, the family made its entrance. Old Mama was allowed to sit at the table; she looked haggard and tired. The daughters stood around in a circle and immediately a babel of voices broke loose. Had it not been for the smiling faces and the uproarious laughter one might have mistaken it for an outburst of family wrath.

Under the cover of this terrific din, Kit and I slipped from our places unobserved and went out into the warm, still night. Around the Port all was asleep, the ships swaying gently at their moorings. We walked to the end of the jetty and looked out over the Mediterranean.

For a long time we stood silent too, hand in hand. We were filled with a great happiness.

CHAPTER II

FROM KIT'S DIARY

I

EVERYTHING IS BEAUTIFUL, everything is fun. We are together and the world is ours. The days are bright and fine, with a magic that our love has put on them; it touches the small things as well as the great: my heart bursts to see G. opening his morning egg with so much painstaking, unnecessary effort, and it is filled with a bustling, nearly maternal love at the sight of a suitcase full of his ancient socks, record of the long life of a bachelor.

We have been here a week now. Part of the time we have spent on the beach; the sand is silver-clean and fine and the sun has warmed it deep below the surface. The water is clear green near the shore, and it is warm too.

At one end of the beach, pink and yellow fishermen's houses sit with their feet in the sand, and big bright-coloured dories are drawn up almost to their thresholds.

The long brown nets are spread out in the sun to dry, and there is a multitude of half-naked children scampering and shouting, and a man cross-legged on the sand, weaving lobster-pots from reeds.

Sometimes we walk through narrow cobbled lanes, shaded by walls higher than our heads, up into those green, softly curving hills that rise behind the Port. There we found, one day, a tiny white village, so small that its street was covered by a single great pergola, a mass of deep green grape leaves flung from one house to another across the way. And so the whole village was protected from the blazing sun, and our road, that had been so hot, plunged gratefully into the dark shade.

There was a little wine-shop, a *trattoria*, with benches under a cool archway. Geraniums and a heavy fuchsia grew in old wash-basins, tomato-tins, and even a night-pot, long past their original use but beautiful in their new incarnations. And there was a proprietor of extraordinary volubility and friendliness. We sat on a bench and leaned against the whitewashed wall of his house, and he brought us glasses of new wine from his vineyards, and we shouted all three together with great goodwill but without much understanding on either side.

When we went away, he shook hands and bowed many times, and swore he was our servant and friend. As we crossed the street under the great pergola, he ran after us panting, and pressed into my hands a little leaf-lined basket of fruit.

That was the day we got lost—beautifully and not at all dangerously lost. Instead of sliding down the cobbles of the steep lane that led to the Port, we found we were wandering through a maze of vineyard paths. The vines grew tall above us, rising in their fertility to ten or twelve feet, and we saw the sky only in rare, vivid blue patches. The sun filtered through the leaves as cool and green as water; everything was still, and it was as though we were walking on the bed of a deep and limpid lake.

Following always the down-slanting land that must lead us to the shore, we came out by a tiny pink church, with a big green door and a little belfry tower. The bell was ringing gently, and its slight song hung on the air, and tangled itself in the glossy leaves of the lemon-trees that stood round about. The lemon-trees must be good Christians, growing up in such close friendliness with their little pink church, bearing their fruit in its shadow, adding the perfume of their white, sweet blossoms to the incense over the altar.

II

Black-haired Angelina and I are great friends. She thrills to our being newly married, and plies me with intimate questions. She won my heart by declaring that G. is *bellissimo* (followed by a giggle to show that there is no danger from her quarter).

Her elder sister, married, surrounded by a flock of grubby 'little pigeons,' as children are fondly called, says that 'when one marries, one takes up one's Cross.' But she says it with a guffaw, so that her burden becomes vaguely spicy, and one wonders if it is not the husband, rather than the pigeons, who must be borne with.

However, though Maria is disillusioned, Angelina and I are not, and, if I have had to bear anything, it could only be the almost overfull sweetness of these days together and the beauty around us.

Yesterday Angelina clattered into our room in her wooden mules, a large white bundle under her arm. She laid it on

31

the bed and undid it. Inside were layers and layers of close-woven heavy linen. She picked up the top one and shook it out: a long shapeless nightgown. It was her trousseau, she confided. She began making it eight years ago; now it is almost complete; three dozen of each sort of garment.

I didn't know what most of them were; they had sleeves of an unfortunate length and a neat round neck. All were variations on the same theme, truncated at different lengths. It was an irony that each of the stiff, shapeless garments was decorated with a wealth of the most exquisite embroidery, half a life-time of work.

I asked her why she had made her clothes so big and wide; they will make her look like a sack of meal. She was very surprised. 'But some day I shall be an old woman, *signora!*' – and she made an expressive gesture, both hands held out supporting an imaginary paunch, then laughed uproariously.

She said she was engaged – *fidanzata*; it's been going on for four years. She grew troubled at this, and for once stopped laughing. He wants to marry her, but his mother for some reason won't agree, and, as she holds the purse-strings, poor Angelina seesaws between hope and despair.

However, she continues to work on her trousseau; it must be ready in case things take a turn for the better, for the first act of the marriage ceremony is always a visit from the prospective mother-in-law, who comes to see and appraise every asset of her son's *fiancée*. On that day everything that the girl has prepared for her married life is laid out on view, and the older woman comes with any relatives and friends who want to see the show.

The woman then examines each nightgown and camisole; she judges the fineness of the embroideries, the quality of the household linen and kitchen utensils, and when she has

IL SOCCORSO
FORIO
RM

Its white walls were dazzling in the sun

p. 40

finished she makes a list of every article of the girl's possessions, with the price that she thinks each is worth.

If this shows her that the girl is clever, industrious, and
well enough endowed to be a good match, she will give her
consent to the marriage. The bride, sensible creature, keeps
the list, so that in the future no bitter tongue can accuse her
of having come to her marriage empty-handed.

Angelina said shyly, clacking her wooden shoes on the
floor in embarrassment, that she had brought me her
trousseau thinking I might like to order a few dozen of the
garments for myself. Hastily I said that I had just bought
a trousseau; then, seeing her crestfallen, and casting about
wildly for something to say or do to show my appreciation,
I picked up the wrapping of her bundle, a lovely creamy
white towel of soft, knotted linen. She said it had been her
grandmother's and had been in use ever since she was a
bride. This linen is made in one of the island villages, the
little hamlet of San Dominico. There is an old *religiosa*
there who weaves it. She, the religious one, is to come to see
me about making some towels as soon as someone has a
journey to make to her village, and can take word to her.

III

Yesterday we set off house-hunting in the wake of Salvatore. He is a Neapolitan son-in-law of the Bonifacios and is
out of a job. Once he held office in a bank under the
splendid title of *Capo-Ragioniere*, which, literally translated,
means head reasoner. This verbal magnificence implies
really very little, for he was a simple accountant. Unfor-
tunately, the bank did not survive his 'reasoning,' and, in
spite of his handsome credentials, no other concern has so far
dared to take him on.

Salvatore is more than useful; he is amusing. He sings Neapolitan songs, his eyes flash, his teeth gleam, he laughs happily at everything and nothing. He is incredibly lazy, and thoroughly enjoys his enforced leisure. Having appointed himself our guide and interpreter, he had promised to show us a 'most darling little villa.' As we followed him through the street of the Port our hearts were full of high hope.

Outside the village there were thick forests of umbrella pines, growing sometimes down to the road and throwing a blot of dark shade like an oasis on the hot cobbles. Once we passed a little walled-in field full of jumbled black lava, where wisps of white steam were rising gently into the air from cracks in the earth. They seemed too fluffy and innocent to be related to the devastating volcanic forces under the island.

All along the road there were houses pretty close together, little white ones in the shade of the pines, little pink ones half hidden in groves of shining orange-trees. We wondered which was going to be ours, but Salvatore led straight on, and the fine dust spurted like smoke under our feet as we followed him.

Suddenly he turned to the right, and there was an ugly little brand-new matchbox of a house, sitting bolt upright on a bed of bare black rock. It had not even the grace of a coat of whitewash to cover its nakedness, and a pretentious double stairway led up to the unpainted front door.

Inside were bare white rooms furnished with black iron beds – six beds in the first room, five in the next, one even in the kitchen thinly disguised with a length of calico. Over all hovered the bright, expectant eyes of the owner, a tall coachman. He could hardly believe that we wanted the *whole* house for ourselves (he was right; we wanted none of it), since it appeared that he had furnished his villa with a view to housing an entire vacationing Neapolitan family in each room, making most of his year's income in the few summer months.

I would rather draw a veil over the dreary time that followed. Salvatore, puzzled but undaunted, led us from one 'villa' to another; our feet ached, our sense of humour gave way. I have kept a kaleidoscopic picture of pampas grasses, fierce, mildewed family photographs, gilded pine cones, creaky pianos, box-like rooms crowded with black iron beds. These, in Salvatore's eyes, are the fitting accompaniments to the life of a 'rich foreigner.'

We grew brusque with eager owners, forgot our dislike of abrupt departures, and no longer edged our way out of each house, pretending to like it immensely but saying that we must 'think it over' before coming to a decision. Finally we even turned against Salvatore, bewildered and drooping by then, and mumbled uncomplimentary things behind his natty back.

'We've seen enough,' we said. '*Basta* – we're going home.' And back to the *albergo* we trailed, footsore and silent.

We washed, and then we went out to sit at a table on the sidewalk of the little café opposite. We chose between coffee *espresso* and vermouth, their two drinks, and sat sipping the latter slowly. One drink, and we didn't feel quite so badly. We had another, and decided we would look for houses in the villages at the other end of the island – Lacco Ameno, Casamicciola, Forio. On our own this time.

The street was very gay; it was Saturday night, and no work to be done. Fishermen don't go out in their boats on Saturdays; the café tables were full. Those who hadn't the price of a drink walked up and down, arm in arm, from one end of the village to the other, and back again. Carriages going through the street had to do a great lot of whip-cracking to clear the way.

From where we sat we could see in through the lighted windows of the barber's shop next door. There was a long line of young fellows, the bucks of the village probably, waiting outside. When their turn came, they climbed into the barber's chair and with the greatest satisfaction watched their own reflections in the mirror, while the barber skilfully put a fine Saturday night wave into their hair. One by one they came out, pompadoured and proud.

IV

When you want to go for a *carrozza* drive in Ischia, don't wait until it is over to fix the price. We have learned that to our cost. Taximeters have never got nearer to the island than Naples; *prezzo fisso* is so foreign to the nature of all Italians that it doesn't exist. The size of cab fares, like every other price on the island, depends on your shrewdness.

To-day we stepped triumphantly out of the novice class and made our bargain before the drive began. 'How much to take us to Forio?' The answer was astute and inevitable, 'Please yourself, *signore*!' We named a price a good deal lower than we expected to pay. The coachman countered with another a great deal higher than he expected to get, throwing in a few apparently random remarks – 'Hills very steep. Very fine grey horse.'

There was a compromise to the satisfaction of all, and away we rattled, everybody happy, including the grey horse, who seemed to enjoy taking the hills at a gallop.

It was a fine drive; the sun was lovely and the view splendid. We galloped along the shore through the fishing-village of Lacco Ameno, a sweet jumble of pastel-coloured

houses. G. looked at their white, domed roofs. 'Now if we
could find something like that to live in . . .' he said.

'Oh – er – *cucchiaio!*' He engaged the coachman's attention.

I nudged him. '*Cocchiere*, dear,' I whispered sibilantly.
'You're calling him a *tablespoon.*'

'*Cucchiaio!*' he repeated firmly.

'*Sissignore*,' the man answered, turning around on his box
to face us and leaving the galloping horse to its own devices.
His face was impassively polite.

'*Cucchiaio*, do you know where we could find a house to
rent, a nice little house like these of the fishermen?'

'*Sissignore*. There is one at Forio, an old convent . . .'

'Take us to it, Tablespoon!' G. shouted. The lash fell
on the horse's back and away we flew, holding on to each
other to keep from being jolted out of the carriage.

We trotted down a long slope toward Forio. We were
on a low flank of Monte Epomeo, and over there, beyond
the sprawling white of the town, the sea was blue and open,
for we were at the end of the island.

There were not many trees; probably they had been cut
away to make room for the great vineyards that covered
the earth like a rippling green quilt as far as we could
see, even up to the high slopes of the mountain where its
rocky peak began. This is, as my little guide-book eagerly
says, 'a passionately cultivated district'; the name Forio is
derived from *fiorito*, a flowering place.

We clattered into the white town and stopped our driver
in the shade of the Torrione, a brown old watch-tower.
Under the pergola of a little *trattoria* we ate *salame* and salad,
and washed it down with the dark red wine of the country.

Afterwards, with the sun still at its hottest, we walked
through Forio's narrow, twisting streets, thinking of things

past; of the days when the town was still uncrumbled and great, when the fine doorways, with their stone coats of arms, had seen splendid costumes instead of these draggled brown children, and the sheltered harbour, down below the cliffs, had been full of fine vessels and rich merchandise.

In the fifteenth century, just about the time that Columbus was discovering America, Forio had no less than twelve fortified watch-towers in and around the town. They were garrisoned by Forian men, then famous for their bravery, and they fought many a battle against the Corsairs, those fierce Mussulman pirates who, drawn by the prosperity of the town, made repeated attacks, sacking, pillaging, and carrying off men and women as slaves.

Of the twelve towers, the Torrione is the last left standing, and it was hard to imagine, when we stood in its shadowy, round upper chamber, that it had ever known hours of grim battle, that once its unwieldy artillery had spat fire through the slits in its walls, while men sweated for their very lives to ram home the charges in their cannon.

Now flowers climb gaily over the scarred battlements, and inside the tower the chalky, lifeless plaster casts and bas-reliefs of a Forian sculptor, who once used it as his studio, have taken the place of the hard-pressed soldiers.

Already in Roman times the town was famous for its miraculous thermal baths. To the Aqua di Citara the Vestal Virgin Cecilia Metella is said to have come at the beginning of our Christian era, recovering her youth and health after repeated baths in the mineral water. Since that early day the spring is reported to have performed innumerable cures; as one doctor claims : '*Essa non solo ristora le forze indebolite, ma le rende anco alle amorose battaglie molto piu potenti e robuste.*'

So great is the power of these waters to fit bathers for

'battles of love' that the author of the guide-book writes a discouraged little paragraph in hot defence of the now neglected spring. 'The present state of these . . . Baths of Venus,' he says – his writing is punctuated with these expressive dots – 'is most deplorable. This divine fountain which, among other things, could ruin Dr. Voronov and all the other inventors of rejuvenating specialities, is now completely abandoned; and in the ugly little house adjoining a miserable stable, where it rises, we find but four cement tubs, one beside the other. These four . . . coffins make a lugubrious impression.'

Venus was busy at this end of the island. Another spring at Panza is said to cure ' gout, frigid passions, etc.' However, I'm afraid we saw none of the miraculous fountains, and all my knowledge of them comes from my little book. But as we walked through the crumbling, deserted streets of Forio, where not a soul was to be seen during this siesta hour, we could well believe that the fame of the springs, like that of the town, belonged to another century.

On the high cliff above the sea we found the tiny old convent. It was bare and windswept, with blank, white outer walls and a great blue door. Its little courtyard was exquisite; an open stairway curved up to the roof, sheltering two wrought-iron well-heads in its shadow, and four fat, whitewashed columns, standing comfortably in beds of red geraniums, enclosed a miniature cloister. There was a walled fruit-garden too, and a view from the seaward windows of blue water, and a little white church on a higher spur of the cliff, silhouetted against the brilliant sky.

The owner was sleepy from his interrupted siesta.

'How much for the summer?' He knit his brows, muttered under his breath, counted on his stumpy fingers.

He hazarded doubtfully, 'Fifteen pounds?'

'And for the year?' asked G.

More mutterings, with fingers stiffly outspread. Then he shook his head impatiently, like a horse bothered by flies. 'Eh, *signore*,' he said, 'fifteen pounds for the year, too.' A pause, then he added hopefully, 'You know, one of the wells contains a most efficacious natural aperient water.'

The little convent had something that no other house we had seen possessed: all the charm of Ischia. It was bitterly disappointing that it was not a possible place to live in, for its rooms were as bare and windswept as its walls, and one cannot live by charm alone; a little furniture is also needed.

The owner was wide awake and friendly now. He talked garrulously. We were too depressed to say much; with this house our last hope was snuffed out.

'Perhaps the rent is too high?' the owner said tentatively, misinterpreting our silence. 'I might make a better figure . . .'

'Thanks,' said G. 'We'll let you know. *Arrivederci!*'

Very discouraged, we walked through narrow alleys until we came to the high, flat piazza in front of the little church we had seen from the convent windows. Its white walls were dazzling in the sun; the whisper of the waves far below mingled in the warm air with the drowsy murmur of praying voices from the open door.

In its dark, incense-scented interior there were a score of peasant women, handkerchiefs on their heads, babies in their arms, praying with the fervour of people to whom their religion is not a duty, but a need and a familiar recreation. As we entered, all heads turned with one accord toward us; the fervent praying continued. When we began to move quietly about, looking at the statues and votive offerings, the volume of sound sank; one by one the worshippers abandoned the service, and before long the entire congregation, the priest included, was happily showing us the points of interest.

The church was dedicated to Santa Maria dei Soccorsi, the kind Lady Saviour who watches over ships at sea. Through many centuries those who have been saved have, in gratitude to her, placed some votive offerings in the church. There were paintings: ships lashed by mile-high waves, on whose decks the crew, naïvely shown as being as high as the masts, knelt in prayer. Above, through a round hole in the storm clouds, the face of Santa Maria looked down with a beautiful smile of reassurance. These simple artists may have been ignorant of the law of perspective, but their faith was real, and they were able to make their Mary's face truly beautiful and serene.

On the plain whitewashed walls hung, too, wooden models of the vessels that had been saved. There were ships old and new, one-masted wine traders, *trabaccoli*, and great square riggers with their high poops; each one was finely and carefully carven, perfect to the last detail, even to the little pennants standing out stiff and proud.

A big peasant woman, tears of earnestness in her eyes, took me to a little chapel, the only ornate part of the church, to show me the crucifix that hung above the altar. It was fine; dark bronze and very strong, and the woman said it was miraculous. It had been found on the sands of Forio, she said; it had swum alone all the way from Turkey.

I asked her if it performed many miracles. She threw up her hands, 'Oh, *signora*, it is enough that He looks on us, that all our troubles disappear!'

The priest slowly lighted the candles on the altar from a long taper; the bronze face of Christ glowed softly in the yellow light. The eyes of the peasant women gathered in front of Him looked up lovingly out of their rough, worn faces. Perhaps He saw them and loved them, too.

We drove home quietly through the thickening dark, till our carriage hung on the high road above the Port. There we got out, and walked home arm in arm through the vineyards, guided by the riding lights on the sleeping ships below.

CHAPTER III

HAD ANYTHING EXCEPT MY CIGARS disappeared I would probably not have noticed it, but man, careless as he may be about the important things in life, is quick to resent any intrusion upon his personal pleasures. It is the nature of the beast.

My little stock of cigars, a choice one, was strictly limited to my needs. It stretched to occasional gifts, but was not calculated to stand the strain of petty pilfering. There was an unmistakable thinning out of the ranks, and, as nothing else was missing, neither socks nor shirts nor even handkerchiefs, it was evidently the work of a single-track mind.

We could not bring ourselves to believe that the theft could be laid to the door of any member of the Bonifacio family. They had too much pride and inborn honesty, too great a contempt for the Neapolitan, for whom such things, they said, were a fine art, to indulge in his tricks.

Nevertheless, our enthusiasm had been dampened and a fragment of our pleasant feeling of confidence shattered.

A nasty little imp, smoking my favourite brand of cigar, danced on top of my chest of drawers, exclaiming airily: 'Well, what about it?' We could not catch him, and it was some time before we managed to chase him away. There was nothing to do but to lock up the remaining supplies and forget about it.

This discovery added itself to our discouragement at being unable so far to find a home on the island. House-hunting is distinctly a lovers' pastime, and even then it must be indulged in moderation. If you are old and haggard and have to house-hunt with someone with whom you have quarrelled for half a century, and don't want to live with anyway, it must be a nightmare. Even our radiant enthu-siasm was now assailed with deep misgivings, and also our bones ached. At the end of each day, no matter how willing the spirit might be, our legs refused to climb any more steps to admire any more panoramas from the roofs of any more houses devoid of every convenience except black iron bed-steads.

From the Bonifacios we had heard much of the mineral springs of Ischia and their miraculous revivifying qualities, and we felt that it was a unique opportunity to put them to the test.

Living upon a volcanic island had its disadvantages but also its advantages. We might have been blown up at any moment, although authorities said that the Epomeo, whose last eruption had taken place seven hundred years before, was now extinct. But the awakening of extinct volcanoes was not unheard of, and a few centuries of sleep were often only a nap in the lives of these fiery monsters. We might also have been swallowed up in the bowels of the earth, for Ischia had provided in recent years one of the worst land-slides in Italian history. But we *could* have boiling water –

all we wanted of it – at any time, and free of charge.

Under the whole of the Port and its surrounding areas lay a vast natural reservoir with a never-ending supply of boiling mineral water. It was just below the surface, and its depth was unfathomable. All one had to do was to make a hole in the ground and pump it up. This natural gift had been known to the inhabitants since time immemorial, but, because the Ischians did not make much use of hot water for bathing purposes, there was never any question of the supply running dry.

Not the least remarkable feature of the Albergo del Porto was its bathing facilities, produced by harnessing the Bonifacio brains to the forces of Nature. At the end of the billiard-room some tiles had been lifted, a small hole dug a few feet into the ground, and an electric pump installed to do the rest. The Bonifacios had quite enough work to do without being obliged to pump water for other people's baths. Once in motion, the pump chugged and chugged away valiantly, leaking a good deal and adding its din to the general clamour of the room, but getting nevertheless a good percentage of the water into the pipes.

At first the water came up lukewarm ; then, as the deeper levels were tapped, hotter and hotter, until it emerged hissing and steaming at 100 degrees Centigrade. Here again the Bonifacio ingenuity stepped in to prevent clients from being boiled alive. Part of the water was pumped up and left to cool in a tank on the roof, from where it could be drawn by the bather through a tap luxuriously labelled 'Cold.'

Much more than this, however, had been provided by the Bonifacios for the pleasure of bathers. As I have already mentioned, the large room back of the dining-room was a combination of *sala da biliardo* and *sala da bagno*. The centre of it was occupied by a full-size billiard-table around which

45

the entire youth of the village assembled in the evening, and at one end of the room stood the grand piano that provided an outlet for the musical genius of Angelina's sister. Along one wall there was a row of ten cubicles, each containing a bath-tub, a chair, and a rush mat. The billiard-room was brilliantly lit by electricity, but no illumination had been provided in the cubicles, so we concluded that the bathers preferred to make their ablutions in the more homely atmosphere produced by leaving the door open. It was certainly more conducive to general conversation, and it banished any feeling of loneliness, of which the Italians have a well-justified horror. If you were a foreigner, and insisted upon closing the door, then you had to content yourself with a candle in the neck of a bottle, and a blackbeetle or two for companions.

But, the reader will exclaim irritably, why take your bath at such a rowdy time? Why not take it upon rising, for instance, or even during the day, when the billiard-room was not in use? Because the electric light company won't let you! The Bonifacios, in conjunction with Nature, were always ready to oblige, but the providers of the all-important current, without which the pump refused to work, were not. To the lucid Latin mind of the company's director, no suitable reason had ever occurred as to why electric current should be required in the daytime. In degenerate, sophisticated places like Naples or Capri, where there were many foreigners, that was another thing, but in Ischia, never!

At five a.m., an hour when all honest and even dishonest Ischians were up and about, the current was switched off, and the company officially retired to slumber until sunset. Frequently it overslept. If we wanted a bath in the morning, it meant rising before dawn; we preferred the rowdy hour.

When we decided to take our first 'public' bath we were confronted with a problem. Should we undress very uncomfortably in the narrow cubicles (with the doors shut), or should we appear before the assembled audience in our dressing-gowns? We chose the latter course. Kit said she did not mind provided we made our *entrée* together. The pump had been working for some time, and this, we told each other, would prepare the Ischian mind for the fact that a bath was about to be taken, and our costumes would seem perfectly natural. However, when Kit, clad in a gorgeous Chanel *négligé* of peach-coloured satin, with long medieval sleeves, said she was ready, I lost all hope of slipping quietly through the crowded room unobserved.

Lifting her train in one hand and holding her turkish towel and sponge-bag in the other, she led the way, her heart fluttering somewhat nervously beneath all this finery. A terrific dispute had most mercifully broken out, drowning all other noises, and, we hoped, absorbing all attention. But we had under-estimated our powers of attraction. Not even the Royal Carabinieri could have restored order more rapidly than our appearance did. Insults were swallowed, bitter words left unspoken; jaws dropped, and bulging, unbelieving eyes followed us as, through a hasty parting in the crowd, we made our way to our cabins. Fortunately they were next to each other. Then it must have dawned upon our audience who we were, for no sooner had we closed our doors than a chorus of '*Buona sera! Buon bagno, signori!*' burst out, to which we replied with equal cordiality.

These heartfelt, earnest wishes for a good bath put us at our ease. They gave the event a delightfully sociable touch. Nor was there any hesitation on their part in following up this warm welcome. The piano was called into action; a chorus of song – not all the same song – broke out from

various parts of the room, and the billiard-balls went cracking gaily up and down the table. There was peace and goodwill among all.

Whatever might be the secret of Nature's brew, this
volcanic water was very potent. The small amount which,
through incautious splashing, found its way into my mouth,
was both bitter and salty, probably due to the combination
of iron and infiltrations from the sea. Like sea-water, it
refused absolutely to lather, but what a miracle it worked!
I had not been in the bath more than a few minutes before I
felt relaxed, yet tingling with new energy, quite prepared to
set out house-hunting afresh.

That evening, as we lingered on at table after dinner,
Salvatore joined us for coffee. As usual, he was full of
magnificent plans for the renting of mythical *palazzi*, some
of them apparently still under construction or requiring for
their completion a mere trifle in the way of funds, to be
supplied by us. We listened with only half an ear to his
inexhaustible flow of words, and as soon as we could do so
without hurting his sensitive feelings we rose and bade him
good night.

At the door, prompted by some obscure instinct, I glanced
back into the room. Salvatore was still seated at our table, a
dreamy smile on his face, while with the aid of his hand a
packet of my English cigarettes was disappearing into his
pocket. It was not, I am sorry to say, his habitual brand.
He smoked the local 'Macedonia' when he had nothing
better. I tapped my pockets to make sure, and found them
empty. There was no longer any need to wonder where my
cigars had disappeared to.

The abominable rascal!

Twin arches opened from the garden into a loggia

p. 51

CHAPTER IV

FROM KIT'S DIARY

I

THESE DAYS HAVE BEEN TOO DREARY to write about. With the failure of our last effort to find a house we decided, sadly, that we were not going to be able to live on our island after all.

We said we would stay a few more days with the Boni-facios, take our favourite walks again, and see everything for the last time. The loveliness of the island hurt, and we felt we were being turned out of Paradise.

To-day we are hopeful again, and this is why:

We were walking this afternoon when suddenly we found ourselves on a new stretch of beach, long and white and extraordinarily beautiful. From where we stood it was as though we were in the centre of a great lake, fringed by shores of mythical beauty. Far across the water were the mountains of Campania, ethereal in the distance; there was

49

Vesuvius, sending a soft muff of smoke into the evening sky, where the sunlight still hung; there was the coast of Sorrento, violet in the twilight, and Capri. To our right the Epomeo rose to its sharp summit, its solid rock grown opalescent, almost translucent, in the pale green light.

It is strange that we have never been to this lovely point of land before; it is more beautiful than any place we have seen. Everyone at the *albergo* has spoken slightingly of that part of the island, for it is within the boundaries of Ischia Ponte, the old town which lies under the protecting shadow of the castle, and there is a fierce rivalry between the two communes. Salvatore told us that there were no houses fit for *signori* in Ischia Ponte, only peasant *casette*; damning it in his own eyes, if not in ours.

We walked on. Our path plunged under the thick shade of a big wood of umbrella pines. The trees were tall and dark, and the branches grew out abruptly at the top, making a dense roof and leaving the fine straight boles free, so that the inside of the wood was like a temple of many columns, sweet with the incense of dry, red-brown needles.

The castle came suddenly into view, a towering mass of medieval masonry, holding the sunset like a cloud.

Then our path turned abruptly inland, following the high, white, ivy-covered wall that cut short its progress. Should we go on? It was late, and the mountainside was darkening. While we hesitated, G. went to a wrought-iron gate let into the white wall and looked through.

In a minute he called excitedly, 'Come here!'

I stood beside him, and through the scrolled ironwork saw our dream, anybody's dream, of an Italian garden made real.

A path led away under a stone-pillared pergola to the verdant tangle of a miniature vineyard beyond. Wistaria grew thickly on the pergola, drooping clusters of flowers earthwards, like fragrant bunches of grapes. To one side there was a fat little balustrade enclosing a flower-garden, bright and sweet scented. The balustrade had once been washed with white, but here and there it had flaked off, showing the colours of previous washings – rose and soft blue. There was a line of terra-cotta vases of odd shapes and sizes on it, and in them geraniums bloomed abundantly.

On either side of the balustrade a tiny stairway led up into the flower-garden, and there, beyond the twisted trunks of two Spanish jasmine-trees, we had a glimpse of the house, low, white, and sturdy. Twin arches opened from the garden into a loggia, and in the shadows we could just see that its inner walls were coloured pale rose.

We must have both fallen in love with the little house at the same moment, for when I turned to G. he was looking startled and excited; that was the way I felt, too.

With one accord we shook the gate, which was locked, and pulled the string that rang a ship's bell hanging inside. Nothing happened. There was no sign of life.

After one more look at the twilit garden we hurried back along the beach to the *albergo*.

The Bonifacios were gathered, as usual, in the kitchen; we pelted them with questions until they were quite sure which house we had seen, and until they had told us that it was the property of a certain old Colonello Buonocuore, and that he let it every year. He lived in the Square of Mount Calvary in Naples. We would have to write to him about the house.

We are afraid to hope, but not strong-minded enough to prevent ourselves from hoping. To-night we have been very gay, and have drunk a good deal of wine in our excitement.

51

II

Ischians are either ignorant of the advantages of the postal system or else have a distrust of it. Whichever it is, they do not buy a fifty centesimi stamp except when it is strictly necessary, but instead entrust their letters for the 'continent,' as they say when speaking of Naples and the mainland in general, to a courier.

These couriers leave Ischia almost before it is light, return by the afternoon boat, and deliver their commissions in the evening. They are all that is obliging, and will do any errand for their clients, from delivering a letter and waiting for an answer, to choosing a length of *lingerie crêpe* or transporting a bullock to the island for slaughter, or buying half a dozen bananas.

After we had written our letter to Colonello Buonocuore, we sent it off to Naples by Enrico, a courier who had been recommended to us because he was so *svelto*. When the afternoon boat came in, we were on the quay to meet it. First off was Enrico, justifying his reputation, and he came straight to us with a letter in his hand.

We hurried back to the *albergo*, where we could read it quietly and carefully. G. was quite as excited as I, though his man's dignity forced him to appear nonchalant. He is for ever twitting me on my 'woman's pride,' which I mention at times, but I don't think there is much to choose between it and manly dignity.

The colonel wrote that his *villino* was for rent. He would, he said, come to talk matters over with us as soon as possible, but as he suffered from sea-sickness he would wait until the sea was less *mosso* than it was at present.

We were unbearably impatient at the thought of a delay that could end only with the calming of the elements.

Really, it is strange how differently you can feel about the same thing at different times. Only the day before we had found that one of Ischia's greatest charms was its lack of bustle and hurry, the feeling that if a thing were not accomplished to-day it would be just as well done to-morrow or the day after.

However, the sea calmed itself eventually; yesterday morning Colonello Buonocuore arrived and sent us a card saying that he would be honoured to receive us at four in the afternoon. His card was interesting. Beside the handwriting, which was so tremulous that the shortest inked line contained an infinity of minute uncertain waves, the title appended to his name was intriguing: 'Colonello di Marina in Riposo.'

So we were doubly curious when we went to the Villa Buonocuore yesterday, almost as anxious to make the acquaintance of the owner as of the property itself.

A tiny old woman with bare feet opened the gate at our ringing. She shuffled softly up the little steps into the flower-garden, beckoning us to follow. Our eyes were very busy. The garden was even sweeter than it had seemed from our former post at the gate. It was so fragrant, so green, and now that we were within its walls we were as much cut off from the alley outside as though the latter had ceased to exist, and the only real thing in a beautiful world was this little isolated kingdom of Buonocuore.

We crossed the loggia, which was cool with shade, and even cooler at one end where a deep canopied well gave out its freshness. We followed the old woman up a low flight of stairs from the loggia to a door; opening it, she ducked her head inside and announced to the *Signor Colonello* that the *Signori Inglesi* had arrived. Then she disappeared, and we were left to enter the room alone.

We had both, actually, been intensely curious to see the interior of the house, but whatever curiosity we had felt was put temporarily to one side by the figure of the old man who came forward to greet us. He must have been nearly eighty years old, rather short and stocky but still strongly erect. He was dressed all in black, after the manner of Italians who wish it to be understood that they are gentlemen. His hair and short moustache were grizzled, and he had one of the kindest and most penetrating pairs of eyes that I have ever seen. Somehow I had the impression from them that he was studying us for our suitability just as much as we were examining his house to the same end. Later, when he showed us his little property, I saw that he loved it, and I think he would not have wished to let it to people whom he did not like.

He was polite in a charming, courtly way. He took my hand and raised it to his lips, and as he did so I could feel what I had not seen: the tremulousness of an old man. He was proud to be able to talk to us in our own language, rusty old phrases of English learned, he said, on his voyages with the Navy, and since then, I should think, seldom drawn forth from the storehouse of his memory.

After a period of gallant conversation, during which I, to my great delight, was referred to as G.'s 'consort,' he showed us the *villino* and the garden.

No house could be more simply planned, none more charming. The four principal rooms are built in a square block, like four child's bricks placed close together. Each room opens into the two others adjacent to it; no space is wasted on corridors. The rooms themselves are square and high, flooded with sun and air, and the ceilings, spotlessly whitewashed, have the exquisitely graceful dome characteristic of the island architecture.

Such a simple description of the shape and size of the house gives no picture of its unique charm. It is full of quietude and the smell of the sea. Like its old owner, it belongs to another era, out of date in furniture and decoration as he is out of date in speech.

On tables and mantels are shining glass globes. Some shelter stiff, prim bunches of faded wax flowers. Others cover little images of the saints, dolls dressed with a touching care and attention to detail in the brown habit of Sant' Antonio or the blue satin and silver stars of the Virgin.

The windows are tall, and framed by stiff lambrequins of old faded cretonne. On the walls hang a few oil paintings, dim seascapes of this very gulf that stretches out beyond the garden wall, and a portrait of a fine strong face framed in the severe black and white of a magistrate's gown. The furniture is demurely Victorian – little easy chairs with fluffy chintz skirts, good old pieces of heavy mahogany, no sign of the welter of beds that greeted us in the other houses we visited.

There are three bedrooms, and between each pair of beds hangs a little wooden plaque with two hooks on it. These, the colonel explained grandly, are for the convenience of married people like ourselves. Quietly, side by side, the two wedding-rings can hang on the hooks all through the night, whilst the 'consorts' slumber peacefully beneath their benediction.

I think we both made an instant decision as to which should be our room. (There never seemed any need to make a decision about taking the house.) It has pale apricot-coloured walls and green shutters that open on to a miniature balcony with an exquisite wrought-iron railing; from it you can look off and away, over the little walled garden, out across that glowing expanse of blue water, to the shores of the mythically beautiful 'continent.'

While we stood there, lost in the view, incredulous to think that we would be renting it as part and parcel of the house, almost as an adjunct to the furnishings of our bedroom, Colonel Buonocuore drew our attention to the bathroom. It is his pride. It lies at the bottom of a little flight of steps leading down from our apricot-coloured room. It contains a noble monument in white enamel, decorated generously with painted red roses. On the wall beside it hangs a plaited straw ring, to be taken down and used as a seat. Four enamelled basins on iron stands range along the wall, with an attendant flock of water-jugs. We should have no excuse not to be very clean in spite of the lack of running water.

Across the garden we were led by the *colonello*, who gallantly offered me his arm with a remark that sounded like 'Can I yelp you?' spoken with cosmopolitan aplomb. We had wondered why we had seen no kitchen in the house; even our enchanted minds could not imagine that a charming *villino* and a magnificent view could entirely dispense with the need for food. Now we were to see it.

Under the pergola we caught a glimpse of a small white house, almost hidden in a cascade of lavender wistaria. On the colonel's arm I went down a flight of steps and found myself in the most lovely, dim, cool dining-room. It was half below the ground level, so that the windows were set unexpectedly high in the walls, and, these windows being round and rather small, of the sort called 'bull's-eye,' it had the effect of being a cabin on board ship. Perhaps the colonel arranged it so that he would not feel too lonely when he became just a Colonel of the Navy at Rest.

No house could pretend more whole-heartedly to be a ship. The walls of the kitchen, adjoining the dining-room, are built on the lava rock at the water's edge; if the sea were

ISLAND IN THE SUN

rough it would pound against the little house in its effort
to enter the garden. The roof makes a fine terrace, with an
unbroken view of beauty in all directions. Standing on it,
we felt as though we were at the prow of a ship, cutting the
waters of the gulf.

We thought not only of the visual attractions of the little
house, but of the aural ones as well. If we should be lucky
enough to find a cook and a house-boy, they would be able
to shriek at each other in gaiety or in anger, one being as
noisy as the other, whilst we, separated from them by the
whole length of the garden, could remain quietly undisturbed. We should also be spared the pungent perfumes
of such foods as tripe and *baccalà*, which, though ultimately
delicious, smell unbelievably awful in the process of preparation.

Down the pergola-covered path, across the garden from
the entrance-gate, we came to another, smaller gate cut in
the stone wall. When the colonel opened it, there lay a
little crescent-shaped beach, golden and completely cut
off by walls going down on either side to the water's edge.
On this side it was the garden wall of the Villa Buonocuore
that hemmed it in; on the other it was sheltered by an old
building, crumbling and picturesque.

'*Questa sara la loro spiaggia privata*,' said the colonel. Our
private beach! How heavenly to possess such a thing through
these long, hot summer days!

The old building opposite was the local prison. 'But
do not let that make an impression on you, *signora*,' said
the old man easily. 'The only inmates are perhaps three or
four youths each year, who have been caught stealing rabbits
or a hen. As for them, they are overjoyed to have a week
or two in jail; they always say it is a real holiday for them,
for they have their loaf of bread and their bowl of soup

57

gratis every day, which is more than they have to eat when the fishing has been bad, and they have no work to do!'

As he spoke I heard a lusty voice singing a Neapolitan song to the accompaniment of a guitar, and presently the singer, presumably one of the inmates of this pleasant prison, strolled out on to the broad roof of the building, and, still singing, looked down at us with the same open and candid interest that all our future neighbours have shown. For of course the Villa Buonocuore is ours. 'Villa Good-Heart'; it is a good omen to start our life in a house with a name like that. We were too pleased even to bargain over the rent; it would have been awkward, anyway, with someone so nice and so very gentlemanly as the colonel, though I think it is always done, and no doubt he expected it. He explained the size of the rental—which, though high for Ischia, is not more than the half of what we should have to pay at home—by something which he called the *ubicazione panoramica*. It alone, he said, was worth the whole sum.

Neither of us knew what an *ubicazione* was; it sounded a little bit dangerous. With the help of our dictionary, however, we find that it means, vaguely, 'a delight.' And, knowing that the colonel was talking about 'a panoramic delight,' I'm not at all sure that I don't agree with him about its value.

We move in ten days. That time will be devoted by the colonel to arranging his house to the pinnacle of his taste; in any other state he declares he would not allow himself to let it. We shall try to capture the Ischian conception of the inconsequence of Time, in order to curb our unruly impatience.

CHAPTER V

I

OUR ISCHIAN FRIENDS professed themselves delighted that
we were going to settle in their midst, even though our
choice of a villa without cement statues, gilded railings,
and other accessories of gentility was frankly distressing.
How like *forestieri*, they thought, to have chosen, from all
this wealth of beautiful houses shown us by Salvatore, one
which was little better than a native dwelling, and with a
garden where vines grew as in a peasant's courtyard.

Now that at last we had a home, said Kit, we had to have
linen. She had been awaiting with undisguised eagerness this
opportunity to make gigantic purchases. Across the water
between us and the mainland lay the island of Procida,
where, in the great penitentiary, the finest linen in Italy was
hand-woven by the unfortunate inmates. Most of the
Bonifacio linen came from there, and Angelina and Maria
had generously offered to act as guides to Kit.

Who could write about Procida and do it justice? It is

a painter's paradise, not an author's. Long, low, and narrow, the island itself possesses no particular charm, but boasts of amazing fertility. It is called the fruit and vegetable garden of Naples, and is especially renowned for its lemon-groves, protected by high walls from the winter winds. The product of these trees is so monstrous in size that it looks like something a hashish eater might expect to see dangling before him in his dreams.

On a great jagged rock is the ancient castle, now the penitentiary, an incredibly sinister and hopeless-looking pile which, as it catches the red rays of the setting sun, seems to sweat with the blood of its unfortunate inmates. At its feet lies the old town that must be the envy of every artist. No more dilapidated picturesqueness exists anywhere in the Mediterranean. The long narrow quay is lined with a solid row of houses of every conceivable colour. There are blue, white, and pink houses, mauve, green, and beige houses, red, chrome-yellow, and terra-cotta houses. Many of them bear witness in size and architecture to having been built in more prosperous days, but are now divided between two or more families. Each family has painted its section a different hue in sign of independence, but with an inborn taste for general harmony. Decayed by the sun and centuries beyond all repair, only a spirit of fraternity seems to prop them up. In reality each house is so tightly wedged in between its neighbours that there is no place for it to fall. The wharf, with a weird collection of old fishing-craft, both sail and steam, is hardly less picturesque than the row of houses back of it.

Our ship anchored in deep water, and small boats put out from the shore to collect passengers and cargo. A sailor immaculate in white, and a soldier in green plus-fours with a hen's feather protruding from his soft felt hat, both heavily armed with carbines and revolvers, patrolled the quay, but as our boat approached they halted and eyed us with deep suspicion.

They were not, as you might imagine, interested in our movements, our political tendencies; they did not want to inspect our passports or follow us around to make sure that we had not come to plan the escape of some poor unfortunate wretch imprisoned in that dismal fortress on the cliff. They were not really interested in us at all, but in the other occupants of the boat, mostly natives of the island. They belonged to the *Guardia delle Finanze*, one of the most important armed forces of Italy, whose members are to be found in every city, town, and village in the country. These 'guardians of finance' are customs officials, and they are there to see that the natives do not smuggle goods from one town or village into another.

They want to know, for instance, exactly what is inside that little package wrapped up in an old newspaper which you are perhaps carrying under your arm. If you have bought it in Naples or Ischia and expect to take it quietly back with you to Procida, you are vastly mistaken. This does not apply to foreign goods imported from France, England, Jerusalem, or Honolulu; it applies to that little funnel you bought at the tin shop for thirty centesimi.

You cannot show a permit, eh! 'Come this way, please.' They are polite but firm. Two guns, two revolvers, and possibly some hidden daggers guarantee your obedience. Between them you are marched into an office, where another finance officer, this time probably a fat one with stripes on his tunic, sits behind his desk. With an air of vast importance he listens to your offence, which sounds pretty serious as the men tell it. He examines the funnel and cross-questions you as to where and why you bought it, and if you are

ISLAND IN THE SUN

quite sure that it was thirty centesimi and not ONE LIRA AND
THIRTY CENTESIMI you paid for it. He then takes down your
name, your father's Christian name, your mother's maiden
name, together with a lot of other vitally important information. This he does in triplicate; it covers reams of paper and
takes considerable time. Virtually a prisoner, you spend this
time gazing apprehensively at the opposite wall, where a
menacing picture of Il Duce glares back at you with popping
eyes. Meditating on your unhappy fate, you are roused at
last by a harsh command to pay ten centesimi, representing
double the tax due, and are warned that you must not be
caught a second time trying to defraud the customs.

How much it costs to maintain the vast army of the
Guardia delle Finanze only the Government knows, but
it is the small items that bring in the large sums, and no
doubt it pays.

Procida at close quarters depressed us. Its dilapidation,
its exotic odours, its indescribable filth, closed in on us on
every side. The town seemed also to be in the clutches of
the Church, for priests abounded in the narrow, dirty streets,
and the shop windows displayed in large letters such signs
as 'Long Live Jesus!' and manifestos proclaiming the excellence of the entire Holy Family. Commercially, these
religious advertisements had the advantage of drawing the
attention away from the mouldy display of goods for sale:
fly-covered cheeses and *salame*, faded packets of spaghetti,
a fancy box of chocolates whose gay ribbon was discoloured
with age.

Inside one shop, a fat priest was seated. There was
nothing mouldy or poverty-stricken about him. From the
top of his black plush hat, ornamented with silk tassels, to
the immaculate shining buckles on his shoes, he bore the
stamp of prosperity. Behind the counter, in an attitude of

62

respectful attention, the shopkeeper stood with a smirk on his face, no doubt inwardly thankful that he had plastered his walls and windows so plentifully with Holy Manifestos, thereby clearly showing the extent of his piety.

Angelina told us that Procida was very rich. It was easy to see where the money went. The inhabitants were considered such excellent and generous children of the Church that, once a year, for the celebration of the local *festa*, no less a personage than the Cardinal-Archbishop of Naples came to the island to attend it, surrounded by a flock of important prelates. There was, Angelina said, a great procession, much illumination, and very much feasting off the fat of the land!

Kit, Angelina, Maria, and I started our climb to the penitentiary in the broiling sun. We had intended to take two carriages, our load being too heavy for one horse, but, as the coachmen wanted twenty-five lire each, we could not waste the afternoon beating them down. The climb was almost vertical, and involved much puffing and blowing, especially on the part of Angelina, who was what the Ischians called *bella grassa, grassa*. Furthermore, she had exchanged her habitual wooden sandals for pink silk stockings and tight, high-heeled patent leather shoes, which did not aid her progress. Much of her 'beautiful fat' must have dissolved during the ascent, though there was still plenty left when we reached the top.

At the forbidding door of the prison we rang the bell. A little, heavily barred peep-hole was opened, and, after explaining our business, we were admitted. The sales-room was a vast whitewashed hall, the walls of which were lined with glass cases filled with great bolts of cream-coloured linen in various degrees of thickness and quality. Three men, half jailers and half shop-attendants, were in charge.

Here Kit and the Bonifacio sisters immediately ran riot. In less than three minutes they had all the cases open and almost the entire contents of the room piled high on the counter. From under this mountain of linen they spied a little piece at the bottom, yanked it out, thereby causing a magnificent avalanche; stretched, rumpled, rolled, and scratched it, held it to the light, sniffed at it delicately to make sure of its absolute genuineness, submitted the attendant to a volley of searching questions about its durability, then suddenly lost all interest in it, having discovered a fresh piece protruding from an even more inaccessible pile.

This linen, all hand-woven by the prisoners, was sold under Government guarantee. Because there were no middleman's profits, and above all because the workers were paid only a minute sum, its price was far below what it would have been in any shop. Little as the prisoner received for his labour, he eagerly welcomed this chance to escape the old and, in some parts of Italy, still prevalent method of solitary confinement, where in a dark, damp cell he was left alone with the terror of his thoughts. In these workshops, in the company of fellow prisoners, he was able to forget for a while the slow passage of time, the months and in many cases the long years which had to come and go before he could hope to walk in freedom again.

While we were there, a prisoner entered carrying a load of material fresh from the looms. He was an old man with white hair and a peaceful resigned face. Thin and horribly pallid, he wore a brown and white striped prison suit and a little *berretto* of the same material. Having consigned his goods to one of the officials, he stood with the patient look of a dumb animal while a chit was being made out for it, then, turning softly on his heel, he left the room.

The sails of some trader . . . moving slowly out to sea

p. 80

Whatever crime he had committed, it seemed as though he had long since atoned for it, even if not to the letter of the law. It hurt to see him, especially when the official, with the satisfied smile of a tamer in a circus, announced in a loud voice: *Un condannato.*

I would not like to be the inmate of any prison, but least of all of any Mediterranean prison. I shuddered when I thought how easy it was for a foreigner in Italy to find himself behind the bars merely for having wagged his tongue a little incautiously about a certain person to whom we always prudently referred as 'Mr. Jones.'

The feeling of this gaunt penitentiary clung to me all the way back. I was glad that no such grim reminder of the ugliness of life existed on our island to mar its beauty.

II

Meanwhile, at the Albergo del Porto great preparations were being made for the marriage of Rosina to Gaetano Strombozzi, a youth from Sorrento. For some time past the Bonifacio family had been in a state of feverish activity, and only our personal preoccupations had so far prevented us from appreciating the full importance of what was going on around us.

The entire ground floor of the *albergo* had undergone a change, principally the billiard-room. Its habitual function as public amusement hall had been temporarily suspended. All doors had been locked, mysterious hammerings could be heard from inside, while an endless caravan of tables and chairs borrowed from all over the house, including our verandah and bedroom, moved towards it. As a special favour Kit and I were allowed a private pre-view.

The vast room had been transformed into a palm court,

65

and it was evident from the imposing seating accommodation that a great many guests were expected. The main object, however, was to exhibit the bride's trousseau. And what a trousseau it was! For quantity it would have held its own in a Mayfair or Fifth Avenue wedding. It consisted chiefly of undergarments, and there were dozens of each variety, piled high on tables that staggered under the load. Solidity rather than fashion had been the prime consideration of Rosina, who for eight years had been working on them. These garments scornfully repudiated any connection with the flimsy feminine French name of *lingerie*, and were better described by their Italian name of *biancheria*, a term which likewise applies to bed-linen and washing; but then, as we knew, they were meant to last a lifetime.

In this room were also displayed the wedding presents from the family and from relations. Kit and I were frankly amazed at their abundance. We had nothing like it at our marriage, though, judging from a certain twitching in Kit's sphinx-like mask as she politely examined the *biancheria*, I do not think she regretted it.

On a great centre table, around which lesser tables were gathered like satellites around a planet, was a pyramid of silverware, chinaware, glassware, kitchenware, and clothing, all jumbled up in an intriguing way. Silver spoons protruded from the instep of patent leather shoes; cooking utensils and a richly embroidered silk shawl lay entwined, gathering into their embrace gold-rimmed coffee-cups and an alabaster effigy of the leaning tower of Pisa. Sooner or later the eyes were bound to reach the top of this mountain of domestic felicity, where, tied up in a magnificent red silk sash, was a cheque on the Banco di Napoli, bearing in a bold signature the name of Enrico Alessandro Bonifacio. As there seemed to be no indiscretion in examining it more closely, I saw to my astonishment that it was made out for five thousand lire.

There are three great occasions in the life of a southern Italian middle-class family which call for a display of un-bridled extravagance. They are birth, marriage, and death. No matter how poor the family may be, no matter at what a crippling cost, no matter how humbly they may have to exist in the intervening periods, appearances must be kept up at these events. The Bonifacios were far from poor, for, in addition to the *albergo*, old Alessandro was the most prosperous wine-merchant of the Port, but Mama confided to us that even they could not afford two marriages the same year, and that if Angelina wanted to follow her sister's example she would have to wait.

If she were going to have a send-off like that, I told her, Angelina would have something well worth waiting for, adding, perhaps unwisely, that she was a fine girl and that the husband she chose would be a lucky man. Clutching my arm and giving me a searching glance, Mama whispered with a deep sigh, 'Had God been willing, *you* might have married Angelina.' I did think that Kit had no business to be at the other end of the room, well out of earshot, at a moment like that.

In the dining-room, tables were being laid for the marriage breakfast on the morrow. Although it was her own daughter's marriage, much of the cooking fell to Mama. Perhaps it was her wish. Perhaps she wished to prepare, with her old wrinkled hands, those traditional wedding-cakes that are part of the island customs.

Some hours later, as we passed the half-open kitchen door on our way out, we had a glimpse of the old woman seated on a rickety chair before the fire. For once she was not busy; her hands were folded quietly in her lap, and her face, grey with fatigue, had a look of infinite sadness. She was so deep in her thoughts that she did not hear our footsteps. Was she thinking of the daughter she was going to lose, or of a certain day in her own life, long, long ago, when she herself had stood radiant and pretty on the threshold of a life that had turned out very differently from her dreams? It was no secret on the island that old Alessandro had been unfaithful to his wife for many a year, and still to-day was said to have a mistress in the great city across the bay where his business so often took him.

III

Rosina and Gaetano Strombozzi were now married, and staggering from the effect of a gargantuan *pranzo di nozze*, they had taken their departure on the afternoon boat to spend their honeymoon in Rome.

The feast had been of great interest to us because of the variety of island specialties which it assembled together, such as fresh-water eels cooked whole and served in a tureen of lukewarm olive oil – not too good to unaccustomed palates – and clotted pig's blood thickened with sugar, a dish which it took diplomacy to get away from. There were, on the other hand, a great variety of delicious island dishes we were already acquainted with, and to these we brought a hearty appetite.

The feast was also extremely instructive in its display of native society manners at their best. Opposite us sat two formidable middle-aged ladies, one massive in the Ischian fashion, the other thin, sallow, and short, but with the most terrifically villainous face. She had a menacing brow, so low that the jet-black hair and the bushy eyebrows almost met, and her lip showed more than a suspicion of down. Her eyes were gimlets, and she used them to bore holes in us. As a professional poisoner she would have been a credit to the Borgias, at least as far as looks were concerned.

Neither woman exchanged a word or a smile, and it seemed evident that they were not on friendly terms. I imagined them to be heads of rival gangs, but I was mistaken. As the meal progressed, the poisoner speared a piece of eel on her plate with a fork she had just taken from her mouth, and, glaring at her neighbour, she slapped it down in front of her. The neighbour returned the glare, and, harpooning the slice, tried to slap it back where it belonged. But the poisoner would have nothing more to do with it. Back and forth it flew, getting limper and limper in the fray, and abundantly scattering the table-cloth with oil, till finally the victim had to give in. Fascinated, we watched her gulp it down, half expecting to see her suddenly collapse writhing on the floor, but nothing of the sort happened. Later, when she in turn had eaten all she could digest of a plate of fried baby octopus, she plunged her fork into a choice morsel complete with tentacles, and deftly landed it in the enemy camp. Again there was a swift passage of arms, after which the tit-bit was accepted and swallowed.

Excellent friends after all, they were merely on their best behaviour. As the occasion was a formal one, it would not have been seemly to laugh or joke, nor above all to accept this neighbourly exchange of delicacies without polite protestation.

The feast ended for us upon a fine note of bravado. Several times during the meal I had been aware of Salvatore's glances, although whenever our eyes met he looked rapidly aside. Since Kit and I had discovered the Villa Buonocuore without his help, a certain tension had reigned in our relations that were already strained enough over the cigars. His friendliness was no longer stimulated by the prospect of the fee we had promised him if he found us a house, and the mask of urbanity, though still worn, was no longer so carefully adjusted that it did not betray an occasional glimpse of what lay beneath.

As we stood among the assembled guests after dinner, Salvatore, flushed from extra-generous libations, advanced smiling with the proffer of a moist hand to shake. It was not, however, the only thing he proffered. Producing two nice little cigars of familiar shape and colour, he said, '*Volete un sigaro, caro signore?*' And, handing me one, proceeded slowly to light the other. '*Roba da poco* – cheap stuff, you know,' he added, with a gleam of amusement in his eye. 'But then, of course, I am a poor man.' Cheap stuff, eh? My own cigars!

It was impossible to grudge Salvatore a certain admiration. Who else could have had the immoral nonchalance of such a gesture? Desperately I cast around for something witty and shrivelling to say, but Salvatore did not wait. With a happy, carefree laugh, he excused himself on the score of having to entertain his father-in-law's other guests, and departed. Defeat stimulated my brain into action; the plan of revenge I had been longing for suddenly dawned upon me.

Going over to Kit, I drew her aside. 'Darling,' I said, 'where does one buy gunpowder?'

'Why, at the tobacconist's, of course,' she replied sweetly.

This was our little joke. You could buy everything at the tobacconist's: tooth-paste, brilliantine, curling-irons, highly coloured post-cards, stamped paper for legal documents, salt, and even tobacco. Why not gunpowder?

Then I saw that she was perfectly serious. 'Inside the fireworks, dear. All you want of it.' Why, of course. How clever of her. *Feste* in honour of local saints were always taking place somewhere on the island, and every *tabaccaio* kept in stock a variety of fireworks, from the squibs that urchins held in their hands to the big rockets that went off like a bomb.

As soon as we could, we slipped away from the party and I outlined my plan to Kit. She dissuaded me from buying a rocket. It would be too conspicuous. We purchased instead a bag full of small fire-crackers, and at another tobacconist's higher up the street a stout piece of cardboard.

Armed with these, we made our way to a certain deserted beach closed in by high rocks, where we felt safe from intrusion. Assembling our instruments on the sand, we sat down to work. First, we emptied the crackers of their gunpowder, then with the aid of a penknife and a cigar piercer we carefully inserted as much explosive as would go into the centre of each of three cigars. When we had replaced carefully the loose tobacco it was almost impossible to see that they had been tampered with.

As we were not living in the Renaissance, we dared not place such heavily loaded vengeance in Salvatore's path without first testing its violence. This was where the cardboard came in useful. By cutting a hole in the centre, just large enough to wedge the small end of a cigar through, it was an effective guard – or at least we hoped so – for the experiment. At that point Kit became restless; she did not, she said, relish becoming a widow even before we moved into our new home. I assured her there was no danger, wishing nevertheless that I had some vague notion of how much gunpowder it was wise to put into a cigar if you wished to survive the experiment.

Kit wanted to sit beside me and share my fate, but as it was necessary for an observer to be posted some distance away to see what happened on the other side of the shield, she finally consented to this rôle. Wedging the shield between boulders and tilting the cigar well upwards, as the gunner points his cannon for long-range firing, I lay flat on my stomach in the approved style and not without difficulty lit the cigar.

Nobody could say that this revenge was a thoughtless one! With beating heart I puffed away and counted the seconds. I had to keep on puffing or the cigar would have gone out. Nothing in the world burned so slowly or tasted worse.

'Look out!' Kit called. 'It must be about due.' I stopped puffing and lay low. There was a loud report, and Kit came running toward me, her face flushed with excitement. 'Magnificent,' she said. 'The end shot clear away and into the sea!' And she pointed toward the vast horizon, where there was nothing whatever to be seen beyond sea and sky. Still attached to the guard was a neat stump; it was nervously chewed at one end, and blown to pieces at the other.

That evening we placed our two remaining cigars in the drawer, removing the others. He would be sure to take one, and it did not matter in the least which one!

We had underrated Salvatore. He did not take one after all. He took both of them. We made this discovery after our morning stroll around the Port the following day, and, as we gazed spellbound at the empty box, a certain horrified feeling of having set in motion the inexorable wheels of Fate overwhelmed us. Up to that moment we had felt ourselves masters of the situation; now there was nothing we could do to prevent Salvatore from setting light, in his own good time, to the dynamited cigars. We could not rush out into the street in search of him, and with tears in our eyes implore a dishonest Neapolitan to cast away his stolen goods. And we did not want to. Our feelings were akin to those of a convinced but inexperienced Nihilist who has just lit the fuse of his first bomb and stowed it away in the grand-duke's carriage; apprehensive but without remorse.

At lunch, unable to bear the suspense, we enquired after Salvatore's health, and were assured by Angelina that it was excellent. He had, she told us, gone with a friend to make what the English called *un picknicko* in the latter's wine-cellar. That explained the two cigars; one of them was to be in payment for his friend's good wine. We could visualise them sitting astride their barrels, munching cheese, tomatoes, and garlic, drinking to their hearts' content, then settling down to a good smoke at the foreigner's expense. If all went well, we said to ourselves, there would be no siesta that afternoon; then we imagined the next morning's papers, with headlines about a mysterious explosion in an Ischian wine-cellar, and again we felt acutely uneasy.

Altogether it was a miserable day. Salvatore, the wretch, did not come back till supper-time, apparently unhurt. Fortunately he did not read the relief in our faces, for, though he entered the room with a brave swagger, his eyes carefully avoided ours, and there was about him the air of a grown-up dog who has been chastised for reverting to the habits of his puppyhood. We shall never know what happened in that cellar, but at least we know that it *did* happen.

CHAPTER VI

FROM KIT'S DIARY

I

MY POOR HUSBAND is in bed. Strangers to the Mediterranean sun do not realise its strength, and he is crimson and feverish.

'Sunstroke,' the Bonifacio family says. The word has an appalling sound; I was worried enough before hearing it. I hope I shall be able to perform all my other wifely duties as well as I do the worrying; I am really awfully thorough about it. I suppose it is rather a good index to the state of my heart.

Everyone has applied his or her favourite remedy to poor G.; the air of our room reeks with the conflicting smells of the various treatments.

First came Angelina, quite grave for once, with a plate of rancid butter. Only the cafés have ice brought over from Naples, and private supplies of butter are good or very bad

75

according to the season. Angelina anointed all G.'s burnt parts – a large area, excluding only the small space that had been covered by his shorts. She retired, smiling again, assuring us that all would now be well.

She was followed by Maria, bearer and rubber-in of pungent vinegar. Next came old Mama with a tureen full of egg-whites, with which she painted G.'s scarlet skin. The egg hardened; G.'s eyes looked out startled from an inflexible mask.

With rising fever came a whole deputation bringing a sickening-looking drink. I asked what it was: castor oil floating heavily between two layers of banana liqueur. It would cure the fever. The liqueur, very fine, was in honour of the foreign *signore*; perhaps he was not accustomed to castor oil, as were all Ischians, who took a large dose of it, a *purga*, regularly once a month.

G. thanked them nervously; when they had gone I disposed of the filthy concoction in the one way that could not hurt their feelings.

In times of trouble we don't want interesting novelties, we want the good things we are used to ; and G., thirsty with his fever, was obsessed by the desire for the simple comfort of a cup of tea. I was happy to have something to do; I promised I would bring it to him – 'Soon, darling, and I'll make it myself so that it will be just right.'

There was no tea in the *albergo* ; Angelina thought, though, that I might find some in the village. I set out quickly, hopefully, and entered the first shop that looked somewhat like a grocer's, one tiny room stocked with tins of tomato, brooms, fans for charcoal stoves, and a great pile of wooden mules.

I wanted some tea, I said confidently. The fat woman plaiting straw for fans behind the counter looked at me curiously. What did I want? Tea? 'Never heard of it,' she remarked flatly. She said I might find it in the big shop up the hill, under the church of San Pietro.

This time it was a fat man with bushy eyebrows who told me he had never heard of tea. Perhaps at the tobacconist's, back yonder near the Albergo del Porto, I might find it; tobacco-shops sold salt, snuff, and quinine, and it might be that they dealt in this tea as well.

The *tabaccaio* knew about tea but he did not sell it. He strongly recommended my trying another tobacconist at the opposite end of the village, and the way in which he suggested that the other shop might sell such a thing could not have been anything but an insult to his rival.

For an hour I ran, increasingly desperate, from shop to shop. I had not known there were so many shops in the village. The last recommendation brought me to the chemist's. I went into a little room lined with old blue *faience* jars, and through a half-open door saw the ancient, dusty chemist asleep in a back room, his spectacles pushed up on his forehead, his feet on a table.

'What do you wish, *signorina?*' he asked drowsily when I had wakened him by pounding on the counter. To be called 'Miss' after all the disappointments of my chase was too much. I have been 'Mrs.' for more than a month now, and do not like to have it ignored. With my left hand on the counter, so that the wedding-ring showed up well, I answered his question coldly:

'I want some tea for my husband, who is ill.'

The old man was not crushed. He hummed and hawed, and my spirits rose when I saw him poking around among his blue jars.

'Do you want camomile or Indian?' he asked.

I emerged with a small paper bag full of a mixture of tea

and the dust of ages. I brewed it in a coffee-pot in the kitchen of the *albergo*. I carried it up to G., and he drank it manfully after an initial grimace of his egg-stiffened face.

He said it was good and that it had made him feel much better. He thought I had not seen the grimace. He is a dear.

II

I have had a visitor. Yesterday a tall, robust old woman in a black cotton dress and white apron strode into the room accompanied by Angelina. It was the nun from San Dominico; she had come to show me samples of the linen she weaves. Her bare feet were dusty from her long walk through the summer lanes; her weather-beaten face was burned red-brown; her carriage was splendid, and on her head she carried a great bundle of linen, so heavy that she needed the help of Angelina to dismount it. Angelina said she was very old, but it was hard to believe it. When I asked her, she said she could not remember her exact age; she supposed she must be about seventy.

Before exchanging any words, she blessed me. The blessing was long and difficult to follow in the dialect, but I heard her call on the Virgin, and on Santa Restituta, and on Sant' Anna, and when she had finished she traced the sign of the Cross on my forehead with her finger.

When that was over she was ready for business. She unpacked her bundle of linen and showed me the towels she had woven. When they are new they are dark brown and very rough; I could hardly believe it was the same cloth as the old creamy, soft towel Angelina had showed me, but she assured me that it grows more beautiful every time it is washed, and that our grandchildren will be able to use it for their trousseaux.

The old woman promised to weave as many towels as I wanted, but I must allow her time. She has the flax to spin into thread before making the cloth, and she cannot work at it all the day long; she has her prayers to attend to as well. I asked her to what order of nuns she belonged. She had no order, she said; she was just a nun, had dedicated herself she could not remember how long ago; the years passed by so swiftly with spinning, weaving, and praying.

We parted great friends, though neither of us had understood much of what the other had said. She gave me another blessing, ending with an unexpected grin. 'She wishes you a hundred years of life and twenty male children,' Angelina translated, laughing.

They carried the linen down the stairs together; the old nun was going to refresh herself in the Bonifacio kitchen before she went home. The roads were hot, and a bottle of good wine would cool her before starting on her return journey to the hills.

III

I have been feeling a little queer these last days. I suppose that, like G., I have had too much sun, but the Bonifacio family does not agree. They do not approve of our anti-fly measures; they consider that the spray is more dangerous than the flies, and they tell me in no uncertain terms that I have been suffering from 'too much Flit'!

G. is better, but he says that his legs are still wobbly and that he must have his arm around me all the time for support. I think I love him very much.

IV

Street scenes in Ischia are as full of colour, music, and movement as an operetta. The same excessively foreign look gives them atmosphere; the sun, pouring down from an unbelievably blue sky, animates the scene like a giant floodlight.

Our little balcony is a box in the theatre; shaded by gnarled wistaria vines, it overhangs the stage. From it we can watch the unending play below: the innumerable actors playing their parts, comic, melodramatic, or tragic. Small parts abound; coachmen in blue dungaree jackets, perched on the high seats of their little *carrozze*, whip their old horses across at a gallop; little donkeys and long-legged mules, a wine-keg strapped to either side of their backs, lope by at an ungainly canter, led by barefoot boys with ragged trousers and brown bodies.

In the wings to the right is a vendor of fruit and vegetables, a young woman with black hair and a red dress. Her stall stands on the paving of the street; it is bright with giant yellow lemons, red apples, oranges, purple plums, scarlet tomatoes, and black shining cherries.

Through the wings to the left comes a glimpse of blue water from the Port, bare masts of ships at anchor, the sails of some trader freighted with fragrant wines moving slowly out to sea, and fishermen mending their russet nets among their vivid dories.

In the centre of the stage stands the little café with small iron tables, covered by bright cloths, spreading out into the street. Here, many an evening, we have acted our small part in the play, sitting together, drinking a vermouth, feeling the fresh breeze of the night coming in over the water.

A large male chorus stands about in true operetta fashion, with little to do seemingly but break into song at the proper moment, or cry *'Bravo! Bis! Bis!'* in applause of the principal actor.

It is not difficult to see who is this principal actor. He

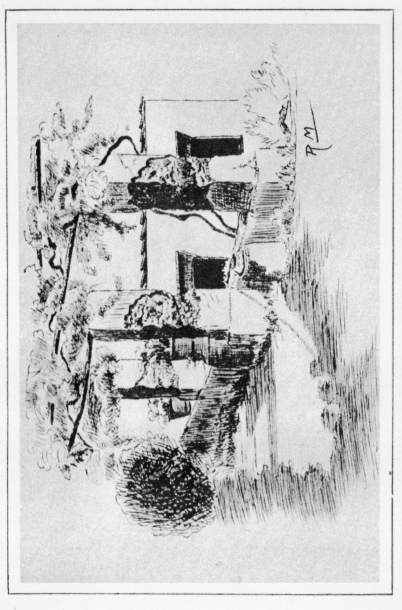

It looked like a little temple to Bacchus

p. 86

comes out of the barber's shop that is built close against the café, and takes up his stand in the centre of the stage. Perhaps you would not think him a hero; he is not tall and lithe and dark like the Neapolitans of operetta; he has not sleek black hair nor a handsome face.

He is a young man, scarcely more than a boy. He has a round, brown face, a tilted nose, and merry eyes.

He does not walk; he cannot. His legs are paralysed. He sits on a common folding-chair and moves himself from place to place with surprising dexterity, hitching the chair forward by jerking his body from side to side.

When he has brought his chair to the right spot in the hot sun of the street he will sing. He has a splendid voice, clear and strong and sweet, and he seems to have the same joy in using it as a bird. He sings all day – there is so little else that he can do – and often late into the night, and he is pleased with the applause from his chorus. I think he is always happy while he is singing; there is gusto in the way he throws his head back, and his mouth is always smiling.

He has many songs, full of sweetness or melancholy or laughter, but there is one to which he always returns – the crowd's favourite, and his own: 'La Vita é Bella.' I do not think the exquisite irony of his choice has ever occurred to him, or he could not sing it. 'Life is Beautiful.' The words would choke him if they were anything but music to him, a medium to use that voice that gives him so much joy. His voice will never be trained now; it might have been, but it is too late. The paralysis that has already robbed him of his legs is not content with that. It will creep every day a little higher, until it has taken the life of the singer itself.

Nothing can be done to avoid this fate; it will not be long in coming. He knows – all Ischia knows and takes for granted – that nothing can save him. Soon he will not be able to sit on his chair, the chair that is substitute for the crutches that his parents are too poor to buy, and then I hope the end will soon come.

Yet still he sings – not sadly, but full of joy.

As we leave our balcony in the late evening, and with our shutters close out the street scene below, his full, strong voice still reaches us, and we can feel the smile on his face and see his merry eyes as he sings: 'La Vita é Bella.'

CASTELLO
d'Ischia
M.

CHAPTER VII

AT LAST THE TIME HAD COME to take possession of our new home. After ten days of preparation, fresh colour-washing of walls both inside and out, tidying up of the garden, and generally leaving things, as he had said, according to his own taste, the old colonel had departed for Naples on the early boat, leaving the keys with a caretaker to hand over to us at our own sweet pleasure.

This opened a new chapter in our lives, the fulfilment of our hopes in coming to this beautiful island. We had enjoyed every moment of our stay at the Albergo del Porto, with its pageant of native life, but we could hardly contain our excitement and our impatience to be off.

Yet it was a day of mixed feelings, for it meant saying good-bye to the Bonifacios, who, especially Angelina and Mama, had welcomed us into their midst with much more than the rich resources of their store-cupboards and cellar. They had shown us a rare hospitality, opening their hearts to us, sharing in our disappointments and joys, aiding us with their invaluable advice, which constituted an indispensable passport to the ways of the island, treating us as privileged children of the family, and even finding us a cook who was waiting at the Villa Buonocuore to prepare our first dinner.

Of course, we should see them again whenever we came to the Port, and they promised to pay us a visit some day when they were not too busy, if such a day ever came. But our new home lay in the commune of Ischia Ponte, in the midst of a different population, and we knew that, although it was only a couple of miles away, invisible barriers of rivalry existed between the two communes and their respective inhabitants. In this sense we were moving into a new world.

We delayed our departure till late afternoon, when the sun was casting long shadows and the air was fresh from the sea. Judging from public attendance both at the start and finish of the short journey, it must have been the day's outstanding event. Grape-vine telegraphy is ancient history to the Ischians, who impart and derive most of life's news by its swift and inaccurate service. Nothing of any interest to the islanders occurs that is not immediately known from one end of Ischia to the other. Foreigners leaving the Albergo del Porto to take their permanent residence in a villa on the island was a spectacle worth knocking off work to see. All Ischia knew without doubt not only which villa we had taken, but how much we paid for it, and how much too much that was!

Although as many as six or eight youths, when they could muster between them the necessary fare, would wedge themselves inside a native *carrozza* for an evening drive up and down the street, there was really only room for two people and none whatever for luggage. Like most newly weds, we had arrived with an overwhelming amount of the latter, adding to it steadily during our stay on the island. Nothing less than five *carrozze* proved sufficient for the move.

With a long experience of processions, our Ischian coachmen knew instinctively how this one was to be conducted. When we were informed that everything was ready, and we emerged at last from the house, accompanied by most of the Bonifacio family, the five carriages were standing in a row, four of them piled high with our belongings, but with the middle one vacant and neatly drawn up before the door. In this manner we had both a vanguard and a rearguard as well as a compact mass of onlookers on the opposite side of the street.

Amid waving handkerchiefs and waving hands, and with a great cracking of whips, we drove off at a furious pace, nothing less than breakneck speed being in keeping with the occasion, rumbling and clattering over the uneven cobblestones, swaying violently, clutching at each other and viewing with the gravest anxiety our mountains of luggage as they rocked, heaved, and tottered, yet somehow miraculously kept their balance.

At a certain moment in our progress we came to a halt; the coachmen drew in their reins and, springing from their seats, seized their horses' heads. We had come to the place where our route left the main road to follow a narrow alley leading to the sea and to our house. It bore the sonorous name of Via Rougemont, but the word *via* was purely a courtesy title, for nothing in the world could more inappropriately have been termed a road. Large chunks of lava rock jutted from the centre of it, forming a miniature mountain range complete with crevasses, landslides, and desolate valleys where dishwater from the neighbouring fishermen's houses lurked in grey lakes.

Nimbly, like mountain chamois, the horses picked their way over the obstacles placed by Nature to impede our progress, pulling the unwilling carriages that groaned and writhed on their meagre springs. In contrast to the black outlook underfoot, strings of gaily coloured underclothes, product of the day's washing, flapped jauntily overhead. Their owners, who at the sound of our approaching caravan had assembled on their doorsteps, pointed gleefully at our vanguard of luggage, and, when our turn came, shouted a lusty *'Buona sera!'* with as much cordial simplicity as though we had always lived among them.

At the bottom of this excruciating lane was a little piazza, where we were forced to alight and continue on foot down a still narrower path to the water's edge. This we did with pleasure. Suddenly we had stepped into a new world, a world of undisturbed peace, stately umbrella pines, smooth yellow sands, the unruffled loveliness of deep blue sea. To the right, its gate wide open, our home stood ready to welcome us.

When the coachmen had been paid off and the caravan had departed, Kit and I, hand in hand, made a rapid, excited tour of inspection. We wandered through the high vaulted rooms where everything was spick and span and smelt wholesomely of fresh paint and whitewash, where everything was cool and peaceful. From the loggia, with its tall graceful arches, flanked in Florentine style by little orange-trees in terra-cotta pots, we looked out across the garden, where the mellow late afternoon sun was casting long shadows over the other little house by the sea. Covered with wistaria in bloom, cool and inviting, it looked like a little temple to Bacchus and the god of spaghetti, whoever he may be.

At that moment we caught sight of a figure in the

doorway, waddling toward us. It was Mary, the cook. Her presence came as a shock, for we had forgotten all about her. One glance was sufficient to convince us that Mary was a blot upon the landscape, an intruder in our peaceful paradise. It was not her excessive fat, her *bella grassa, grassa*, so dear to the Ischian male heart, an attribute so pleasantly demonstrated in the Bonifacio family, that disturbed us. It was not even her ugly face, whose prolific hairiness found vent in nasty little spurts of beard that grew in patches to incredible length. It was everything about her. In a word, she was not *simpatica*.

In our first words of conversation, she informed us that she had spent a year in America, at 'Brokolino' (Brooklyn), and was consequently well acquainted with the ways of foreigners, in whose honour she had changed her name from Maria to Mary. She spoke English to the extent of one word: nice, which she elongated to a wheezy, greasy 'naeece,' and she enjoyed the sound of it so much that she refused to speak or understand her native tongue.

What did this matter, provided she stayed in the kitchen and turned out the usual variety of savoury island dishes? She could cook, couldn't she? Kit asked suddenly. Mary heaved her bulk in a succession of miniature convulsions and replied, 'Naeece.' Kit left her to prepare whatever she thought best for this first evening's supper. The cook problem was the only difficult one, it seemed, in Ischia. Most of the native ladies had their own families to attend to, and, even if they did not have other mouths to feed, the fact that they were ladies made it impossible for them to cook for other people. Mary, having been to America, was, however, emancipated, and, according to the Bonifacios, we were lucky to get her.

By the time we had cleared the loggia of our luggage and

87

unpacked in a leisurely way, interrupted by much sitting down and talking as well as by an occasional cigarette, we were quite pleasantly prepared for Mary's raucous summons to table.

It was rather a bare-looking table, as our dining-room linen was not yet finished. Soup plates, kitchen glasses, and tin spoons sat bleakly upon the plain wooden surface, but what did such details matter to two healthy, hungry, and happy mortals, ready to do justice to a hearty meal? Did I say two? We saw with horror that the table was laid for three. Mary was evidently going to eat with us.

Oh, no, she wasn't! Kit's authority as mistress in her new house made that quite clear. Grabbing the third party's utensils, she marched into the kitchen and deposited them firmly where they belonged. Mary did not mind; she was good-tempered and patient with our idiosyncrasies, and thought that we should probably feel better after we had eaten our share of the big dish of steaming macaroni she set before us. She was to be disillusioned, and so, alas, were we. Accustomed to the succulent cooking of Mama Bonifacio, we had thought that all the islanders were born chefs. This was plain boiled macaroni, as free from artifice as a new-born baby, macaroni without seasoning, without butter, without tomato sauce. To make matters worse, it was almost raw. Frankly, it was hostile and refractory to all advances.

Mary, sent for in a hurry, was pained but not put out. That toughness we complained of constituted a great Neapolitan delicacy, she said. It.was *ardente*; one felt it between the teeth; it was the only real way to cook it. 'Naeece,' she concluded.

'Well,' we said, realising that further discussion was futile, 'bring in the next course.'

Mary looked blank, then burst out laughing. Next course?

There was no next course. She sat down on the vacant chair we had failed to remove and fanned herself with the straw-plaited fan used for the charcoal fire. She was perspiring freely. 'An old Neapolitan proverb . . .' she began.

'Mary, get out!' we yelled. 'Get out!'

Puffing, she heaved herself to her feet; she was really hurt. She made for the kitchen, then her better nature got the upper hand. Her broad whiskered face lit up with a warm smile. She stopped, turned to Kit, and with a greasy forefinger chucked her under the chin. 'Naeece,' she said, and bounced out of the room.

We took refuge from our stormy emotions by unpacking a bundle of sheets and pillow-cases and making our beds. We did not relish the thought of Mary's fat, dirty hands smoothing down our beautiful new linen. Mary would have to go. That fact required no lengthy discussion. Her out-standing characteristics were too overpowering for us, and, besides, we needed a cook. She did not sleep in, having her family in the village, and it was with a sigh of satisfaction that we saw her large black bulk ambulate from the kitchen, where she had been grieving at our ingratitude, and dis-appear through the gate into the night. At least, this first night we were going to have our home to ourselves. When morning came, some solution would surely be found to our difficulties, and with this sublime confidence we turned in.

At first we did not notice it, then we sensed that the exquisite freshness of our sheets was not entirely natural; they were, in fact, wringing wet from their recent hurried laundering. Had it not been for our slightly feverish con-dition over Mary's vagaries when we made the beds, we should probably have noticed the fact. There was nothing to do but to remove them. We remembered two brightly coloured table-covers we had bought in Capri; they were pure wool, woven in stripes of every conceivable hue, and, like everybody else, we had bought them because they were picturesque, not knowing what to do with them. In this crisis they became very useful. We wrapped ourselves in them and lay down again to capture sleep. Kit had just succeeded in doing so when there was a terrific crash. Jumping up, I saw her startled eyes peering up at me from the floor. Her bed had collapsed, and it required only a glance to know why. The spring mattress rested by a neat trick of balance on the two ends of the bed, like logs on andirons, but not so securely. We had ruthlessly violated this fine adjustment in making the beds, so that, like the mousetrap, it had required only one incautious movement to bring about disaster.

With odds and ends of string we tied the unwilling parts together, and as a further measure of precaution did the same to mine.

For the third time we were ready to retire, but by then we were so wide awake that we had to resort to scientific methods to lull us to sleep. We lay flat on our backs, closed our eyes, breathed deeply, and relaxed. Instead of sheep, we counted goats, these being the island's most popular animals. At last, in despair, we indulged in a little Couéism with as much conviction as we could muster, but our efforts were in vain. Finally we sat up and decided to make the best of things. Why waste time lying awake? Let sleep sulk by itself in the corner while we explored the night.

Kit clad in her nightgown and I in my pyjamas, we pushed open the tall shutters of the French windows on to the loggia and walked out into the soft radiance beyond. The moon was low over the water, its waning light mellow like the patina of old ivory. The water had lost its inky blackness, becoming silvery, and on the horizon appeared faint streaks of colour. On hurried wings the night was swiftly flying from the pursuing dawn.

Crossing the garden, we climbed up the crumbling steps to the terrace above the dining-room and listened to the waves lapping gently against the base of the walls. Out at sea the big fishing-boats were drawing in their nets under the light of their powerful lamps. Suddenly, and so silently that we did not hear it approach, one of these boats glided by almost at our feet, manned by four stalwart youths, who in true Mediterranean fashion rowed forward and standing up, with a rhythmic splash of their long oars. They were returning home from their night's work, tired and silent.

Suddenly also the water tempted us. Down from the terrace we scrambled, and through the gate on to our private beach. There, shedding our few clothes, we plunged into the sea. It was Kit's element, for she is a splendid swimmer. No sooner had she felt the contact of the water than she was out of sight, leaving me puffing and blowing in the background while she turned somersaults gaily, stood on her head, disappeared to reappear in totally unexpected places, her laughter ringing out clear and fresh in the morning air, performing these aquatics as joyfully and gracefully as a dolphin.

Had our private beach not been surrounded on three sides by high walls, our exit in the nude and our dash for the house would have been a little *risqué*, for the Ischians were early risers. Invigorated more than by eight hours' sleep, we dressed and descended once more to the little house by the water's edge, this time to make ourselves some breakfast. It was half past four, the sun was well above the horizon, and all the island was golden. We lit a little charcoal fire, and, while I fanned it into a nice blaze, Kit prepared coffee. Never did its rich aroma smell more deliciously.

ISLAND IN THE SUN

On a round stone table beneath the pergola, surrounded by grape-vines and a riot of wild morning-glory, we breakfasted on black coffee and hot buttered toast, happy and proud of our achievement as only two inexperienced dabblers in the art of cooking could be. The whole world seemed suffused in golden splendour.

It had been a glorious night after all.

CHAPTER VIII

FROM KIT'S DIARY

. . . MARY ARRIVED about four hours after our early morning breakfast. She was wheezily amused to think we had done the cooking ourselves. I still clung to the belief that so large a woman must have some use (though G., at my elbow, was muttering, 'Sack her! Go on and sack her!'), so I asked her if she would do our laundry as well as the cooking. She looked surprised. Her tiny black eyes gleamed with reproach.

'*Signora!*' she said, heavily indignant, 'how could you expect poor me to do any washing with a stomach like mine? Why, I can't even get near enough to the wash-tub to reach the water!'

Sacking her was easy; she thought it a fine joke, like everything else we did or said, chucked me once more under the chin and waddled away. Probably she was glad to go back to her own house, where she could sit and fan her moist bulk

93

in peace, with no foolish foreigners to make demands on her.

As the gate clanged shut behind her, a sense of peace descended on our house. But my mind wasn't altogether easy. I'm not much of a cook, and I had no desire to experiment on anyone as important to me as G.

I spread our wet sheets out in the sun and worried quietly.

After a while the garden bell rang, and G. let in a lanky, pale boy, seventeen or eighteen years old, in a black suit a good many sizes too large for him and no collar. He was wriggling with embarrassment.

" I am Giovangiuseppe!" he announced tremulously.

Well, we asked, what of it? We weren't in a soft mood.

He wanted, he said, to become our *cameriere*, a glorified name for a waiter and general handy-man. He had never been in service; he'd always worked in his father's vineyards in the village of Fiaiano up in the hills, but ever since he could remember he had cherished the one ambition: to become a *cameriere*. He would serve us devotedly, he said, with or without pay. (This I did not believe, but as an argument it was attractive, of course.) I was rather touched by this tremulous eloquence, but G., made of sterner stuff, was severely practical.

'Listen!' he said impressively. 'What good is a *cameriere* to us since we have no cook? Now, I will make a bargain with you, Giovangiuseppe. If you can find us a cook – a good cook, mind you, who knows how to make something better than underdone spaghetti – and if you can bring her here in time to cook our midday meal, we will engage you both and give you a fair trial. If you are satisfactory . . . But there's time to talk of that later.'

After a minute's frowning concentration Giovangiuseppe gave a flashing, reassuring smile, said a cheerful '*Arrivederci*,' and disappeared through the garden gate.

It wasn't more than an hour before he was back again, all his timidity forgotten in the new importance of being aide-de-camp to a foreign family. After him came a short, rather fat woman, not very young, with a mop of short black curls and big black eyes.

'This is Dominica!' announced the boy proudly.

'*Buon giorno, signori*,' said Dominica. She had a gentle, husky voice, and kept her eyes steadily on the ground.

Giovangiuseppe expatiated on his find, as though she were not there, and also rather as though he had created her himself for our especial benefit. She was the most celebrated cook on the island, he said, and rattled off a string of superlatives – *fantasiosa, mondiale, bravissima* – which, at the moment, we were in no mood to believe.

When he had finished, Dominica held out the basket she was carrying. 'I stopped in the market, *signora*,' she said, 'and bought a few little things for your dinner. I hope it was not a liberty.'

Then she went quietly down the steps into the kitchen, and soon I heard her shovelling charcoal into the tiny box grates of the stove, and before long the garden was sweetened by the most beautiful smells of cooking.

Giovangiuseppe, meanwhile, was bustling about in shirt-sleeves. I heard sounds of water being drawn from the well, of sweeping; I found our beds neatly made and the clothes we had taken off for our swim folded tidily on a chair. When he heard that our table-linen had not yet arrived, he darted out of the gate and came back a minute later with a spotless cloth of rough, home-woven linen, borrowed who knows where, and laid the table in our marine dining-room.

At one o'clock he announced, still with a slight wriggle, 'We are ready at table, *signori*.'

I descended on my husband's arm, and we sat down to a

95

meal that no words can describe. There was a plate of eggs, stuffed with savoury herbs and spices, then a vast platter of little fresh anchovies, dipped in a light batter and fried until each fish puffed up into a superlative small balloon. Roast kid followed, with delicious fresh vegetables, after which there came a salad with just the right amount of garlic, a great bowl of fruits, and cups of strong black coffee.

When he was not serving us, Giovangiuseppe stood stiffly to attention by the kitchen door, looking, in his old clothes, as little as possible like a butler. Of Dominica there was no sign, but once or twice I saw the bright gleam of an eye through a crack in the kitchen door; she wanted to know what reception we were giving to her 'few little things.'

We never believed that such a halcyon state of domestic affairs could continue. Life at home had destroyed our faith, if indeed our generation wasn't born without such a thing, in the satisfactoriness of servants. But, with the exception of a few interesting ups and down about which I will write later, Giovangiuseppe and Dominica continue to be perfect.

The boy has become butler, gentleman-chambermaid, valet, gardener, and handy-man. He is a whirlwind of activity; he sweeps with fine enthusiasm the house, the garden, the roofs; he waters the garden, and waters, too, for coolness, the clean tiled floors of all the rooms. And he has learned that devastating, nerve-racking method of serving us at table, holding platters and dishes high up in the air on three fingers in the best *wagon-lit* style. We have had a few suits of white duck made for him; he keeps them immaculate, and the poor country lad of a few weeks ago is transformed into quite a dashing figure.

We pay them each about thirty shillings a month; this is considered princely on the island. The only extra item is the allowance of a quart of wine a day, to which they are

From the garden gate of our new home it was framed
in all its medieval beauty

p. 105

each entitled by an unwritten law. That the letter of this law isn't always observed we have already discovered. Only to-day Giovangiuseppe came, breathing hard and full of the self-righteous indignation to which I am afraid he is rather addicted, to tell the master of a horrid crime on the part of Dominica. That barrel of wine that the *signore* had bought only ten days ago from the *illustrissimo* Cavaliere Bonifacio. It was gone! Gone? G. asked. Well, he had meant to say that the barrel was still there, but its contents had disappeared. When he had gone to fill our decanter for dinner he had found the barrel quite dry.

We were more intrigued than angry. The local barrels hold forty-four litres – about twelve or thirteen gallons. Of that we have drunk not more than a bottle or two, having laid in a special red wine for ourselves. Giovangiuseppe, Dominica admitted placidly when I questioned her, drank nothing but water. So the fact emerges that she alone has disposed of an average of four and a half quarts of wine a day. This is all the more remarkable because we have never seen her looking drunk. The only indication of the number of bottles consumed seems to be an increase of imagination in her always excellent cooking.

In spite of costing us more in this way – though, as the price of wine is only a penny a quart, even this ten days' indulgence has not been very expensive – Dominica is more than worth her thirty shillings a month to us.

She sleeps at her own home, gets up at four-thirty in the morning, and goes to the market to do our day's shopping. This is a duty that no 'lady' may undertake without loss of caste, though possibly this social significance is only an out-crop of the undeniable fact that no lady is physically fitted for the fierce strife of the open-air market, where fixed prices are unknown, and success in the pitched battles of bargaining depends mainly on lung-power and dogged tenacity; also, I think, not a little on one's talents as an actor, for there's a great technique in the art of bargaining; the simulated amazement and anger at the opponent's tactics, the feigned departures in search of another vendor, the protestations at any price a *soldo* over one's limit. Italians excel in these exercises and enjoy them.

Dominica is full of pride in the pennies she has saved when, every evening, she dictates her long list of minute purchases to me. She cannot write, and perhaps on that account has developed a prodigious memory. Often her shopping-list will have twenty or thirty items: a halfpenny for six lemons, a farthing for a cornucopia of pepper, twopence for the fish we ate for dinner, and so on. Each item is the monument to a colossal vocal struggle which is retold to me as I sit in the dining-room doing accounts, while she stands near by.

Besides these duties, she does our washing to perfection. Yet she never appears to be hurried. Most often I see her standing in front of her stove, fanning it gently and singing the melancholy songs that they love so well around Naples. But the work is always done, and well done. So far she has refused to take even an afternoon off, though I, being used to another sort of servant, have urged her to. She merely answered politely that it was more 'wearing' to get ready and go out than to stay quietly at her work in the kitchen.

Dominica is not a beauty. She has, as the novelists say, 'more than a suspicion of a moustache' on her upper lip, and it extends generously, moreover, on to her chin. We have noticed this with special interest because of its periodic character. Through the week it is allowed to develop unchecked, but on Saturday night, some time between our supper and the time she goes home, a metamorphosis occurs in the kitchen, and she emerges to say good night to us with smooth cheeks and chin, and a layer of white powder – flour maybe – spread thickly over her red face, giving it a curious lavender tinge.

She has a talent for story-telling. I remarked once that she was the only woman on the island I had seen with short hair. At that she recounted a dramatic tale of how she had been, one day, on the roof terrace of her sister's house with a little niece, when the child had clambered on to the balustrade, and, before the horrified Dominica could reach her, had fallen into the void below. Terror for her fate had given Dominica what she called a 'strong displeasure,' and the result was that all her hair, which seems to have borne the burden of the shock, dropped out. 'Leaving me like an egg, *signora!*' she ended with tragic eyes. The child, of tougher fibre, landed on the cobblestones but was none the worse for it.

Another day I had the story of her infancy. Her father, it seems, deserted her mother when Dominica was only a month old, emigrating to America, the Mecca of all Italians. One cannot help understanding his behaviour, even while not approving it, for the mother is a truly villainous-looking old woman with a single yellow fang, black beady eyes, and a great bulk of a body. The only reason we can find for liking her is that she always addresses us by the satisfying title of 'Excellency.'

With the desertion of the father, the maternal milk also vanished, and the babe Dominica, pining and wailing, refused to take any other nourishment. She grew daily thinner; everyone gave her up for lost. On the day when her strength was almost exhausted, she was left lying somewhere in the kitchen – probably, considering the length of a month-old arm, on the stove itself. When no one was looking, the feeble creature stretched out a minute hand which, from accident or design, encountered a casserole that was steaming near by. From it the indomitable infant plucked a potato, and, under the amazed eyes of her mother, proceeded to eat it.

From that minute the tide turned and the babe was saved. She flourished. She lived mostly on haricot beans.

'I tell you this, *signora*,' said Dominica respectfully, 'because it may be useful to you when your own *piccolo* comes.'

CHAPTER IX

ALTHOUGH GEOGRAPHICALLY the Villa Buonocuore was situated half way between the Port and the old town of Ischia, it was in reality in the latter's territory. Dominica was a native of the old town, and our entire economic life, from the purchase of olive-oil to shoe-strings, depended upon its resources. Henceforth our destinies were also linked with it.

We had taken many drives and walks in the course of our house-hunting, yet, though we were so near, we had never made the acquaintance of the town that gave its name to the island, except for a fleeting glimpse of it from the motor-boat the afternoon of our arrival from Capri. After we were settled in our new home, it was natural that our first walk should have led us there.

From our house there were two ways of setting out. One was to retrace our steps up the narrow alley past our garden wall and on to the main road, and the other way was along the beach. We chose the latter because it looked more picturesque.

In contrast to the vast deserted beach on the other side of our villa, this approach to the old town was thickly populated. Along one side of it, apparently built on the soft sand but no doubt on a solid rock foundation, was a long row of fishermen's houses painted every colour of the rainbow, and, sandwiched in between them, an ancient little chapel.

Drawn up almost to their front doors were the great sturdy fishing-boats, even more gaily painted than the houses. Their prows, which rose curiously to a tall slender column of wood, were characteristic of all Ischian boats, remnants and wholly unconscious symbols of the ancient phallic cult practised by the Phœnicians when they were masters of this part of the Mediterranean.

The Ischians took great pride in the beauty of their boats, in their slender graceful shape, and not only kept them in excellent repair, but were perpetually lavishing fresh coats of paint upon them. Each was a galaxy of colour, the hull being one colour, the interior another, while around the edge ran a frieze of several contrasting shades blending perfectly with the general scheme.

At first sight they looked alike, but upon closer examination – and nothing gives an Ischian fisherman more pleasure than that you should admire his boat – we saw that no two were the same. Each family had its own particular scheme of colours, as distinguishing as a coat of arms. The names, in large letters under the prow, were equally picturesque. The Virgin Mary and the saints, who are innumerable, claimed a good share, but here and there, in place of a name, good sound Ischian philosophy appeared in such quotations as, 'Ask no questions and you will be told no lies,' or, again, 'Occupy thyself with thy own affairs,' both of which were revealing tributes to the island's insatiable love of gossip.

These fishermen of the old town were truly wedded to

their boats. Not only did they spend the greater part of their twenty-four hours in them, trying to wrest a miserable living from the increasingly understocked Mediterranean, but their leisure moments were spent in leaning against them in groups, smoking and discussing their mutual luck. As these boats represented considerable capital, and required from four to eight men to row them, the sons joined their father in his enterprise, and, if there were not sufficient sons, the vacancies were easily filled from the unlimited supply of brothers-in-law, cousins, and other relations.

Here and there, scattered over the beach, men were busy plaiting reed lobster-pots, or mending the long nets which also represented important capital, and, further on, others were dying new nets. Over wood fires sheltered from the wind, big cauldrons were filled with a boiling concoction of tree bark and tannin, and into this mixture the nets, which were the natural colour of flax, were plunged, emerging a deep russet brown. This dye not only remained permanent, but protected them during their long immersion in the water. On high poles they were hung out to dry in the hot sun, and their strong, pungent odour mingled not unpleasantly with the salty air.

From the men we talked to, it looked as if the future would be no less hard than the present, and the present was hard enough. Often the total haul of one big boat barely filled one small basket, which, at the market, did not fetch even sufficient *soldi* to buy the family's meagre rations of bread and tomatoes, which was what the poorest lived on. As there were no seasons when fishing was either restricted or prohibited, the poor fishes, unlike the Ischians, had little opportunity to procreate and rear large, healthy families. As each year saw a noticeable decrease in the haul and a noticeable increase in the number of future fishermen, one could well understand that the islanders felt some anxiety for their livelihood.

Yet to us, the most remarkable thing about the island was the absence of beggars. We had not come across a single one, young or old, although the population was desperately poor. Accustomed to the hordes of children, studiously attired in rags, who in Capri fastened themselves on us and on everybody else, whimpering miserably for *un soldo* and only to be shaken off upon payment of a ransom, this was a great surprise. More than ever we were glad that the sophisticated tourist traffic and the so-called benefits of modern civilisation had passed Ischia by, and that these simple, generous people had not yet learned, among other unpleasant tricks, that it was more profitable to beg than to do an honest day's work.

At the end of the beach, a path joining the main road from the Port led up to the old town. Like the Port, its activities were centred on the main street, with its shops, cafés, and churches, its colourful crowd of barefooted peasants, mules saddled with wine-barrels, baskets of fruit and fish and all the island products. Unlike the Port, however, Ischia Ponte, as the old town was called, showed many signs of former splendour, great gaunt *palazzi* better meriting the name than the pretentious modern buildings erected by the few prosperous Ischians. One of these was the Archbishop's palace and another was a seminary. Through their stern portals we caught glimpses of slender wrought-iron gates, and, beyond these, of abandoned gardens full of orange-trees and wild morning-glory.

At the end of the town, after a short bend, we came suddenly face to face with the castle. On its jagged, isolated rock, joined to the island by a long narrow causeway, it was magnificent. Although we had often seen it from a distance –

and, indeed, from the garden gate of our new home it was framed in all its medieval beauty – this was the first time we had seen it at such close quarters.

Dominating the old town at its feet, dominating the entire panorama, this fantastic ruin, crowning the summit of precipitous rock that fell on three sides sheer into deep water, was a beautiful and impressive sight. Apart from this, it was the nucleus of the island's interest, its one undying claim to fame, for this castle, and above all the rock it occupied so grandly, boasted a history that no other in this ancient land could rival.

According to legend, Ischia was the island where Ulysses, on his way home to a far too patient Penelope, dallied for seven years with Nausicaa, and in recent years a well-known French archæologist has produced a monumental work to prove that, contrary to the accepted theory, Homer had Ischia and not Corfu in mind when he mapped out his hero's immortal journey, thereby giving good foundation to the belief.

Whatever legendary fame Ulysses and Nausicaa may have conferred upon the castle rock, it is certain that, as far back as a thousand one hundred years before Christ, the Phœnicians founded upon it a colony, leaving profound traces in the blood of subsequent populations. In 474 B.C. the advantages of this rock as an inaccessible stronghold were again recognised by the famous Geronimo of Syracuse, who held it and the island in the name of Greece, and added Grecian blood to its Phœnician strain. In both cases the rock held not only the ruler's palace, but an entire town, which was the chief and possibly the only settlement on the island. As in those days there was no causeway, it formed an independent citadel which was safe from all attack.

When Greece in turn succumbed to the might of Rome,

the island sank into oblivion, passing finally as private property into the hands of Augustus, who, finding it too large for a playground, exchanged it for Capri. With the fall of the Empire, Ischia shared the same turbulent fate as the mainland. Its stronghold was first seized by the Saracens, those fierce Mussulman invaders, already masters of Spain and Sicily, who were rapidly conquering the Mediterranean for the glory of Islam, and later by the Normans of the Third Crusade, for whom the Pope sent in a hurry to drive them out.

When these Crusaders made themselves kings of Naples and Sicily, founding the dynasties of Anjou and Aragon as a self-conferred reward for their successful campaigns, Ischia re-entered the limelight. Upon the rock that had been the site of Phœnician, Greek, Roman, Saracen, and Norman splendour, Alphonso I of Aragon built in 1441 the medieval castle whose ruins are still standing. He also built the first causeway joining it to the island, and, following the example of his predecessors, he re-created an entire citadel complete with churches, monasteries, convents, barracks, and the inevitable dungeons. By this time the island had become well populated; an important medieval town had sprung up by the sea, and the castle citadel was chiefly intended as a place of refuge in such dire extremes as invasions, cholera epidemics, or a possible eruption of the then still active volcano, the Monte Epomeo.

The days of invasions were not over, and in 1541 the dreaded Turkish corsair, Barbarossa, admiral of the fleet of the Sultan Souliman the Magnificent, gave the Christian world as much cause for panic as the Saracens had done. His real name, Cheir-ed-Din, was unpronounceable to the Italians, and he became known as Barbarossa on account of his flaming red beard. He pillaged the coast, carrying off the pick of the population – the men as slaves, the girls as candidates for the harems of his royal master and his own. Compared with Naples in flames and Capri almost completely depopulated, Ischia suffered little; that is, if one leaves out the feelings of the four hundred men and women he removed from the island as hostages.

In spite of its great past, the castle of Ischia's chief claim to fame to-day is its long association with that most brilliant woman of the Renaissance, Vittoria Colonna, the friend of Michelangelo, who in 1501 was married here to Don Ferrante d'Avalos, and who for sixteen years as his wife, and for a further eleven years as his widow, made it her chief residence. Descendant by birth from one of the oldest, richest, and most powerful princely families of the Peninsula, she became the outstanding literary figure of her age; her sonnets were read throughout the courts of Europe, and the prestige she gained as a poet, added to her great social position, enabled her to assemble around her on this isolated rock some of the most brilliant people of her time.

Against the background of this sleepy little white town it was almost impossible for us to imagine the pageantry of the past, but as we walked slowly across the long causeway, and the great mass of the castle loomed up nearer and nearer, it became intensely real. As we passed through the first gate on to the rock, we felt at once that this had been a world of its own.

Everywhere there were ruins, but ruins on a gigantic scale that spelt unlimited fantasy, unlimited wealth, and unlimited labour. Battlemented walls, deserted grass-grown courts, barracks and guard-rooms, occupied the base of the rock. Looking up its almost perpendicular sides, we could see, at the distorted angle of a skyscraper viewed from the street, the castle and the citadel at a great height above us, and with no apparent means of approach. A little further on, however, we came face to face with a high, narrow gate hewn out of the rock, and leading into a cavern-like obscurity. As we passed through this second gate, a long, winding, tunnelled ascent became dimly visible.

The ascent was an easy one, with long wide steps over which horses could go, and must, indeed, have often been ridden. High up in the roof of the passage, through narrow slits overgrown by shrubs, a soft green light filtered. Here a great stillness reigned, and there was in the air a dank chill. Our senses were awed, for here lingered, not one past, but an infinity of pasts, the rise and fall of three thousand years of human might.

Riding up by the side of his young bride, Don Ferrante d'Avalos must have promised her a surprise when they reached the top, the same surprise that awaited us. Suddenly we emerged from this tunnel in the rock to find ourselves on a crenated terrace high above the sea, with Ischia Ponte, a neat little array of white cubes across a stretch of indigo water, at our feet. On the island a little apart from the old town stood the ancient tower commonly called Torre di Michelangelo, because, according to the islanders, the great sculptor came there to live in order to be able to look up at the castle where the woman he loved resided. Charming as it sounds, there is not a particle of evidence to prove that he ever set foot on the island, and the friendship that united them dated from later years, when Vittoria Colonna had withdrawn to a convent in Rome.

The terrace where we stood was not the summit of the rock; it was only half way up. We climbed a last dizzy flight of steps and sank down gratefully in the shade of an olive-tree to look around. What a marvellous site to live upon! But also what a sad, dilapidated, crumbled, twisted, distorted mass of ruins! It looked like the combined efforts of an earthquake and an air-raid. Out of the conglomeration of buildings, hardly one stood complete. Where walls existed, roofs were missing, the fallen masonry being scattered on the ground. Gaunt empty windows stared vacantly at us as much as to ask why on earth we had come up all that way to look at them. On every side were terraces, courtyards, archways, parts of houses, all decayed and abandoned. The actual castle, clinging to the extremity of the precipice, stood on a still higher level, and to our surprise it appeared to be the only existing relic of the Renaissance. The other buildings had evidently been restored in the eighteenth century, which in southern Italy was an unfortunate age of pink and white stucco, the work of the last lords of Ischia, and hopelessly out of keeping with its medieval approach.

While we sat gazing over this depressing scene, a sheepish, watery-eyed youth advanced out of nowhere with a book of tickets in his hand, and informed us that we could have the pleasure of being shown over the place for the price of two lire apiece. This, he explained hastily, was the Government tax. Tax on what, we could not imagine; it could certainly not have been for the preservation of the ruins. The panorama alone was, however, worth the price, so we paid our money, wondering if the Government would ever see it, and fell into step behind our guide.

He showed us a whitewashed church where Vittoria had been married; he took us down into endless crypts and dungeons, along endless subterranean passages to the accompaniment of showers of falling masonry. He asked Kit politely if she was about to become a mother, and, on being informed that this was not the case, took us to see the burial-place of the nuns. This was an underground chamber in pitch blackness, where, with the aid of a match and an old newspaper, he showed us how their bodies had been propped up on stone seats with holes in the centre, so that, when they had sufficiently decayed, their flesh fell through, leaving the dry skeletons, still clothed in their habits, rigidly upright.

Our guide was a thorough one. 'Leave no stone unturned' was evidently his golden rule. After we had walked through miles of ruins, internal, external, subterranean, and above-ground, we begged him to take us to some nice terrace as far as possible from all this decayed grandeur, where we could feast our eyes on the panorama. His face registered disgust at our lack of historical appreciation, but, as this was compensated for by the prospect of a tip, he promptly led the way into the sunshine.

The place where he finally took us was very beautiful indeed. We sat on the ground, propped our weary backs against a tree, and stretched our aching legs over a parapet into the void. We offered our youth a cigarette and asked him if he showed many people around, and he admitted that he did not. Foreigners were rare, and Ischians, he said, had no interest in antiquities. I could not imagine the Bonifacio family toiling all the way up, to pay two perfectly good lire when they got to the top, if they ever did. Then how did he come to accept such a job, we asked him, and where did he live? He looked at us in surprise. Surely we did not think he was a mere guide! That rôle he assumed when the occasion demanded, just out of kindness to the Government. He was secretary to the owner of the castle, and resided permanently there.

What! we exclaimed incredulously. Was it possible that this jumbled heap of ruins belonged to someone, and above all to someone who actually lived among them? Our eyes turned to the castle standing above and aloof from the rest, and we conjured up visions of an old and impoverished nobleman, a last descendant of the princely house of Avalos, loth to abandon his tragic heritage. The guide, who had followed our gaze, shook his head and pointed to a tiny house which had escaped our notice in the mass of ruins. The story he told us was an extraordinary one.

The owner was in no way descended from the lords of Ischia, but was a native of the island, of peasant stock and a lawyer. He had bought the castle and the entire rock from the Government as a speculation. That was before the war, when the country was full of wealthy *forestieri*, and Capri, under German tutelage, was at the height of its prosperity. Directors of a big German hotel company were scouring the Bay of Naples for a spectacular site upon which to build a super-palace hotel. They came to Ischia, set eyes on the castle, saw in its fantastic ruins and in the island's unspoilt beauty all the elements of success. They would turn Ischia into a second Capri and these grim relics of the past into a gold-mine.

When the news of the project leaked out, as such things do, this Ischian lawyer conceived the brilliant idea of stepping in first, buying it from the Government, and reselling it to the German hotel company at a huge profit. For twenty-five thousand lire – then the equivalent of a thousand pounds – he could secure the title to it. It was a paltry sum, but he was far from possessing it. However, he was not a lawyer for nothing. By a small first payment, the castle became legally his, and long before the second instalment became due he would have realised, as the guide said, a profit of several millions on it.

He would have done, yes – if things had gone differently. But that was in 1914. A few months later war had broken out, and, although Italy was not yet involved in it, the German hotel company promptly vanished. The gold-mine was metamorphosed back into a grey, lonely mass of ruins, and now it was a millstone around his neck. As the time approached for his second payment to the Government the consequences of his wild gamble became terrifying. At last, in despair, he shot himself. The bullet did not kill him. It blinded him.

That was long ago; in some way the Government's claim was settled and the blind man became undisputed master of the castle. By selling old iron from the crumbling buildings, it was said that he had even recovered the purchase price, but at what a penalty! With this youth to look after him, he lived in two whitewashed rooms salvaged from the surrounding wreckage.

This story obsessed us all the way down from the castle. Was this the vengeance of the proud spirits who, for thirty centuries, had held sway over this mighty rock, vengeance upon this Ischian upstart who had tried to sell these venerable ruins for a vulgar speculation? Or was it merely an indifferent and ironical Fate which gave this once magnificent dwelling to such a master? One thing at least was certain: the castle would never suffer the disgrace from which it had so narrowly escaped, for the Government had finally decreed it a national monument.

With the swiftness peculiar to the south, night had fallen when we stepped out again on to the causeway. Looking up once more at the great deserted mass of masonry, we could just see the flickering light of a candle in a window.

CHAPTER X

IN SPITE OF THEIR FLOWERY SPEECH, it often struck us that the Ischians had more accurate descriptive powers than we did. Thus, Kit having explained to Dominica the northern mystery of the poached egg, a mystery which she solved to perfection after the first trial, it became known as egg *a l'occhio di bue* or bull's-eye egg. On little *canapés* of hot buttered toast, they formed part of our morning breakfast on the loggia, accompanied by delicious green and purple figs from the garden, island honey, and that excellent coffee which the Italians make so well everywhere except in hotels.

It was characteristic of Giovangiuseppe's inborn tact and psychology that he waited until we had finished breakfast before placing in front of me a summons to appear before the local police. Had he reversed the proceedings, I doubt if we should have enjoyed our breakfast as much.

Under dictatorial rule there are so many things beside ordinary vulgar crime for which you can be thrown into prison, and as, according to Italian law, you are considered guilty until you can prove your innocence, your stay there may be a long one. An unguarded remark about the head of the Government, a misinterpreted laugh overheard by a zealous listener at a café, are quite sufficient to get you into trouble, to say nothing of the failure to comply with the complicated regulations concerning the sojourn of foreigners in Italy.

About the latter we had done absolutely nothing since our arrival on the island. That we had forgotten the existence of the police was the greatest tribute we could pay to Ischia's unsophisticated charm, but what was the penalty going to be? It was evident that the authorities were fully acquainted with our arrival at the Albergo del Porto, our move to the Villa Buonocuore, and our failure to register our names with them, but this was not all. A grave irregularity in our papers made our case more serious.

We had both been residents in Italy before our marriage, and we both possessed the *permesso di soggiorno* which every foreigner is required to obtain and keep up to date. Although the wedding ceremony had been performed by an Italian general who was also a judge, and although Kit now possessed a new passport in her married name, we had failed to have her Italian permit altered. This vital paper still proclaimed her to be a maiden lady travelling in Italy for 'the benefit of study.' In the eyes of the Italian Government, we were living in sin. Failure to report to the police was bad enough; to be living under false pretences was far worse.

Once again, Giovangiuseppe showed how invaluable he could be in a crisis and how well he understood his compatriots. Although the *Municipio* was only a step away, he insisted on our arriving there in a carriage, and also upon accompanying us in order to carry our papers. Dressed in his immaculate white livery, he gave us to understand by his example that the occasion called also for our best clothes.

I think he would have preferred us in black, this being the correct Neapolitan attire for ceremonious affairs, but he was quite pleased when Kit added stockings and a hat to her usual costume, and I exchanged my bathing-suit for white flannels. To be entirely truthful, I put on the flannels over the bathing-suit in my hurry, perhaps with the subconscious hope that, if things came to the worst, we might be able to swim across the Mediterranean to safety.

The boy was right. His presence saved the day. Far from being a mark of servility, his livery became a distinguished uniform which not only raised him above the rank and file, but ensured for us a consideration we would not otherwise have commanded. Jumping down from his seat beside the coachman, and armed with our credentials, he proceeded with dignified efficiency to lead the way. The ropes were familiar to him, because, as he explained, his *fratello di latte* – his 'milk-brother' – worked at the *Municipio*. This was a unique Italian relationship, and implied that the person in question had been raised on his own mother's milk, a relationship which apparently created ties of everlasting gratitude.

In a large ante-room full of busy clerks we waited while he conversed in low tones with his peculiar relative and disappeared with him into an inner sanctum. After a minute he emerged beaming, and ushered us into the presence of an important official behind a desk, who motioned us to be seated. During the interview, Giovangiuseppe stood to attention by the door, in the same manner as he did when we were at table.

The official was grave but not unkind. He listened

patiently while I made pointed references to the marriage certificate and passports that lay open before him, and, when I had finished, he handed them back to me with the discouraging remark that they were of no importance whatever. 'This,' he said, waving Kit's old *permesso di soggiorno* in the air, 'this is everything.'

Humbly I agreed, begging him, even if it was so late, to give Kit a new one made out in her married name. Hardly were the words out of my mouth than he recoiled in horror, as though I had bribed him to set us free.

'Give her a new name?' he echoed incredulously. '*Macché, signore!* Utterly impossible! Change the address, yes, but the name . . . never!'

'But see,' I explained, 'she is no longer a *signorina*. She is married. Her name is . . .'

He held up his hand to command silence. Leaning forward, he fixed a penetrating pair of eyes upon me and, with devastating clearness, slowly asked, 'Was this lady born with a maiden name or was she not?' I had to admit that she was.

'*Ebbene.*' Like a barrister who has just gained a decisive point, he relaxed and smiled. 'Once born with a maiden name, she must live and die with it. That is the law,' he added simply.

Seeing our amazement, and taking it for a deep moral discouragement, he added paternally, 'Do not worry, *signore*; the marriage certificate . . . it justifies everything!' Hastily he scribbled our new address on the papers, motioned to our boy to carry them for us, and, bowing to us most affably, signified that the interview was at an end.

'A great and very strong lawyer; the finest on the island,' Giovangiuseppe told us on the way home.

So it was all over and we were free.

A day begun with such an upheaval could not end tamely, and before it was over we were to make the acquaintance of a force far mightier and, to the Ischians, far more frightening than the law.

That night I dreamed that we were floating on the crest of a wave. Up, up we went, then down, then up again. The wave grew bigger; we were swept higher and higher, until at last I awoke to find myself sitting bolt upright.

The beds were swaying from side to side; a large picture in a heavy gilt frame above my head swung out from the wall and gently back again; all the furniture became animate, creaking and muttering and querulously throwing its contents on to the floor. Suddenly the door flew open with a bang, started to shut again, and jammed.

Earthquake!

By the time I had roused Kit it was all over. The night was pitch black, but the luminous dial of the clock revealed a quarter to midnight. Standing before the tall French windows that opened on to the garden, we became aware of a distant, confused roar, like the muffled rumbling of traffic in a great city, and increasing in volume every second. Voices, thousands of voices, shrill and panic-stricken, talking at once. We realised that all the men, women, and children in the old town, and probably in every town and village on the island, had fled from their homes and were seeking refuge in the open. More than that, they were hurrying toward us, making for the beaches and probably for the boats. Mobs in revolutions must, we imagined, sound something like this. Excitement and terror were relieved by occasional laughter and snatches of song. Perhaps it was to give them courage; perhaps, being all together, they felt more in safety.

ISLAND IN THE SUN

The shock had been violent but short, and seemed hardly sufficient to warrant such an exodus. In any other place, it is doubtful if the population would have been so panic-stricken, but Ischia was different. On the island there was every reason for such behaviour. Although the volcano Epomeo had been extinct for over six centuries, the island was seething with subterranean forces of incredible violence, in many places held down only by a thin crust of earth. Boiling springs and boiling mud, sands and rocks that smoked, were ever-present reminders of what might happen if they broke loose; but, above all, most of the adult population remembered what had happened only forty years before.

Casamicciola, the big town beyond Porto d'Ischia, was literally buried, with the greater part of its inhabitants, in a combined earthquake and landslide which ranks as one of the worst disasters of its kind on the Peninsula. At that time this town was the best known on the island; its mud baths were much frequented not only by Italians but also by foreigners, and there were several hotels. Terrible scenes were witnessed during the earthquake; in one hotel the ball-room, crowded with dancing couples, was swallowed up completely, the earth closing again over the gap, while people who had been standing on the threshold escaped uninjured.

So great was the impression caused by this disaster throughout Italy, that the name Casamicciola has become synonymous with any kind of calamity. 'A veritable Casa-micciola,' meaning a complete catastrophe and applying equally well to a bank failure or a railway accident, is still used in everyday conversation by many people who have no idea that such a place exists. With this memory still vivid in the minds of the inhabitants, it was easy to understand that the shock which woke us from our sleep sent them flying from their homes.

For a while we hesitated. Should we also seek the open, either in the garden or on the beach, or should we go quietly back to bed? Meanwhile our boy's absence was conspicuous. Was it possible that he had slept through it? His room gave off the drawing-room and the door stood open, revealing its emptiness! Oh, Giovangiuseppe! At that moment he was without doubt heading the crowds, having forgotten our existence in his panic. It did not surprise us; his endearing qualities did not include personal courage, and, after all, earthquakes were not of daily occurrence.

We decided in favour of bed, not to go to sleep, of course, but to lie in readiness to spring to our feet at the next shock. Nothing would be easier than to get out of our house in a hurry, since it was all on one floor and the windows opened on to the garden.

We must, however, be simple, unimaginative souls, for the next thing we felt was the hot sun streaming across our beds; we had left the shutters open to facilitate our escape. It was scandalously late.

Giovangiuseppe had orders never to call us in the morning. We appeared when we were ready for our morning swim, and our sleepy descent to the beach was signal for breakfast to be prepared. This morning we wondered if we were staffless; wondered, indeed, if there were any inhabitants left on the island or whether they were all at sea. Everything was still and the day was serene. Only a long crack in the wall by our beds bore silent testimony to the night's events.

Nothing, however, was changed in the household. The breakfast-table was laid as usual on the loggia, and our boy was fussing around in the background. He was not in the least embarrassed when I asked him how he had slept, and, as he seemed genuinely delighted to see that we were alive and cheerful, we left it at that.

One of his daily duties was to pour jugs of cold, fresh water over us after our swim, and this morning, as we stood bare-footed under the pergola, the human shower-bath was bubbling over with information which he poured out at the same time. It had not been an Ischian earthquake after all. The island had merely shuddered out of sympathy for Naples, poor Naples which had been largely destroyed. A great fire had also broken out, devouring the few houses that had been left standing, and it was said that Vesuvius might erupt at any moment and bury the city in ashes. This was terrible news. We waited anxiously for the arrival of the morning papers. Fortunately, when they arrived we discovered that the story was merely another product of our boy's colourful imagination. It was true that the city had felt the shock, and that a few crumbling tenement houses had collapsed, but nobody had been killed. The real shock had taken place in the Abruzzi, causing considerable havoc and loss of life, but about this Giovangiuseppe knew nothing.

Nevertheless, wild excitement continued to reign on the island. A stream of neighbours called at the gate to ask how we were, and also why we had not turned out with the rest of them. The Bonifacios sent around a small boy to tell us that on no account must we think of sleeping a second night in the house, for the Vesuvius observatory had issued a bulletin announcing the possibility of another and far more severe shock taking place within twenty-four hours. This bulletin was actually issued, and was not of island fabrication. Like everybody else, the Bonifacios were going to spend the night in the open, and, if we wished, we could share their tent. It was one more instance of their thoughtfulness, but we declined the invitation as tactfully as possible. Having been foolhardy enough to return to sleep the previous night we were quite ready, in spite of the official warning, to try our luck again.

As the day wore on, the island's preparations for the night were started in earnest, and, when evening came, we went for a walk along the wide beach separating us from the Port. The beach, usually so deserted, was this night crowded. Not the most popular seaside resort in the height of the season could have competed with it.

Progress was impossible without stepping over recumbent figures of both sexes and all ages. The sea was like a mirror, and along the water's edge tents were erected in thick rows. They were flimsy affairs, consisting chiefly of bed-linen rigged up between poles, but the interiors were comfortably furnished with mattresses, chairs, and tables, and a great variety of ornaments representing the most valued possessions of each family.

A constant procession of new arrivals swelled the crowd, laden down with more bedding and more valuables, the heavy furniture being carried by the women on their heads. Before each tent a charcoal fire burned brightly, and over them suppers were being cooked. A thousand dishes of spaghetti, covered with rich sauces of tomato and garlic, filled the air with their fragrance.

Ischia took the warning seriously but also philosophically. Village wits were busy, judging from the uproarious laughter on all sides, while here and there a mandolin player accompanied some surprisingly fine voice singing Neapolitan songs in which the magic words *amore*, *mare*, and *sole* rhymed in eternal refrain.

It was an impressive spectacle, this great crowd camping on the sands like some ancient nomad tribe, and unforgettably picturesque. Village acquaintances whom we came across cordially invited us to share their supper, and everybody took it for granted that we should also be coming with our bedding later on.

Something was certainly expected to happen before the night was over, and, scoff as we might between ourselves, it was equally certain that this mass demonstration of the disadvantages of staying at home and being buried beneath the debris of one's villa had its effect on us. What if there *should* be another earthquake, and a more violent one? What if the crack in the wall above our heads were to widen? Perhaps it would be wiser, after all, to wedge ourselves in somehow, somewhere, among the crowds on the beach.

When we had crossed the threshold of the Villa Buono-cuore, into the cool, deep shade of our lovely garden, so still and so delightfully *empty*, when we had entered the house and seen our comfortable beds neatly turned down and ready, our lazy scepticism again waylaid us. For a moment we thought of compromising, of sleeping in the garden, but we abandoned the idea. There was almost as much masonry in the nature of old walls, pillars, and gates to fall down on us as in the house, and far more likely to do so, being given their advanced state of dilapidation.

At supper, Giovangiuseppe had admitted that he was going for a walk along the beach, a walk from which, as we well knew, he would not return before morning, and as Dominica did not sleep in, there was no use expecting any outward assistance in case of disaster. As we stood undecided what to do, torn between comfort and prudence, Kit had a brain-wave. We should get a bell, she said, and suspend it above the beds. It would automatically warn us at the first shock. The only bell at our disposal was the one at the garden gate, a particularly loud one which dangled at the end of a coiled spring and went on ringing for a long time after it was pulled. Taking it down was easy enough, but the secret of success in our scheme depended entirely upon the delicate adjustment in hanging it. This we managed by simply tying it with a handkerchief to the electric light bracket jutting out from the wall. If the wall shook, the bell would ring, and if the bell rang nobody on earth could possibly sleep through it unless, of course, the wall collapsed at the same time.

We had, in addition to the bell, a detailed plan of what we were to do when it rang. We were to wake each other – which meant that I, being the lighter sleeper, was to wake up Kit – and then we were to vault gracefully through the open window and run down to the beach.

It was not without a thrill, and also a qualm or two, that we finally courted sleep. On the entire island we were probably the only people settling down for the night indoors. Sleep came nevertheless; a sleep undisturbed by nightmares, earthquakes, or even by the terrific gale that sprang up in the night.

This story, I am afraid, has no moral at all; in fact, quite the contrary! The wind howled and raged with such force that in the morning breakfast on the loggia was out of the question. In between gusts, Giovangiuseppe explained that it was a volcanic wind, a statement nearer to the truth than most of his utterances. For the people on the beach it had been a *notte terrible*! At the first gust of the gale all the tents had collapsed, while subsequent gusts had lashed the calm mirror of the sea to fury, driving the campers to take meagre shelter behind the rocks. There, voluntarily homeless, the poor people had huddled miserably until the hour had come for the day's business to begin. This, for the Ischians, was in the neighbourhood of four o'clock.

The twenty-four hours' warning sent by the meteorological authorities having finally elapsed, with no danger signals ahead, the inhabitants had been busy ever since struggling home against the gale with their bulky belongings.

As for us, our comfortable, peaceful night's slumber could only be called the Unjust Survival of the Foolhardy.

CHAPTER XI

FROM KIT'S DIARY

I

PETER ARRIVED YESTERDAY from Rome, where he has been waiting *en pension* until we sent for him. Such a dear dog, and we love him even more since he flattered us so outrageously at this reunion. His first taste of liberty, after a short lifetime spent in an apartment, intoxicated him; he went into a frenzy, and did a series of wild circles around the garden, each one bigger and faster than the last. Small yaps of joy came from him, more and more breathlessly; finally he flopped down at our feet, panting and laughing up at us with his eyes and his lolling pink tongue.

I bought him before we were married at a dingy little shop in Via delle Botteghe Osscure in Rome, where the dogs offered for sale were kept in the owner's blowsy bedroom. Most of them were *lupetti* – small dogs that have been used since time immemorial to sit on the wine-carts coming into the city from the Castelli Romani and guard the kegs when the drivers have disappeared into some *trattoria* for refreshment. Among them all (and the bedroom floor was teeming with them) the young Peter was the smallest, a brown woolly bundle hardly four inches long. The shop-keeper declared that he was a dwarf *lupetto*, fully grown. 'See!' he exclaimed, swooping down like Nemesis and enclosing the entire small dog in one hand, 'look at his teeth! They are of the second set!' And he drew back the minute black lips to show teeth like ivory needles.

'He is *tascabile* – pocketable,' said the man proudly, and Peter disappeared suddenly into the depths of his dirty pocket.

I don't know whether I believed that shopkeeper, but I bought Peter, and for a little while he was *tascabile*. I had an azalea in a flower-pot on my balcony, and he used to walk on the soil as though the plant were a big shade tree and the flower-pot a good garden.

Now he is the size of a fox-terrier, with a character as intricate and interesting as any human's. He is dauntless with men and with dogs many times his size; swaggering in the way he throws out his paws when he trots; and decidedly vain of his long silky coat, the ruffles of fur with which Nature has provided him so generously and handsomely, the immaculately curled tail which lies neatly across his back.

But, like many people's, his face when he is asleep betrays him. The black lips have a pathetic curve, and the little muzzle is just a shade too short to be quite so brave and determined as he pretends. He takes his punishments like a gentleman, but a loud noise, such as a stick hitting the ground near him, reduces him to a mass of nerves. He cowers down, his eyes screwed tight shut, his lips twitching, his whole body trembling . . . our poor arrogant Peter!

Here, 'Love me, love my dog,' is amplified to 'Serve me, serve my dog.' From Giovangiuseppe and Dominica, Peter receives the attention due to the pet of a ruling monarch. They find his name difficult. In spite of our permission to translate it to Pietro, they continue to attempt the English version, which Giovangiuseppe makes 'Peetre,' and Dominica simply 'Pee.' Dominica is as anxious to please his palate as ours. To his spaghetti or macaroni, the usual diet of well-to-do Italian dogs (the lower classes subsist on stale bread and water), she adds savoury sauces of tomato or fish or meat to tempt him. When she has succeeded, she tells me with beaming pride that Pee has licked his plate clean.

One hot night we had finished our dinner and Peter's had not appeared. I went into the kitchen to see if it had been forgotten. Dominica was nowhere in sight. I went out of the kitchen door into the darkness of the garden, and eventually found her standing by the wall. Here, where a fresh breeze came in over the water, she had taken Peter's dinner. She had set his plate up on the wall, and with energetic strokes of her fan was hastening Nature's cooling of the fragrant, steaming dish.

II

The house begins to look like our own home, though we have done very little to change it; the days are too beautiful to be indoors, and we do more sun-bathing and swimming than interior decorating. We have put away a few of the glass globes with their saints and wax flowers, and replaced them with some of our own things. Among others is a photograph of Rembrandt's famous painting of his old and very ugly cook cutting up a carrot. It was given to G. by

127

the owner of the painting, and Giovangiuseppe's reaction to it was characteristically enthusiastic and inaccurate. 'Oh, *signore*, how beautiful is your mama!' he exclaimed fervently.

We eat in fine style since the embroidery of my table-linen has been finished, and we do not need to borrow cloths from our neighbours. The linen has a simple monogram, K. B. H., which looks pretty exciting to me after twenty-four years of K. S., but it was not easy to confine my embroiderers to such a plain inscription. They were eagerly anticipating something more fanciful, and asked me only out of courtesy whether I preferred 'Hearty Appetite!' or 'Good Dinner!' in large letters in the centre of the table-cloths. When I said that I wanted neither they were disappointed and incredulous, and probably only consoled themselves when they remembered that they were dealing with foreigners, who are well known to be eccentric.

The hand-woven towel linen has also been delivered by the old nun of San Dominico. She was such a long time in making it that we drove up one day to ask her to pray less and weave more until our order was made, both of us having grown tired of drying ourselves on handkerchiefs and odd towels produced by Giovangiuseppe's conjuring.

We found the old woman eating her one meal of the day. This, a large bowl of spaghetti with tomato sauce, was resting on the taut surface of the linen that was stretched in the loom. It was easy for the old nun, sitting in front of the loom, to put her dinner down beside her on the floor and go on with her interrupted weaving for our benefit. And it was also easy for me to understand, when she delivered the finished roll of cloth a few days later, why the entire length of the stuff was punctuated with red patterns of tomato. We were even able to calculate, by the distance in

A charming villa on the hillside

p. 133

between the spots, how much weaving she had done in a day, and which days had been especially devoted to prayer. A simple but expressive diary.

Yesterday an old woman came to the gate to ask for work. She had on a shabby black cotton dress, and she said she was Eufrasia Perla. Dominica says that surnames like Pearl, Ruby, and Beauty are given to the nameless little orphans who enter the great foundling homes in Naples. The orphans are known, touchingly, as 'Children of the Madonna.' They have no one else to call mother. I wonder if the authorities give them their poetic names because they want to put a touch of beauty into the pathetic little lives? I doubt it; it is more likely that they are afraid of trespassing on ones already in good use.

Eufrasia is going to help with the laundry.

I have just been across the garden to tell Dominica that in the future the master would like his octopus served in disguise. The first time it appeared, a tentacled derby hat standing dreadfully upright and covered with bright red sauce, it caused a major digestive disaster.

Dominica, said Giovangiuseppe, was on what we used to imagine he called the 'elastic' but which we have since identified as the *lastrica*, the terrace on the roof of the kitchen. She was hanging out a complete set of underwear, voluminous bloomers, camisole, and all, which she appears to wash every day at some time during her working hours.

As I came back to the house I looked over my shoulder and saw her plump silhouette on the 'elastic,' outlined against the blue afternoon sky. She was holding something in her hand that seemed to be a garter, and she was waving it with the energy and meaning that are put into wig-wagging.

A minute later a big fisherman's boat slid out from the

patch of water at her feet. One man was in it, rowing lazily. He was young, big, and brown; his strong toes gripped the ribs of his boat.

He was grinning broadly.

CHAPTER XII

ALL BIG BUSINESS begins in a small way, rising with time and patience to impressive proportions; the same applies to hobbies. Our hobby – a totally unprofitable one conducted on the most up-to-date and humane lines – was no exception to this rule. It was livestock, and originated one morning with the rabbit which Kit had ordered for lunch.

Giovangiuseppe brought it in alive for us to inspect, holding the poor little creature by its hind legs in the habitual fashion reserved for poultry and game, although it was neither one nor the other. It was brown, soft, and fluffy, and was, he informed us, a *bellissima femmina*. From the lunch viewpoint, this was a great mistake. Neither Kit nor I could possibly face a meal in which such a 'beautiful female' played a part. We were about to send her home again when we realised that this would only mean her ending up on someone else's table, and that idea was equally unpleasant. We realised at the same time that we could not give shelter to all the rabbits on the island, but this one, at least, should never make the acquaintance of the *cassaruola*, seasoned with garlic and surrounded with a rich brown sauce.

The first thing to be done was to make a home for her, the second to give her a name. We explained this to Giovangiuseppe, and sent him out in search of a wooden crate, some wire netting, some straw, and anything else that might be required to make her comfortable. One of our boy's endearing qualities was the rapid way in which he entered into plans that were to him complete exhibitions of foreign folly. He not only brought his alert native intelligence to bear on the problem, but also a readiness that was most engaging and a flashing smile of genuine pleasure. This left you with the feeling that your plan was both charming and witty as well as original. Giovangiuseppe was, in a word, a born courtier, with just the right amount of grace and astuteness to save his face when he got into trouble.

But to return to our lady-rabbit; we christened her Penelope. There was no deep-rooted *arrière pensée* in this, no subtle reference to Ulysses and his misconduct on the island; we merely thought the name suited her. Unless approached too closely, she was disarmingly tame, and when we let her loose in the garden she progressed down the path with little leaps and bounds, her ears twitching with excitement, indulging on the way in an orgy of geraniums and periwinkles.

Giovangiuseppe returned from the village with a beautiful crate. Not being a woman – in other words, not an inferior creature – he had been unable to carry it himself, and had been forced to hire a *carrozza*. Knowing the island standards, we were not surprised. We knew that such an immaculate white livery could not be demeaned in the eyes of the villagers by anything so closely resembling manual labour. Inside our garden gate he at once stripped off his jacket and set to work with a variety of tools borrowed from who knew where, and in no time had erected a really charming little *palazzo*. Catching Penelope was more difficult, and necessitated all hands being called in to help. Dominica, on account of her corpulence, acted as goalkeeper, while Kit, the boy, and I did the actual rounding up. Once inside the cage, her belly distended with leaves and flowers, she sat placidly content.

During lunch, which had apparently not suffered from the absence of Penelope in dish form, we discussed her future. Kit, with the well-known feminine weakness for arranging marriages, said that she must be wedded at once. It was, she said, every woman's right, and, besides, a husband would be company. More modestly she murmured something about children and the popular saying about breeding like rabbits. That, no doubt, was also her right.

A few days earlier we had made the acquaintance of an elderly lady who lived in a charming villa on the hillside and kept a variety of pets. Kit wrote her a note, explaining the situation and asking if she could lend us a husband for Penelope. This note she sent around with Giovangiuseppe, who in due course returned bearing a magnificent, ferocious-looking specimen, and also some verbal instructions. A week, the lady said, was the habitual honeymoon period, and under no condition were we to be perturbed if during this time we heard piercing screams. They merely denoted conjugal bliss.

If that was the case, this couple must have been supremely happy, although they certainly did not look it, especially not the husband. From the first meeting, it was evident that Penelope had the upper hand. She chased her borrowed husband all over the cage, biting him viciously and for preference in the ears, which were prominent, but not disdaining a large chunk of fur from his back when she got the chance. Indeed, it seemed that for the next two days we never set eyes on Penelope without noticing traces of her husband's silky coat lingering about her gentle lips.

As for him, poor creature, all signs of masculine domination had disappeared. He sat in the corner, huddled and cowed, while from the opposite corner Penelope glared at him with red hostile eyes. We were worried for his condition; we felt that he would never be the same again, and, after all, he was, in a way, our guest. Without waiting for the full week to elapse, we thought it better to return him to his owner with a letter of profuse thanks, hoping that she would not be mortally offended when she set eyes on his dingy remains.

The next morning, to our surprise, a messenger brought another rabbit from her, accompanied by a letter in which she apologised for a most deplorable mistake. No sooner had the husband come back, she said, than he had produced a litter of eleven beautiful babies. But we could rest assured that the one she was sending now was a *real* husband; we could see the difference for ourselves.

Silly woman, we said. Imagine not being able to distinguish between a male and a female rabbit, and when she lived in the country too! However, when it came to distinguishing the difference ourselves we had to admit that there did not seem to be any. If anything, the new, the *authentic* husband looked rather milder than his predecessor.

'Penelope, look at the nice gentleman who has come to stay with you!' Thus introduced, we closed the door on them and hoped that this time things would be different. They were. They *both* fought, and with what spirited fury! Round and round they went, and at such a speed that it was impossible to say which was chasing the other. With fur flying and teeth imbedded deeply in each other, they both uttered piercing screams.

'She's a feminist,' said Kit disgustedly, 'and, what's more, a misanthrope. Look at the way she behaved toward that poor expectant mother!' At this moment there was another violent collision, followed by more blood-thirsty noises.

'Oh, let's leave them alone,' I said. 'They will probably settle down when they know each other better.'

On this second honeymoon we left them longer together, and I noted with satisfaction that the intrepid woman also suffered in the fray. After another tempestuous quarrel we found her with one eye completely closed, and limping badly. That was too much. Once again we returned the borrowed husband and medicated Penelope with boracic acid and cotton wool. Leaving her in peace, we waited patiently for the days to pass and the arrival of the family to which we felt, by now, fully entitled.

Weeks passed, and her recovery was amazing. She became again her own sweet self, but that was as far as she was willing to oblige us. Reluctantly we had to admit that Penelope was extremely disappointing, or, to put it more strongly, a disgrace to her sex. At last Giovangiuseppe, who was deeply interested and felt himself to be indirectly responsible for her conduct, became alarmed. It was, he said, unheard of in the annals of the island. We must call in the wife of one of the fishermen who lived higher up our alley, and was noted for her knowledge of rabbit midwifery. She could tell, he said, just how many *piciun* – the dialect for children – we had a right to expect, and, furthermore, whether they would be boys or girls.

She arrived, and turned out to be a typical elderly

Ischian woman, enormous, comfortable, and competent, with snow-white hair and, what was very rare on the island for a woman of her age, a surprisingly youthful and pretty face. She picked up Penelope and, gazing into space, prodded her with dexterity. After a while, her serene countenance clouded over and a frown settled on her brow. She was perplexed. She held Penelope at arm's length, shook her, then started all over again from another angle. Suddenly her countenance cleared and a smile danced in her eyes.

'*Macché!*' she pronounced with scorn. 'This rabbit will never produce a family; it is not even a female!'

We laughed aloud, then, remembering that it was all our boy's fault, we scowled heavily at him. He was responsible, for he had told us emphatically that Penelope was a *femmina*, and, of course, we had taken his word for it. Now, unless we believed, like an old Swiss lady I once knew, that there were three kinds of rabbits, some male, some female, and some that were just rabbits, we had to set about to procure a wife for Penelope. We were forced to reconsider her status, but, like the gentleman at the *Municipio*, we refused to change her name. She had been christened Penelope, and, even though she had now turned out to be a man, this name should remain.

Needless to say, the story got round, and was undoubtedly the cause of many a hearty and none too refined joke in the village. But the Ischians were the soul of generosity. Indeed, their desire to give pleasure by making gifts quite out of proportion to their humble means was almost embarrassing. From then onwards a stream of rabbits of all ages and both sexes, securely tied up in huge blue chequered cotton handkerchiefs, found their way to the Villa Buonocuore from Giovangiuseppe, Dominica, the Bonifacios, the midwife up the lane, and from the lady who had lent us Penelope's husbands.

In this manner we acquired Mr. and Mrs. George Black, Mrs. Moore, Eleanor with the blue eyes, for whom our dog Peter developed a sentimental weakness, sitting on his haunches and gazing mournfully by the hour, and the Duchess.

The Duchess was a charming creature only a few weeks old, the first and only rabbit to whom I ever gave a bath. It was not, as Kit informed me, a bright idea, but I was sure that, once properly cleaned, she would make an ideal house pet. She emerged from the big tin bucket full of warm soapy water, forlorn and dangerously limp, and it was only after wrapping her up in a Turkish towel and putting her into the hot sun to bake that she recovered. After powdering her with Kit's best talcum and combing out her fine golden fur and ornamenting her neck with a bright ribbon contributed by Dominica from her undergarments, she was as pretty as something in a pastoral scene by Watteau.

In spite of these attentions, she was not grateful. Her first act was to disappear under a quite immovable wardrobe in our bedroom, from where it was only possible to coax her after three days by scattering the floor with fresh vegetables. By that time we had built up quite an impressive rabbit colony with a big communal run, wired in, but commanding a splendid view of the Bay of Naples, and into this we reluctantly confided the Duchess. She did not live long, poor little thing, but her death was not due to any after-effects of her bath. Her neck was broken one day by Penelope, in a fit of temper!

This hobby, so innocently begun, was taking us far from our original idea. It was also through this hobby that we made the acquaintance of our best friend on the island. Our boy, in one of those outbursts of enthusiasm which made him so different from any other servant, announced to us one morning that he had discovered up in Barano, the chief hill-town of the island, a giant race of rabbits that drank water! Why this was remarkable we did not know. We always presumed that our rabbits drank water, but he assured us that they did not. We never enquired what they did drink, as this might have led to embarrassing discoveries. It was already bad enough that Dominica had consumed a barrel of forty-four litres of wine in a fortnight, without finding out that our rabbits had similar habits.

But Giovangiuseppe knew his audience well and scored his victory. We ordered a carriage and set off the same afternoon to investigate, taking him with us. There was nothing he liked better than to accompany us on our drives, when he sat up beside the coachman, with whom he carried on an uninterrupted conversation in dialect. They kept each other company during the hours they had to wait while Kit and I explored our destination at leisure.

The road to Barano branched off half way between the old town and the Port, skirting pine-woods and rising steadily, so that we spent most of the time looking back at the panorama slowly unfolding itself behind us. Driving up this road that led from the sea into the hills gave us the satisfactory sensation of being on a really substantial island; an island that could boast of an 'interior.'

These hills were fascinating, small, round, and green, rising gently back of one another until they led your gaze up to the one solitary peak of the Monte Epomeo. Seen against the afternoon sun, each hill stood clearly detached in an atmosphere of calm infinity. The higher we climbed the more extensive grew the vineyards, until they covered the slopes. The vines grew to a great height, and into their midst little paths disappeared as into a forest. Here and there, but not nearly so crowded as by the shore, little houses of every colour added gaiety and friendliness to this oasis of green.

Bordering the road on one side lay a deep valley strewn with huge blocks of lava. Here the molten river had flowed from the crater in the last eruption of the Epomeo in the fourteenth century, burning its way through this rich land and entering the sea near where our villa stood. It was a wonderful example of Nature's miraculous and eternal cycle of destruction and creation, of death and life, for Ischia, like the slopes of Vesuvius across the Bay, owed its amazing fertility to this same death-dealing lava which, through slow mysterious alchemy, had been transformed into the most fertile soil of the Mediterranean. Lava it was that enabled the tall, stately, century-old umbrella pines by our villa to reach the water's edge; lava it was that gave such amazing vigour to the vineyards through which our carriage passed on its way up the mountain.

A sharp bend in the road revealed Barano, clinging to the mountainside on a variety of levels, its outer fringes straggling off to settle in the vineyards. It was scrupulously clean, a refreshing change from the coastal towns, and, if less picturesque, it seemed more sober and collected, as though the bracing air of the higher altitude had instilled in the inhabitants prouder reserve and a greater self-respect.

Enquiries on the part of Giovangiuseppe brought us to the abode of the mysterious water-drinking rabbits. We rang the bell at the garden gate of a large and rather austere house, not of the peasant type, and this was opened by a youth who ran off in search of the owner. We found ourselves standing inside a lovely terraced garden overlooking a valley.

A tall middle-aged man advanced to meet us. This, the youth announced, was Signor Cesare Giusto, the owner. His face was striking, heavily lined and deeply tanned, and looked as if it had been hewn out of granite. It was not the kind of face one meets in everyday life, but looked rather as if it might have belonged to one of those fierce Phœnician or Saracen warriors who had once terrorised the Mediterranean. From under bushy eyebrows a pair of piercing black eyes summed us up, and when he spoke his voice was a deep *basso profondo* which contrasted with the high voices of the islanders. But there was something else about him besides these startling sardonic features, something extremely pleasing: a frank unwavering glance and a forcible character. To our great surprise, he addressed us in excellent English and with a disarming smile.

We explained our mission, although he was probably already acquainted with it through our boy, and without loss of time he took us to see his monsters. From a long row of neatly kept cages that put to shame our shabby conglomeration of old crates, they glared at us with genuine distaste. Our host explained that he was the only man on the island who bred them, and he did it as an experiment. Their skins were much in demand by fur dealers, who transformed them into imitation ermine, sable, fox, or chinchilla. In this mysterious process they lost their plebeian name of rabbit and acquired some vaguer but more fashionable one ending in 'insky.' The animals were also, he said, uncommonly delicious to eat, although we could not imagine eating, far less digesting, anything so wicked-looking.

Many were champions purchased at the International Exhibition at Milan and originated in Flanders. As he was willing to part with some of them, we made a choice of two magnificent specimens. One was a giant black creature with an incredibly evil leer, which we then and there named Beelzebub; the other, equally massive but of a becoming shade of grey and with a somewhat milder expression, we decided to call Cleopatra. Both of them were expectant mothers, and were guaranteed to supply us with a family of little Beelzebubs and Cleopatras.

Our business concluded, Signor Giusto ordered our new acquisitions to be placed in a basket with a stout peasant handkerchief and plenty of cord to keep them securely down, and handed them over to Giovangiuseppe, who had gone back to the carriage to wait. He then asked us if we would care to see his garden, and led us to a charming, rose-covered belvedere to admire the view. There on a stone table was a tray with three glasses and a bottle of wine! How it got there was a mystery, but with the exquisite courtesy of the islanders he was not going to allow us to leave his domain without refreshment.

This soon proved to be no ordinary refreshment either. We had not imbibed all manner of island vintages – and indeed, before our arrival in Ischia sampled most of the wines of the country – without having learned to recognise an aristocrat when we met one. This one belonged to the kind that held itself aloof from everyday contact and did not consent to sit at the table of anybody but a connoisseur. It was, in a word, the cherished product of an expert wine-grower; its colour, as our host filled our glasses, was a deep golden, and it was mellow with years. Old as it was, age, however, did not alone account for its excellence. No sojourn in a cellar, no matter how prolonged, could have given this wine its perfection had not the original vine been wisely selected, planted in carefully studied and well-prepared soil, tended with constant care, and finally been stripped of only its choicest bunches for the presses.

In answer to our question, Signor Giusto informed us that wine production was his chief interest, the raising of rabbits and other animals being merely a side-issue, and he asked if we would care to go over part of his property with him. Knowing that our boy and the coachman were at the moment also engaged in drinking our host's health, though possibly not in such excellent vintage, and therefore fully at peace with the world, we accepted heartily.

We might have known from the size of the rabbits that this was an estate where everything belonging either to the vegetable or animal kingdom was on a gigantic scale. Guarding the entrance between the garden and the rest of the property was the most enormous goat we had ever seen. She had a shaggy mane that trailed on the ground and a pair of horns worthy of being called antlers. She was also as good as her size in respect to the amount of milk she supplied. Other goats supplied two litres a day and were praised for it; this one, Signor Giusto informed us, would not hear of giving less than five litres, in which capacity she put some cows to shame. With it all, she was a proud beast, and when I tried to pat her she withdrew, not out of modesty, but in order to get up sufficient recoil for a mammoth butt which I escaped in the nick of time and with just the loss of a little dignity.

Further on, we were shown a turnip recently dug up which tipped the scales at ten kilos, or twenty-two pounds. Our host, however, did not pretend that it was an ordinary turnip; he admitted frankly that it was a freak, but, then, I believe that the goat was also one. He led us past model vegetable gardens, past enclosures full of white leghorns, past orchards of plum, almond, apple, and *nespoli* trees, and into the vineyards. These covered both slopes of a valley that faced the opposite side of the island, the side we had not yet explored. Unlike the northern coast, it faced the open sea and was almost uninhabited.

From our lofty promontory we spied a superb empty beach stretching apparently for miles, and at the end of it, jutting out of the sea, was a rock which was almost the facsimile of the castle of Ischia, except for the absence of ruins. There was even a replica of the causeway joining it to the island in the form of a long ridge of sand. At either end of this ridge nestled the little village of Sant' Angelo, with white houses glistening in the sun against the deep blue sea, the only settlement on the entire coast.

Our host told us that there was no road leading to Sant' Angelo, and that except for mountain trails it was cut off from the rest of the island. Once a fortnight a boat from Naples called there on its way to the distant Ponza islands, but if we wished to reach it from where we lived we had either to drive up the way we had come, and on to another hill-town called Testaccio, from where a long flight of steps led down to the beach – with a long walk still ahead of us – or else hire a boat with some stalwart fishermen to do the rowing, and make a day's excursion. The latter sounded by far the simplest and most pleasant way.

From what Signor Giusto told us, this coast was well worth a visit, for there were many curious volcanic manifestations to be found there: smoking rocks and sands, boiling lavender-coloured springs and strange caverns, besides the sheer beauty of the spot.

Viewed from Barano, it was a lovely sight, and so untouched by the passage of time that we could imagine that we were looking down on a stretch of unexplored Mediterranean. It held one spellbound; the little white village might have been an ancient Greek settlement; indeed, the native architecture had changed very little in its essential form since that time, and it needed no great effort of imagination on this clear summer afternoon to evoke the ships of Ulysses making for the shore.

This part of the island, unprotected by trees and facing full south, was much hotter than our side, although Barano, being high up, did not suffer from it. No wonder that this valley, basking twelve months of the year in the sun, produced the best wine of the island. The main output was exported to the mainland to become, probably, 'Vino di Vesuvio' or 'Vino do Capri,' like the wine of old Papa Bonifacio. The best of it, nectar for the gods, was bottled and stored away, to be reserved for the owner and his guests.

On our way through the property, we saw in the steep mountain slopes arched doorways with stout, heavily barred doors. They were cellars hewn out of the rock where the various qualities of wine were kept, and, what was more important, kept cool, for not the fiercest sun could penetrate this thickness of earth and rock. I think we visited them all. I say I *think*, because as in each one we were forced by our host to sample just a little of the contents of the enormous barrels, we could not be *sure* of anything.

Entering these cellars, or *cave*, as they are so appropriately called in Italian, was like stepping inside a giant frigidaire; the air seemed icy by contrast with the heat outside. They were tunnelled so deep into the mountainside that the far ends were plunged in obscurity. All of them were very old, having been built by our host's ancestors, and one bore the date 1665 over the entrance. Along both sides of the cellars great barrels, comfortably propped up on a wide ledge, were waiting to be tapped, and, judging from the number of glasses that met our eyes in each one we visited, they must have been tapped quite frequently. Friendly sampling went on apparently every time a neighbour dropped in. Yet, well

A large and rather austere house, not of the peasant type

out of sight of the casual visitor, in the darkest recess of these *cave*, the special wines were left to mature.

It was certainly a glowing tribute to our gastric juices that at the end of the grand tour we still survived, as in between 'sampling' we had absorbed a rich assortment of pickings from the orchards, fruits which our host had insisted were to be eaten right away.

On our return to the house Signor Giusto introduced us to his mother and his two sisters, who insisted that we accept a cup of coffee before setting out on our journey home. It was excellent, and welcome after our mixed libations, a fact of which the family was probably well aware, being used to Cesare's habit of introducing friends to his cellars.

The Signora Giusto was over eighty; a remarkable old lady with the bearing and dignity of a *grande dame*. Her serene poise, however, did not come from contact with the world, for she had lived most of her long life not only on the island, but up at Barano; it came from a knowledge of the true values of life. There was wisdom and kindness in her eyes, and from the way she looked at Kit I think that she approved of her. I had not realised how tall she was until we said good-bye and she walked with us to the threshold of her home. She wore a long brown dress like a nun's habit, and her silvery-white hair was combed back from her forehead in a severe way that was in keeping with her costume.

As we were leaving, she gave Kit a little bouquet she had gathered while we were in the vineyards, and with the charming grace of a very old lady kissed her on both cheeks.

Signor Giusto accompanied us to the carriage, where the coachman and Giovangiuseppe and the basket containing Beelzebub and Cleopatra were waiting. He agreed to come and see us when he next came down to the shore, and in return made us promise to lunch with them at Barano one day soon.

Although Dominica had dinner waiting when we got home, we had first to inspect the new additions to the family. Cleopatra had evidently made a pact with the devil, for she and Beelzebub were reclining peacefully at the bottom of the basket, resting their heads on each other's backs. To put them into the communal run would have meant massacre on a grand scale for the others, so after supper we rigged up two more houses for them, and before putting them to bed we weighed them. Beelzebub carried off the laurels at twelve kilos, or approximately twenty-six pounds, the other weighing a mere twenty-two pounds. Both of them were ugly customers to handle, and had to be picked up by the hind legs in an unsuspecting moment, for their claws could have ripped your arm to shreds. At the very sight of us they stamped on the ground with a violence that rocked their cages. Giovangiuseppe had said that they drank water, but he had omitted to add that they growled!

Somewhere further back, I mentioned the well-known breeding propensity of rabbits. You started with two, provided that your first selection was better than ours, and by the end of the year the place was simply teeming with young. They darted out from every bush, scuttled across the path at every step until they finally tripped you up and you wished you had never started to collect the species. Well, if I implied all this it was merely in rosy anticipation of events. Day by day, with bated breath, we watched old Beelzebub prepare her nest, tearing out with her large yellow teeth fur from her own breast to line it with. Good old girl, we thought, she could not help her ferocious appearance which hid a heart of gold. When one evening she at last produced

146

eleven sweet little bunnies, we retired to bed as pleased as though we had done it ourselves.

But not so Beelzebub. She spent an active night stamping on them, so that by morning they were all flattened out like pancakes.

As for Cleopatra, when her family made its appearance she did not stamp on them. No half measures for her, indeed. She ate them, fur and all!

Frustrated, we centred our hopes on our more plebeian rabbits. Mr. and Mrs. George Black produced no children, neither did Mrs. Moore, in spite of a liaison with Penelope and a number of other gentlemen. At last it fell to Eleanor, little blue-eyed Eleanor, to save the day. After a lot of fuss, a prolonged diet of our best salads, and many a touching look, she produced what was a record for the entire island. She became the wonder of the species; she gave birth to *one* rabbit.

Time passed. Cleopatra died and Beelzebub, no longer in favour, was returned by us to Signor Giusto in exchange for some excellent wine. Spot, the offspring of Eleanor, was a precocious child, and did not attain maturity. That was as far as we ever got in rabbit farming.

Kit and I were disillusioned; our hearts were hardened. Do not ask what became of the other rabbits, or, if you must, then ask Dominica. She knew better than we did what went into those simmering pots on the kitchen fire.

CASTELLO d'ISCHIA

R M

CHAPTER XIII

EVERY DAY IS *festa* somewhere in Italy. With a more than sufficient number of saints to fill the calendar, there is always one conveniently handy for the occasion.

Almost the same thing may be said for the island. Each of its numerous towns, villages, and hamlets has its own patron saint, whose birth, martyrdom, or miracles are celebrated once a year, so that a continuous round of jollity can be counted upon.

A fierce pride and rivalry is felt over this question of feast-days, just as it is over the saint they commemorate. The natives of each village stand solidly behind their patron. They swear by him in all senses of the word; they pray to him, light candles before his image, praise him when he does what they want, and are appallingly uncivil when he does not. Above all, they have blind faith in his ability to protect them and their homes from adversity, and in his absolute, unquestionable superiority over his other heavenly colleagues.

To the Ischians, escaping punishment in this life and getting into Paradise in the next one is less a question of tiresome virtue than of the ability of their own particular saint to put in a good word for them at the crucial moment. They engage his services in the same way as a client engages a successful lawyer to defend a somewhat doubtful case. The patron saint has to know all about his client's weaknesses and must also possess accurate knowledge of the boundary-lines dividing his commune from the commune protected by a rival saint. A clever saint is much more advantageous to them than a saint who is just a saint.

The inhabitants of Porto d'Ischia will tell you that this was clearly demonstrated in the great landslide of Casamicciola. All the houses on the Casamicciola side of the boundary were ruthlessly destroyed, while not one on their own side was even shaken. A house that happened to be built on the actual frontier of the two communes was cut in half, one half being swallowed up and the other left standing. In the matter of wickedness, they say, there is not much to choose between the two populations; the incident merely proves the superior influence of their saint over that of his Casamicciola rival.

With such a policy of isolation, these *feste* are bound to be strictly local and their prerogatives jealously guarded. Some tiny hamlet, whose handful of houses and a church entitle it to have a patron saint of its own, will suddenly burst into wild exuberance, shooting off fireworks, exploding dangerously large quantities of gunpowder, and lighting huge bonfires which can be seen and heard all over the island, while the surrounding villages, scornful and not a little petulant, will have gone to bed, pretending to ignore the matter.

These rejoicings vary greatly in importance. While little

San Dominico can only afford one celebration in the year, the old town of Ischia commemorates not only its patron saint, but also the Holy Virgin and as many others of the heavenly host as its exchequer permits.

To appreciate the importance of these feasts in the eyes of the Ischians one must realise that, unlike city dwellers, the islanders have no other source of gaiety. Apart from love-making and such purely family celebrations as births and marriages, they are the only bright spots in their hard-working lives.

It seemed to us that throughout the entire summer the inhabitants of the old town were either feverishly preparing a *festa*, whole-heartedly enjoying one, or staggering from its recent effects. The most important of these – probably the most important on the island – was the one given in honour of its patron, San Giovan Giuseppe della Croce, whose birth-place was Ischia, whose miracles were said to be innumer-able, and whose spirit was constantly being seen by the faithful. This feast – 'a world-wide and fantastic event,' as our boy, who was named after this saint, described it – lasted three days and nights without interruption.

With interest we watched the old town dressing up for the occasion. From her store-rooms and old trunks, from her dusty attics and cellars, she was sorting out not only her treasures, but everything that could be used to add to the gaiety. From the balconies of the houses splendid hangings of brocaded velvet, embroidered with gold and silver, superb though tattered silks in delicate shades of blue and old rose, relics of Ischia's more glorious days, hung side by side with modern matrimonial bed covers in gaudy satinette.

Carpenters, painters, blacksmiths, and all other artisans were working busily and free of charge, contributing their share to the general cause, erecting rows of arches beneath which the procession was to pass, decorating them with thousands of acetylene lamps and brightly coloured paper flowers, stretching across the street banners bearing in huge letters a cordial welcome to their patron, erecting bandstands at intervals, and tall poles from which flags in profusion were already waving.

Along the water-front giant bonfires were being laid, while the streets were lined with strings of rockets and fuses, leading up to the big display of fireworks which was to take place on the causeway half way between the castle and the town. Watching the youths of Ischia throwing lighted matches and glowing cigarette-ends in all directions with casual lightheartedness, we held our breath on more than one occasion, waiting for the terrific explosion which would blow us all straight up to heaven, but this was because we were new to gunpowder and the Ischians were not.

Although the proceedings were entirely in his honour, San Giovan Giuseppe, unlike most patron saints, did not make any public appearance, for there was no statue of him, and his rôle in the processions was obligingly filled by the statues of the Madonna and of Sant' Antonio, protector of the fishermen, who both had their own feast-days and in this way enjoyed a double ovation.

On Friday at sunset things began to happen. There was a sharp, loud, crackling fusillade – bang, bang, pop, crash, bang! – followed by a series of explosions. At the same moment, rising above the tumult in the distance, we heard the strains of a band.

Our boy came running across the garden, begging us to hurry. The procession had already started from the cathedral and was making its way in our direction. Leaving the main road, it would proceed down our narrow alley on to the beach and back along the shore to the old town. In this way everybody would have a chance of seeing it, and the whole town would be blessed.

Followed at a discreet distance by our boy and Dominica, we set out for the little piazza back of our villa. The air reeked of gunpowder, the wind was blowing down a cloud of wood smoke, and the heat was fierce. In the middle of the little piazza we found a bonfire blazing away, to the great joy of a crowd of urchins who were dancing around it, while an outer circle of corpulent mothers with babies in arms were gazing at it with equal fascination. Wood was a scarcity on the island, a luxury few could afford, and here a gigantic pile was being offered up in flames to the saint. The people were proud of the sacrifice.

Peter had come along too, wildly excited by the noise, adding his barking to the general confusion and madly chasing stray chickens with even more than his habitual gusto. He may not have known what it was all about, but he did know that something was in the air, that everybody was just a little mad, and that it was a unique opportunity to do whatever he liked without fear of drawing attention to his misdeeds.

The music drew nearer, and people began running down the alley. Cries of 'Ecco viene la Madonna!' rang out on all sides. Almost unperceived, a youth with a lighted taper set fire to a long fuse and a trail of gunpowder exploded in a succession of ear-splitting reports. Immediately following this the procession appeared, filling the narrow lane, headed by a band in full swing, cymbals clashing, trumpets blaring, pistons working, and cheeks puffing, drowning even the noise of the explosions. The band was composed of neatly turned-out youths in military garb, white duck trousers and blue tunics with brass buttons, and each one carried his music score in a little ledge on his instrument.

Behind them came the choir-boys in red cassocks and white surplices, holding tall lighted candles, and following in a cloud of incense came the priests in their vestments, with scarlet velvet capes bordered with white fur, holding more candles and chanting.

Around us the peasants fell on their knees, for there now appeared the statue of the Holy Virgin on her silver throne, carried on the shoulders of four young fishermen, very ill at ease in their Sunday clothes. Towering above the procession of which she was the centre, she was a weird, impressive spectacle; an ancient wax figure with an opulent flaxen wig beautifully curled in long ringlets, and wearing a finely wrought crown of gold. She was richly dressed, and from her shoulders hung in stiff folds a long mantle of magnificent cream-coloured brocade, embroidered in silver, which almost covered the throne.

As the bearers picked their way cautiously over the un-even path, the Madonna lurched and wobbled perilously, only just maintaining her equilibrium, but with an unchanging, beatific smile on her waxen countenance, her glass eyes gazing into space, seeing nothing, seeing everything, according to the degree of faith of the onlookers.

Crude as her image was, there was nothing ridiculous about her. She was indeed venerable and beautiful. Loving, pious hands had curled the flaxen ringlets, and toiled patiently over the exquisite robes; earnest prayers, faith, and pride accompanied her through the streets. Bobbing and swaying, she disappeared down the hill.

Immediately behind the Madonna, and second only to her in importance, came the Bishop, walking under a red canopy. His vestments were elaborate and heavy, and, as he had nobody to carry *him*, he sweated profusely, interrupting his flow of Latin every now and then to mop his ample neck with an enormous pocket handkerchief. Escorting the Bishop were more prelates, and finally the procession was brought to a close by the old men of the Funeral Club.

This unique association, the father of modern insurance, guaranteed its members a respectable funeral upon payment of a regular monthly contribution. The funeral included a first-class coffin, candles, wax flowers, attendance of the clergy, and a suitable following. It also included a certain number of Masses to speed him on his way to heaven, and, if he got stuck in Purgatory, to get him out as soon as possible.

We followed the procession as far as the beach, where we watched its slow progress back to the old town, past the fishermen's boats, the drying nets, the lobster-pots, adding pageantry to a wealth of local colour. At intervals along the route it came to a halt, the band stopped playing and refreshed itself with a glass of wine, the glass being, in this instance, a symbol and not a measure.

Not until nightfall did the rejoicing begin in earnest. For the three successive nights of the *festa* we dined early and joined the crowds in the old town. The arches blazed with thousands of little lights and the street teemed with happy, laughing people. Improvised cafés, with tables and chairs overflowing into the road, had every seat occupied, while the owners of the houses in between had moved their drawing-room furniture down on to the sidewalk and sat with their guests watching the passers-by.

The habitual traffic had vanished; there were no *carrozze* clattering at breakneck speed over the cobblestones; indeed, there would have been no place for them to pass. Like the Piazza San Marco in Venice, the street was a great outdoor *salon*, the reception-hall of the saint, where all his guests knew each other and were there to enjoy themselves. In one of the bandstands the same intrepid youths were playing away, and playing uncommonly well. One could not help contrasting their efforts with those of a village band at home. Like all southern Italians – indeed like all Mediterranean peoples – they had music in their veins, their *tempo* was perfect, and there was rarely a false note.

Being lucky enough to find a table, we sat and drank *caffè nero* and ate *casati* ices to the accompaniment of *La Traviata* and *Il Trovatore*. The street was lined with gaily decked booths displaying under brightly coloured awnings, and by the flare of acetylene lamps, that wonderful conglomeration of wares only to be found at country fairs and Italian *feste*.

There were beautiful Venetian shawls with long opulent fringes, and other shawls equally Venetian, but so appalling that they hurt the eye; little black devils in airtight bottles which, as you pressed on the rubber stopper, glided up and down; there was chinaware; fanciful ladies' garters; fountain-pens; saucepans; coloured pictures of San Giovan Giuseppe, Sant' Antonio, and the Holy Family; dreadful strips of pseudo-tapestry depicting the encounter of Dante and Beatrice – this article, incidentally, was a great favourite in Neapolitan shops – gold, silver, ivory, and coral horns in all sizes, to ward off the Evil Eye, and countless other trinkets.

Other booths were entirely devoted to the perdition of the sweet-toothed, booths laden down with mounds of nougat, dried figs stuffed with almonds and neatly wrapped in vine-leaves, and slabs of *giandura*, a deliciously rich mixture of milk chocolate, honey, and nuts.

Higher up, in a quiet alley, we discovered a Punch and Judy show in full swing; before it a crowd of spectators, which numbered more grown-ups than children, stood engrossed. It was many a long year since either of us had watched this ancient and most popular of all plays; we listened with delight to the amusing, highly Rabelaisian dialogue, half in Italian, half in Ischian, and we laughed hard-heartedly when Punch got hit on the head by his intolerant wife, an international joke which the islanders thoroughly appreciated. When it was over, the solitary actor-manager crawled out from under the stage; a poor devil, hoarse and dishevelled, who passed round the hat in which a few soldi, placed there in advance, jingled hopefully. The crowd dispersed, and, except for the distant sound of music, all was still under the starlit sky.

The cathedral was brilliantly illuminated. Like the entrance to a magnificent *palazzo* on the night of a great reception, the big central doors, draped for the occasion with ornate lambrequins, were flung wide open, and there was a red carpet on the steps. At the top of these steps, on the threshold of the softly lit interior, and on a pedestal surrounded by flowers, stood the two holy figures of the Madonna and Sant' Antonio.

In their glittering setting they combined admirably their deep religious significance with their mundane duties. Visible to their guests, sanctioning the festivities by their presence, they yet held themselves quietly aloof. From the crowded street, a constant stream of silent, reverent people came to kneel at their feet in prayer before continuing the round of entertainments. It struck us that there was an excellent understanding between the reigning powers above and the faithful on earth. Like perfect hosts, the former wished their guests to be gay, to enjoy fully all that had been prepared for them, and as heavenly beings they exacted the reverence which was certainly shown them. A sensible and pleasing conception, if there ever was one!

157

The high point of the feast of San Giovan Giuseppe was reached only on the third night. It was the night on which the giant bonfires on the wharf were to be set alight and the fireworks displayed.

When we reached this wharf where the long causeway led off to the castle, it was, with the exception of a few fishermen and children, deserted. Several bonfires were already low, but here and there great tongues of flame leapt up, weirdly illuminating their surroundings. In the darkness, the wavering bursts of light and their fantastic, flickering shadows brought into sharp relief the age-worn stones, the arches and loggias of the native houses, the ships at anchor, and the rugged features of the fishermen standing near by. On its isolated rock the castle emerged from the night, unbelievably sinister and ghostlike. No modern floodlight could have called forth such magic; it was like the *chiaroscuro* of a Rembrandt etching.

We were sitting on the parapet of the causeway when an Ischian approached and politely warned us to choose another seat if we did not want to be blown up with the fireworks. It was only a few minutes before midnight, and at the stroke of twelve from the cathedral clock the display would begin. Already the half-deserted wharf was beginning to fill up with people.

We took refuge on one of the mooring-pillars, at a safe distance, and waited for the grand finale of the remaining supply of gunpowder which constituted, we supposed, what the Ischians called fireworks. The resources of the old town, already drained by three days of *festa*, could never afford a costly display of fireworks, when even fashionable and wealthy tourist resorts went cautiously into the venture.

Bang! A rocket soared into the air and expired without leaving any trace of its passage. This was about what we had expected. Boom ! Whizz! Another rocket was fired, but it did not end so ignominiously. Spreading out high above us, it fell slowly in a great shower of gold. Suddenly there was a great noise as rocket after rocket soared up, filling the sky with incredible beauty in an endless variety of forms. Little coloured balloons floated lightly down to meet the water, where, with a hiss, they were extinguished, great golden and silver flowers spread out above the castle, lingered for a moment, and vanished slowly into the night. We craned our necks upwards, spellbound, not believing our eyes. When the rockets were over, Catherine-wheels and large ornamental figures sprang to life along the water-front.

Suddenly we all turned toward the Torre di Michelangelo, the old tower that stood a little apart from the town. From each of its three floors a cascade of fire poured down like a gigantic waterfall, smoothly flowing into the abyss of dark-ness at its feet, the smoke rising like spray. The colours changed over and over again, reflecting in the still water a scene of unsurpassable beauty. At last the fire burnt itself out; the tower became engulfed once more in the night from which it had emerged for one brief, splendid moment, and the noise that had filled the air made way for a profound silence. The *festa* of San Giovan Giuseppe was over.

This display of fireworks amazed us not only by its lavish-ness, but also by its beauty. The Ischians might have dreadful notions of the kind of house a gentleman should live in, judging from the modern *palazzi* we had been offered for rent, but in everything connected with their ancient traditions, in the procession, in the decoration of the churches and streets, in every detail of this three days' *festa* which we had just witnessed, including its magnificent ending, they revealed instinctive, unerring taste. It was born in them, together with their sense of colour and their ear for music.

This did not, however, solve the riddle of where the money came from, and our amazement increased when we learned from an official source that in their display of fireworks alone the inhabitants of the old town had exploded the sum of sixty thousand lire! It was impossible that the natives, mostly fishermen and vine-growers so poor that they were unable to afford many of life's so-called necessities, could have illuminated the heavens to the extent of such a fabulous sum.

We had forgotten that the Ischians, like all southern Italians, are great emigrants, the majority going to the United States. Although they may live under alien skies for many years, they remain intensely patriotic, forgetting neither their native land nor their native village to which they hope to return some day to live as real *signori*. Above all, they never fail to contribute to the fund for their local feasts. In this manner they feel they are actually participating in them, and their minds can conjure up a faithful picture of the scenes they have so often witnessed in their youth. Most of the expenses of the *festa* of San Giovan Giuseppe had been provided by these faithful emigrants, the sixty thousand lire for the fireworks being a gift from the Ischians of California. To get some idea of the total sums that yearly make their way across the Atlantic to this little island unknown to most Americans, one must remember that San Giovan Giuseppe is not the only saint to be feasted in the old town, and that the latter is only one of the many settlements on the island.

Do not ask why the islanders do not use this influx of wealth to improve their own conditions; why they do not build an up-to-date hospital, provide proper schools, or introduce modern drainage. This would not be half as much fun as having a *festa*, and as to whether, under such Utopian conditions, especially at the sacrifice of these old-established and much-cherished traditions, the Ischians would be happier, is much to be doubted. There is no telling where modern drains might lead. They might lead to another Capri. Heaven forbid! I, for one, shall continue to contribute my modest offering to local feasts on the understanding that it shall be blown up into the air, even if only in the shape of one of those modest rockets that explode with a bang and leave nothing to show for it.

The day following a *festa* has usually the depressing atmosphere of a Monday, only far gloomier. Having discarded so successfully all their cares, this return to the strenuous realities of everyday life is too much even for the Ischians to take lightly. But the day following this particular feast was a great exception.

Murder had been committed in the old town.

Marietta, a pretty girl of eighteen, whose marriage was to have taken place just after the *festa*, had shot her lover dead with her father's gun. The entire island was ablaze with excitement.

Giovangiuseppe, Dominica, and all the neighbours had a different story to tell, and were determined to tell it, but everybody agreed upon the motive for the crime, and sympathies were unanimously on the girl's side. She had, they said, defended her honour.

In Ischia, as in all other parts of Italy, and indeed in most Latin countries, it is the custom for a girl to bring a dowry when she marries, no matter how poor her family may be.

Marietta's parents, so the story ran, had managed, by years of saving, to put aside ten thousand lire to enable her to make a good match. It was a large sum, more than many girls of better-off families received, and they were proud of their sacrifice. They would have liked to see their only child marry an honest, hard-working Ischian, a fisherman of their own clan, where her dowry might help to purchase one of those little pink or white houses on the beach for a home, or go toward making her husband the owner of the great, brightly painted boat in which he toiled for a living. They would have liked her to settle among them, so that her children might grow up near by, laughing and playing half naked on the beach, splashing in and out of the clear water with the other children, to grow up and one day take their places in the community, and so continue the cycle of their lives. They did not want to lose her.

Certainly, with such a pretty girl as Marietta, there had been no lack of suitors, but she was headstrong. Perhaps she had already fallen in love with the young Neapolitan, a sharp, handsome fellow who was mate on one of the ships that ran the daily service between Ischia and the mainland. Perhaps she was dazzled by the prospect he held out to her of life in the great city, of his promised rapid advancement to the rank of captain. In her eyes it was a brilliant marriage, far above the offers of her Ischian suitors.

There had been months of courtship without the knowledge of her parents; secret meetings in isolated groves; furtive embraces and furtive promises. When the parents heard of it, they were reluctant to give their consent, with their instinctive distrust for Neapolitans; but to Marietta's pleadings they gave way at last, and the date of the marriage had been fixed.

That much was known to the Ischians, but what followed was known only to Marietta. This young Neapolitan did not intend to demean himself by marrying a peasant without good reason. Ten thousand lire was a very good reason. Furthermore, by a little astute blackmailing he hoped to increase this sum. It was one of those cases dear to the heart of the worst kind of Neapolitan, where pleasure and profit could be conducted hand in hand.

As Marietta was madly in love and trusted him implicitly, it was not difficult for him to seduce her. When she confessed, just before the *festa*, that she was expecting a child, he became evasive. Their marriage might have to be postponed, he said. There was the possibility of his being transferred to another line; then, again, it would be a serious handicap to his career if he married on so little. Finally he made it clear that, unless she could persuade her parents to increase the dowry to fifteen thousand, he would 'disappear,' leaving her to face the consequences. These consequences – a broken marriage, an illegitimate child – were enough to frighten any girl, but they were nothing to the bitterness of her disillusion.

Both pride and fear prevented her from opening her heart to her parents, and, anyway, she knew the utter impossibility of obtaining what her *fiancé* demanded. She little suspected that he had no intention of carrying out his threat.

Some days before the *festa* the sharp eyes of the Ischian women had discovered her in church, prostrated before the miraculous image of the Madonna, in fervent prayer. They had attributed it in their kind way to a lovers' quarrel, and this opinion was confirmed when, at the beginning of the celebrations, Marietta and her *fiancé* were again seen together. They said she threw herself almost feverishly into the round of gaiety.

On the last night, when Marietta knew that her parents and neighbours would be out watching the fireworks, she gave her lover a rendezvous in the empty house. It was a rendezvous to which each went with a different idea. Had Marietta's father been curious enough, on any of those days preceding the tragedy, to take up his army rifle and examine it, he would have been surprised to see that it was oiled, cleaned, and loaded.

The meeting took place in the one whitewashed room which in the poorer Ischian houses combined kitchen, living-room, and bedroom. Against the wall hung a large coloured reproduction of the miraculous Madonna, and before it, night and day, a wick in a cup of oil burned with a tiny flame. For illumination, the rest of the room depended on a candle in the neck of an empty bottle.

When the Neapolitan, interpreting this discreet invitation in the manner most agreeable to him, sauntered into the room, he found himself face to face with a stranger. It was Marietta, but not the Marietta whom he thought he knew. What she told him, or what bitter anguish was in her words, no one will ever know. But she spoke, and before he could recover from his surprise, before he could make a movement, she had raised the gun and with terrible accuracy shot him where he stood. In her own peculiar way, Marietta had interpreted the answer to her prayer at the Madonna's feet.

When the cause of the crime became known, feeling ran high, not only in the old town, but all over the island. The deeply rooted dislike of the islanders for the Neapolitans flared up, ready to manifest itself by forcibly preventing the girl's arrest. Only a reinforcement of *Carabinieri* kept them in check.

We were walking along the main street when the little *carrozza* in which Marietta was being taken into custody drove past. By the furious pace at which it was going, as well as by the proud bearing of the coachman as he cracked his whip in the air, it was evident from a distance that something of importance was taking place. As it flashed by, we had a glimpse of two armed *Carabinieri*, their ample cloaks billowing out behind them, the chin-straps of their characteristic Napoleonic hats officially lowered, their white-cotton gloved hands holding the arms of the slender girl who sat wedged in between them. Not that there was any need to hold her, for a more unresisting prisoner could not have been found. Serene, apparently oblivious of everything around her, she sat back with her hands folded quietly in her lap, her eyes fixed on space, an expression of resigned indifference on her face.

People in the street stopped to watch the carriage pass, waving their handkerchiefs to the prisoner and calling out words of encouragement which she apparently did not hear or did not heed. Even the *Carabinieri*, in spite of their unpleasant duty, seemed proud to have charge of such a distinguished prisoner, one who in the public eye was little less than a heroine.

'Certainly she will not be condemned,' everybody told us. 'She has defended her honour. They will not dare to punish her.' Having heard the pitiful story, having had this fleeting glimpse of her on the way to the *Questura*, thinking also of the penitentiary at Procida and whatever its counterpart for women might be, we hoped sincerely that they were right.

After all, he was a Neapolitan, and, remembering the weakness of our ex-friend Salvatore, we felt like joining in the general sentiments of the islanders and crying: 'Down with Naples! Long live Ischia!'

CHAPTER XIV

FROM KIT'S DIARY

I

OUR FRIEND, THE WIDOW TREZZI, says that everybody in the world was created to marry one certain other person. These two, who are so indispensable to one another that each is only half of a complete entity, are cut apart like an apple by *Buon Dio* in heaven, before being sent down to earth to pursue their destinies.

'So,' says the widow, 'the world is full of separate halves of apples, and each half is looking for the piece that completes it. Some get stuck on to an apple that they've no business to be with, and no good comes of that. But you,' she says to us, 'are two halves of the same apple. *Buon Dio* made you one, and cut you apart, and brought you together again, and that is why your life is happy.'

On the 19th, our two months anniversary, the kitchen department of our household quivered with excitement and secrecy. Dominica was invisible. Giovangiuseppe was beaming and mysterious. Early in the morning, having made our beds almost before we were out of them, he asked permission to go up to his home in Fiaiano. We said he might; if we had known the purpose of his trip we would not have agreed so lightly.

When he came back, the door of the dining-room was shut and bolted from the inside; we were requested not to peek, and our midday meal was served on the loggia.

At eight o'clock the door was thrown open and we were ushered into a surprise banquet by a proud Giovangiuseppe. At least, it would have been a surprise except for the sustained mystery of the day.

As we entered the dining-room, both of them, reddening with embarrassment, presented me with large, strangled bunches of flowers and good wishes for many more anniversaries. The room was lit with an extra number of candles, stuck, for lack of something better, in the necks of empty wine-bottles. By their yellow light I saw the decorations that stretched across the room and over the table, so opulent and lavish that we could hardly reach our chairs. For a moment my heart sank, and I had difficulty in producing the cries of delight that I knew were expected of me. For Giovangiuseppe, always anxious to make a *bel effetto*, had hung the room with garlands and garlands of blue morning-glories, and I knew, as surely as if I had seen him do it, that he had stripped our lovely garden wall of its burden of flowers to please us.

However, this was not the moment for regrets, and nothing could chill the warmth that we felt at this spontaneous showing of pleasure in our anniversary. Every Ischian loves a *festa*, but it is a very small *festa* indeed that marks the end of two months of marriage, and only real friendliness could explain all this careful planning, the preparation of special food, the long hours of bustling and secrecy. We felt touched and grateful as we sat down to the feast.

Both of them stayed with us while we ate, refusing to sit down but standing near, entertaining us and telling us about the food; how the wine, a smooth, potent Malvasia, was a present from Giovangiuseppe's parents, and the chicken the outcome of a titanic battle between Dominica and a woman of Campagnana. Dominica had offered three lire for it; the chicken woman had demanded four. The argument ended with a triumphant victory for our side when the bird fell at three lire and fifteen centesimi.

The dinner came to an end, we thought, with a tall cake made in layers *all' Americana* in our honour, and, grossly overfed, we were about to make an effort to stand up when Giovangiuseppe held up his hand in a commanding gesture. With his usual instinct for the dramatic he had chosen the most effective moment to produce his surprise.

'*Signori*,' he said, 'I pray you to remain seated! I have a dish, a *piatto molto speciale*, which my mother has made especially to celebrate this happy day. It is exquisite; it is considered the greatest delicacy that one can eat in Fiaiano!'

With that he vanished. In a minute he came back with a large flat baking-dish which he offered to me, grinning. In it was a sea of brown liquid, in which swam oily globules tinged with red. Monsters of some sort humped up through the liquid. I helped myself, murmuring politely.

G. also took some of the mixture, but he was looking frankly suspicious. We took our first bite. My stomach gave a scream of protest; G.'s face was scarlet and congested under his tan. The pudding, the delicacy from Fiaiano, was made of eggplant which had been fried in oil and tomato, and over this had been poured generously a thick, sweet sauce of chocolate and cinnamon!

I was quicker than G. In a moment, when Giovangiuseppe was out of the room, I jumped on a chair and emptied my plate out of the high window, praying that cats or rabbits or ants might remove the mess before morning light.

But poor G., under the bright, pleased eyes of Giovangiuseppe, put spoonful after spoonful of the concoction into his mouth, doing his best to control the revolt of his stomach, and hide the fierce shudders that shook him.

And so, finally, to bed. And there G. has stayed ever since with a nasty upset, result of the pudding, or perhaps of general overfeeding. He was so miserable and I so worried (as usual) that I called in Dr. Palermo, who had been recommended to us. It was our first experience of local medicine.

Palermo is small and slight, with painfully crossed eyes that must be a great handicap to him in a country that believes in *malocchio*. He dresses in unrelieved black, a sign of distinction which marks him as a *signore*. I suppose he is a Jew, since I have heard that those whose surnames are Napoli, Roma, Genova, and the like, are Jews whose forefathers adopted the names of the towns where they lived, some time after the era when their people were allowed no family names at all.

After examining the patient, the doctor prescribed 'baths of aromatic herbs.' When I looked blank, he asked me if we had no aromatic herbs in the garden. I said I didn't know; I wasn't sure what they were.

So the doctor, with great patience, took me for a tour of our garden. Here was geranium, he said; I must take some of that. How much? I asked. He must have thought me idiotic to want to know the exact number of leaves, but he was very polite about it, and told me that I should take perhaps five. Next we had five leaves from an orange-tree, and five from a lemon, smelling sweet like verbena. Then three sprigs of a little wild mint, a handful of myrtle, and two sprays of fragrant bay.

When these had been boiled together in a muslin they gave out, in concentrated form, the glorious perfume that rises from the rough uncultivated slopes of the island when they are hot under the sun.

The liquor was to be added to G.'s bath every day until he was better. The action of the herbs was to quicken the circulation and restore the health.

As the Villa Buonocuore had no receptacle large enough to bath in, I raced to Ischia Ponte to find one. The great hardware emporium had, apparently, never been called on to supply bathtubs; the largest vessel of any kind was a galvanised-iron washtub, about three feet long and quite nice and deep. I bought it, and rattled home in a carriage to fix the bath.

It was lovely, fragrant, and steaming, and, after helping G. through the rather difficult operation of folding himself up in the tub, I left him to soak and improve his circulation.

Peacefully reading on the loggia, I heard an angry bellow. 'Kit! Kit! Kit!' He was shouting terribly loudly. I threw away my book, upset my chair in my hurry, and rushed indoors, fearing a major disaster.

There was G., still folded up double in the washtub, his knees alongside his ears and his face purple from his efforts to disengage himself from the tub's embrace. I laughed till the tears ran down my cheeks. G.'s eyes popped indignantly, but in a minute he was laughing too, in spite of much grunting and a good deal of bad language.

Finally, after valiant tugging, with my hands under his arms and my foot jammed on the rim of the tub, I prised him loose. By that time there was no need to call Giovangiuseppe to empty the bath; it had quite emptied itself in its aromatic transit round the room.

G. is certainly better, though I don't know whether to thank the herbs, which I have painstakingly gathered and cooked every morning, or the exercise he has had while in his bath.

This is our only personal experience with the local medicos so far, but we did, one day, see something of a cure that has probably been in use through a great many centuries.

We were walking with Angelina through the main street of the Port when the crowd separated, and a procession of priests came through. There were several of them, dressed in white surplices and carrying lighted candles and a cross. Behind them walked four little acolytes in red, swinging censers. They were all chanting in a queer minor key, and this, with the jangling of the censers, made a fairly loud accompaniment to their progress.

Angelina said, as calmly as though she were talking about the weather, 'They are going to cure Pasquale's *bambino* of his worms.'

Evidently the idea of the Mother Church exorcising worms from her small followers was not new or strange to Angelina. When we begged her to tell us how it was done, she laughed good-heartedly at our curiosity. First of all, she said, the purpose of the loud chanting and rattling of censers was to warn the worms that the priests were coming. They had been quite near to Pasquale's house when they passed us. In the house Pasquale would be waiting with the unlucky *bambino* and all the rest of the family.

When the priests arrived, they would commence a long ceremony centring entirely around the by now badly frightened child. It would be a service nicely calculated to increase his terror. The priests, never for an instant ceasing their chant of exorcism, would cross the child's body repeatedly with symbolic strokes of their fingers, up and down, and from side to side. These strokes signified that the worms were to be cut into many pieces and utterly destroyed. They were then commanded to leave the child's body for ever.

Afterwards . . . Angelina shrugged. The worms had died during the visit of the priests – *non é vero?* – and they would soon depart in a way that we could guess. The child whose worms had been exorcised was always completely cured.

Dr. Palermo confirmed this, to our surprise. Like a good modern Italian, he laughed a little at the superstitious method of curing the ailment, and said he could do it more easily with a dose of medicine. But the principle was sound. Only it was the child and not the worms that heard the procession approaching from afar, and it was the child's terror at being the centre of the religious ceremony that produced such a violent reaction among the various juices in his little stomach that the worms died as a result.

II

We have had an exciting adventure, which followed G.'s upset and in a way hinged on it, since if we had not been sleeping in separate rooms things might have turned out quite differently.

He had been having an attack of insomnia, and had moved into the blue room behind ours in order to escape from me. I, it seems, have taken to talking in my sleep, shouting indignant refusals to pay a thousand lire for a coffee-grinder, and other misguided comments not amusing enough to reconcile anybody to being wakened out of a hard-won sleep.

At half past two one morning I was awakened by a gentle tug at the sheet that covered me. I thought it was G., wandering around because he couldn't sleep, and as I sat up in bed I saw the door between our rooms close softly.

'Are you all right?' I called.

'Yes,' he answered very wakefully. 'Are *you* all right?

I was surprised, and said 'Yes' too, and he asked, 'Why are you walking around?'

'But I haven't been out of bed at all,' I said. 'Didn't you go through my room?'

'I haven't been out of bed either!' he said.

Then suddenly we both realised that we were not alone, that there was a mysterious Third Person in the house. Was he a burglar? I think it would be better to call him a footpad (such a charming word), because subsequently we found he had burgled nothing; the only sign of his presence besides that tug at my sheet, which he must have touched in passing my bed, and the closing of the door, was the quick padding of feet that G. heard in the room next to his, going through the living-room and so, we supposed, out into the garden.

It was an odd sensation for which we had only ourselves to thank; we had never locked either the house doors or the garden gate when we turned in at night. I held G.'s arm in a determined grip; I did not at all approve of his fool-hardy desire to have a look around the property.

To make doubly sure that we had not imagined the whole thing, Peter dashed to the stairs leading down to the loggia, barking and growling furiously. Of course, he ought to have done it much sooner, when the footpad came in, and not waited till we were out of bed and the marauder safely gone from the house; but when he is once well asleep I'm afraid he isn't much of a watchdog.

We roused the boy; we thought the brave lad would rush

out of the house and beat the grounds for the intruder. Far
from it. When he heard our story he turned ashy pale and
had to lean against the wall to brace his shaking knees.

In a very trembly voice he advanced the theory that we
had dreamed the whole thing. 'I, too, *signori*, when I have
heavily eaten have similar dreams!' When we pointed out
that it was scarcely possible that both of us and the dog
besides should have had the same nightmare, poor Giovangiuseppe grew paler still and looked at us piteously. I could
hear his teeth chattering.

'*Signori*,' he quavered, 'it is the night of San Giuseppe.
Signori, those were not human footsteps. It was the *munielli*!'

With that he turned and vanished precipitately into his
little room, where we could hear him barring his door and
windows securely, leaving us to wonder what sort of spirit
a *muniello* might be.

We did not find out in the course of that night, nor have
we since. But we lock our doors now, because we do not
agree with Giovangiuseppe that those were not 'human
footsteps.' G. says that they were surely flesh and blood,
large and bare.

A suitable boat with two rowers, capable of taking us to Sant' Angelo

p. 183

CHAPTER XV

WE HAD LUNCHED SEVERAL TIMES at Barano with our good
friends the Giustos. What meals! '*Mama mia!*' as the Ischians
say. How did we survive them?

We had earnestly entreated them not to kill the fatted calf
for us, and this they had promised. But, as Cesare put it,
his sisters could never quite grasp the fact that the English
and Americans ate at frequent intervals all day long and
consequently never had much of an appetite, while the
Ischians had only one real meal, which was at midday.

We protested that our principal meal was also in the
middle of the day, but a close cross-examination by Cesare
revealed that we ate, in addition to it, a late and scandalously large breakfast, a hearty tea, and a supper that was
by no means a mere symbol.

The Giustos, on the other hand, rose at four o'clock in
the morning, or, if they had kept late hours the previous
night, at half past four, and, after a cup of black coffee and
a peach, they pursued their various occupations until twelve

o'clock dinner. Between this and bedtime they had nothing beyond a light supper of bread and cheese washed down by a glass of wine. It was understandable, then, that this midday *colazione* was no occasion for toying with food, but was a solid meal prepared by that excellent cook, the Signorina Margherita, the eldest sister. And what a meal!

Cutting down breakfast the days we went to Barano, in the vain hope of coping with it, was just about as useless as a drop of water is to the sea. Furthermore, after our first experience, we always gave Dominica the day off, knowing full well that upon our return we should be unable to face any meal, and feeling that we should never require her services in the future.

It was not that we arrived without an appetite; on the contrary, our fast, the drive, and the invigorating air of the hills brought us to their table with a fine hunger. It was merely that we did not possess the physical space for storing away such mountains of food. From the first, everything tempted us toward gastric destruction. The lofty dining-room, with its graceful domed ceiling and its high windows in the recesses of the enormously thick walls, was delightfully cool; the snow-white cloth and the neatly laid table, and above all the *saporito* odours that emanated from the adjoining kitchen, sorely tried our prudence.

When the Signora Giusto had said grace, Cesare began uncorking his bottles; first a plain white wine to drink in the place of water, then another simple little wine (his words, not ours) to drink with the *antipasti*. This preliminary dish consisted of raw and cooked ham, pickled herring and anchovy, red peppers and capers, home-made bread and home-made butter. From the way we set about devouring these excellent things, one might have thought that they formed the chief part of the meal, and were not merely the prelude to it. Yet Cesare, with native courtesy, pressed us to second helpings, and, when we refused, would exclaim, '*Non avete mangiato nulla!*' and all the family would look inexpressibly shocked at our lack of appetite.

Things started in earnest with the appearance of a steaming tureen of soup, a savoury, full-bodied essence of innumerable and, alas, most nourishing things, the secret of which was known alone to the Signorina Margherita. This in turn made way for a gargantuan bowl of rich, creamy *pasta fatta in casa* – home-made macaroni – accompanied either by an appetising meat sauce or one made of sun-dried tomatoes. With it, Cesare would produce 'another little bottle.'

This dish was always the beginning of our defeat, partly because it was so innocently deceptive. It slid ingratiatingly down our throats, but, once safely inside, it assumed, like the wolf in Little Red Riding Hood, terrifying proportions. We felt gastronomically paralysed, yet it was the moment we had to exert the greatest vigilance lest the Signorina Margherita or her sister, taking advantage of some remark we imprudently made about the beauty of the view, filled our plates with a second helping! Once on our plates, reasoning or no reasoning, we had to eat it. A lifetime of Ischian traditions were not swept so lightly aside on the feeble excuse that we had no more appetite. '*Macché! Mangiate, mangiate!*' they would urge with fierce smiles.

It was useless to plead for the intervention of Cesare, for he, by then, had disappeared in search of more bottles. He was always extremely serious about the medicinal properties of his wines, although his modesty prevented him from commenting upon their excellence. This time it would be a red wine, stronger and better than the preceding vintages. It would cleanse the viscera, enrich the blood and *far' bene allo stomaco*, and against this filling of glasses there was as little hope of appeal as against the second helpings of *pasta*.

Carrying on a conversation in Italian after all these libations – for only Cesare spoke English – was extremely
difficult, but by then there was no time for talking, as the
chief dish of the meal made its appearance. It might be a
young kid roasted to a tender brown crispness, or one of
those giant rabbits renowned for their delicate flavour, and
of course surrounded by a variety of vegetables.

By this time Kit had been reduced to silence. The corners
of her mouth twitched into an automatic smile whenever she
was addressed, but her eyes were glassy and her hand sought
mine under the table for a squeeze of encouragement.
Slowly, heroically, she munched on, aided only by the
soothing vagueness of our host's wines.

At least, we thought, there could only be cheese and fruit
to follow, and, according to Ischian lights, one was not
obliged to eat them, but this illusion was confined to our
first visit. It might be a White Leghorn, a Rhode Island Red,
or a Plymouth Rock – a nasty name for anything so tender;
perhaps it was just a plain, unpedigreed, but well-fattened
native bird, but chicken it was. Never had I thought it
possible to view so coldly anything so delicious. I heard
myself stammering hypocritical exclamations of delight in-
termingled with abject regrets and excuses, lying statements
about being under doctors' orders and on a strict diet. The
family swept them all aside with the statement that chicken
was *molto leggero* – which by itself was a true enough statement – and that it was, in our case, *molto indicato*.

Oh, no. It was not 'indicated' by any means. Much more
indicated would have been a stretcher to carry us both out
under the shade of a tree, leaving us to recuperate. To make
matters more serious, all the best pieces were piled on to our
plates.

Cheese and fruit we stolidly refused, but when old Signora
Giusto rose from the table and disappeared into another
room to return with a sweet she had made with her own
hands, we knew that somehow, somewhere, we had to find
a little extra place. Do not think it was any ghastly concoction like the atrocity committed by Giovangiuseppe's mother
on our wedding anniversary. It looked, and was, delicious,
yet like Kit, who paled visibly, I felt that it was a pity we
could not politely ask to have it packed up and take it home
for consumption the following week.

It was then that Cesare tipped back his chair, and from
the side-table deftly caught hold of a bottle covered with
cobwebs, which had come to meet the light of day after
maturing for nearly half a century in a dark corner of one
of his numerous cellars. He admitted that there were few
of its vintage left, for the wine had been laid down by his
father before his birth, and, in bringing out one of these
rare bottles for us, Cesare was not only making a hospitable
gesture, but paying a singular compliment to our palates.

The wine was copper-coloured rather than red, and its
medicinal qualities as enumerated by our host would have
sufficed to make a watering-place famous. At the sight of it,
Kit came suddenly to life; the old New England sea captains
in her blood rose eagerly to the occasion. They had sailed
the seven seas, and, in addition to being connoisseurs of
Jamaica rum, which Kit, thank heaven, is not, possessed no
doubt a suitable appreciation for the excellence of Mediterranean wines. Rich as a cordial, mellow with age, it did
possess some of the life-saving qualities which Cesare claimed
for it. At each of our lunches at Barano, a similar bottle
made its appearance as the *gran finale*.

At this point the family withdrew, leaving us with our
host, who invariably offered us the option of a siesta on the

matrimonial bed or a stroll in the vineyards. The former was more tempting, but we knew that if we once succumbed to laying our heads on one of the pillow-cases so aptly embroidered *Buon Riposo*, it would have needed more will-power than we possessed to rise again when the time came to go home. Therefore we chose the vineyards, often sitting down on the shady, grassy slopes under the pretext of admiring the view.

In the late afternoon we would return to the Villa Buonocuore, to be greeted by good old Peter with leaps and bounds. He always wanted to hear a detailed account of what we had been doing in his absence, although, had he been obliged to render a similar account of his own doings during that time, he might have been acutely embarrassed. We would take him bathing with us, and afterwards spend the evening sipping non-alcoholic drinks on the terrace while he sat on his haunches, entranced and mystified by bluebottle flies.

He never succeeded in catching one, but he would sit indefinitely, watching them with beady eyes, his neck describing an almost complete circle in his effort to keep track of their flight. Round and round his head would go, then, when one of them was within easy reach, he would draw back his little black lips, exposing his fine white teeth in a ferocious snarl, spring forward manfully, and snap, snap, snap at it in rapid succession. When the bluebottle sailed heavily away, droning placidly to itself, Peter would return to his former position, defeated but undaunted. He was a patient dog!

CHAPTER XVI

I

WE ASKED PETER ONE EVENING if he would like to come with us for a long boat-ride to the other side of the island; if he would like to scamper, unhampered by hordes of teasing children, along a magnificent deserted beach; if he would like to act as bodyguard to us in the exploration of dark and mysterious caverns. Like all sensible dogs, he understood perfectly, and showed his appreciation by tearing madly up and down the garden. Cesare Giusto had repeatedly offered to act as escort, if we would let him know a day ahead. He often went down to the other coast to fish for octopus, and a friend of his was the owner of the vine-covered rock at Sant' Angelo, so like the castle. If we went by boat, he would meet us on the beach.

We hastily scribbled a note and sent it by a coachman. At the same time Giovangiuseppe was despatched to find us a suitable boat with two rowers capable of taking us to Sant' Angelo and back. This could almost always be managed,

except on a *festa*, by notifying the owner of the boat before
he set out for the night's fishing. Fishermen were glad
enough to be assured of a certain sum instead of being
dependent on their hazardous haul.

Next morning we were up early, and, while we had breakfast, our boy brought Giusto's verbal reply in the affirmative,
and at the same time informed us that a boat was waiting on
our little private beach. Dominica had prepared a copious
picnic hamper which was already on board. The day was
serene, the sea was as blue and unruffled as the sky, while the
boat, which had been newly painted, was a galaxy of colours.

With an eye to keeping trade in the family, our boy had
chosen his brother, who was a fisherman, as one of the
rowers, a splendid youth baked as brown as an African
tribesman by the Mediterranean sun. We set off with Peter
seated proudly and stiffly in the bow. The two men rowed
standing up, with long single oars which they manipulated
with a slow, steady forward stroke.

After a time they asked permission to remove their shirts.
Swiftly and silently the big boat cut through the water, the
men exchanging an uninterrupted flow of dialect and rowing
without any apparent effort except for the rippling muscles
in their strong backs.

When we had rounded the castle, a new world was opened
to us. High, arid, precipitous cliffs fell into the sea, and
continued their downward path, according to the fishermen,
to a great depth beneath the tranquil surface. Where rock
and sea met, the water was a deep cobalt blue. A little
further on, the men swung the boat around with a swift turn
of their oars and made straight for the jagged rocks, which
revealed, at our approach, the great natural arch of Ischia's
one marine grotto.

Our guides were anxious that we should not miss any of

the sights while in their charge. Inside this oasis of shade, the water assumed fantastic hues, reflecting the roof, walls and submarine floor of the grotto, the latter being studded with vivid patches of coral. The water was incredibly clear, and through it we could see what looked like small hedgehogs clinging to the rocks. Our boy's brother explained that they were *ricci*, a species of *frutti di mare* and very good to eat.

With the blade of his oar, he prised one loose and brought it to the surface. It was round, with long, sharp spikes of a deep purple, and seemed as inanimate as the rock it had clung to, but, when it was prodded, the spikes began to undulate gently back and forth, as though swaying in a strong current. With the aid of a bowie-knife, the fisherman chopped it into neat halves. We had expected to see some gruesome display of insides, but to our surprise the interior was as neat as though it had been scrubbed and also immaculately empty! Seeing that we doubted his statement about its being good to eat, he explained that this was not the right season. When the full moon came, the *ricci* would fill themselves with eggs. Since then we have seen many of these *ricci*, and eaten the rich yellow flower-like contents, and we understand also why, together with other crustaceous foods, the Italians call them by the lovely name of 'fruits of the sea.'

Once outside the grotto, the bright sunshine blinded us and the heat was scorching. We were glad of the protection afforded by our broad-brimmed native straw hats, which cast almost as much shade as an umbrella. The rowers did not seem to mind the sun, though they were bare-headed, and their only article of clothing above the waist consisted of a brightly coloured scarf, which they wore around their necks to prevent the sweat from trickling down their backs. Repeatedly we urged them to lay down their oars and rest, but they only laughed. They often went to Sant' Angelo to fish, they told us, not only rowing there and back, but putting in several strenuous hours casting and hauling in the nets as well.

Occasionally we passed fishermen taking a holiday from their regular work . . . by fishing! For this pastime they used rods instead of nets, baiting their hooks with *baccalà*, which was evidently considered as much of a delicacy by the fishes as by the islanders. Lusty greetings would then be exchanged between the two boats, followed by a volley of questions and answers in the obscurest dialect. Smiles and rapid glances in our direction revealed that the idiosyncrasies, past and present, of certain foreigners were being commented upon, and the details of the day's outing discussed, no doubt, more fully than we knew them ourselves. They could say what they liked without fear of hurting our feelings, for this dialect was incomprehensible to us. Our personal affairs were, however, only of passing interest to them; soon they were absorbed in their own affairs and in the distribution of local news.

It was an excellent demonstration of the native telegraph system in full swing. The information imparted and received at this encounter would travel on at the next one; it would be taken home by each individual listener, passed from fisherman to peasant, from seashore to vineyard, and in this way reach even the most remote village in the hills; and only a few hours late at that. No wonder that they had no use for the official telegraph; this was so much more lively and amusing, judging from the smacking of thighs and the gusts of laughter that rang out over the water, and it lent itself to infinite patterns of embroidery on the way, without losing track of the essential facts.

During this exchange of courtesies, Peter, curiously

enough, had been silent. Usually he took an active part in all
proceedings which involved the presence of strangers, even
at a distance, by barking himself hoarse. We looked at him
anxiously. No wonder he was silent, poor fellow, for under
his fine brown manly whiskers he was green! – yes, the pale,
ignominious green of one who is hopelessly, abjectly seasick.
I recognised the symptoms instantly, having frequently
experienced them, although it took more than the gentle
motion of a boat on a glassy sea to produce the effect on me.
All Peter's fire and sparkle, his dauntless courage, his
supreme arrogance, his superb Renaissance vanity, had
vanished. His ruffles no longer had their immaculate
starched appearance; his beautiful fluffy tail, habitually so
neatly curled around his posterior, drooped listlessly; and
from his proud lips he blew faint, despairing bubbles, the
aftermath of a rejected breakfast.

The men laughed heartlessly. '*Si é rovesciato!*' they
exclaimed – 'He has turned himself inside out' – which,
alas, most aptly sized up the situation. Before we could stop
him, one of them had seized Peter by the scruff of his neck
and plunged him into the sea. 'Now he will feel better,' he
said, exhibiting at arm's length a forlorn, dripping wreck
of a dog, and replacing him gently at the bottom of the boat
to dry. These drastic methods were much more efficacious
than our murmured sympathy and patting would have been,
and, after shaking himself vigorously all over us, he came
and settled down between our knees in the warm sun.

Happily we did not have much further to go. Rounding
the eastern point of the island, we skirted at last the south
coast. The cliffs withdrew to make place for the magnificent
beach of the Maronti, and behind them rose the hills leading
up to the Epomeo. Up there were Testaccio and Barano,
and, higher up, Serrara Fontana and Fontana. From the

vineyards of the Giustos we had often looked down on this very spot. Ahead of us, following the line of the beach, was the little village of Sant' Angelo, nestling by the water, with its curious rock.

There was one other boat in sight, manned by two rowers, and, as we appeared, it advanced swiftly to meet us. Standing in the bow and waving to us was Cesare Giusto.

II

Cesare was wearing his summer fishing costume, consisting of a pair of pearl-grey cotton pyjamas and a little white American sailor's hat perched at a rakish angle over one eye. He was most anxious to inspect his octopus pots before we set out to explore this part of the island, so that we might have some fresh baby *polipi* for lunch.

These *polipi* or *calamaretti* are of a retiring, domestic nature and insatiably curious. Like the lobster, they are easily enticed by the appearance of an attractive, uninhabited, and apparently safe home lying at the bottom of the sea, but, while the lobster likes his 'pot' to be made of basketwork, the octopus prefers his abode to be a real earthenware pot. He likes it wide at the bottom and with a narrow opening, so that, once inside, he fills it up completely. He is more than pleased when there are plenty of pebbles in it, for this enables him to get a firm hold with some of his tentacles, while with the others he can reach out and grab any unfortunate fish which happens to swim too near his hiding-place. Once in his grasp, there is no escape, and the octopus then draws his victim into the pot and devours him at leisure.

Like the perfect landlord, Cesare supplied them with all these commodities, and, after the fashion of modern dwellings, all his houses were close to each other in a row, a kind

of Octopus Lane on the sea floor. These houses were, however, not freehold, and their leases were short. They were
suspended from a long stout rope, one end being fastened to
the rocks near the beach.

After allowing the octopi a few days in which to take
possession of their new homes, the rope was raised and they
were rudely shaken out. To do this without disturbing the
position of the line, which was the object of careful calculation, Cesare did his inspection from a boat, pulling up the
pots one by one and dropping them back again into the
deep.

In the famous Naples aquarium, which at one time was,
I believe, considered to be the finest in the world for all
Mediterranean species, there were two giant specimens of
this particularly revolting monster, the octopus. Visiting
the aquarium with my parents when I was ten years old,
they horrified and fascinated me. Revisiting it twenty-five
years later with Kit, the horror was just as great although
the old octopi had been replaced by new ones.

Behind the fortunately thick panes of glass, we watched
them clinging motionless to the rocks that lined the sides
of the tank, their tentacles slowly coiling and uncoiling, and
their bodies, huge, gelatinous, and bell-shaped, from which
protruded hideous eyes, heaving slowly as they breathed.
Hoping for a tip, the attendant offered to feed them for us.
While we looked through the glass, he disappeared and
soon after, from the top of the tank, a bait was lowered on
a thin piece of thread. It was a living frog. No sooner had
one of the sluggish creatures spied it than, with incredible
rapidity, it shot up through the water, straight as an arrow,
and, with the tip of one of its tentacles, whipped hold of
its victim. Slowly the octopus sank to the bottom, and,
covering the frog with its bell-shaped mass, proceeded to

devour it. Hidden from view was a sharp curved tooth like the beak of a bird of prey, with which it tore its food to pieces.

The occupants of Cesare's pots were not of such terrifying proportions, although they possessed in miniature the same revolting characteristics. He asked us if we would care to board his boat before he started the examination of his catch, but, with the thought of a lively family of octopi slithering on the floor and over our bare legs, we declined. Instead, our boat drew alongside, and we watched from a comfortable distance.

The rope was raised, an earthenware jug came up dripping from the deep, but it was empty, and so, to Cesare's great disgust, was the next. The third looked equally empty, but when he shook it there slowly emerged two long tentacles blindly feeling their way; he gave another shake and the whole creature was out. It was extremely lively and immediately entwined itself around his bare arm. In a flash he bent down and dug his teeth into its head; the octopus became limp and was thrown into the bottom of the boat. With a grin, Cesare explained that this was necessary, for if the creatures were left alive, they would soon climb over the side and make their escape.

Up came more pots and the operation was repeated many times. It took accurate knowledge and long practice to know the exact place to bite in order to sever the nerve-centres, this being the usual way of killing them. Every man his price, as the saying goes, but I wondered what sum would tempt me to bite into this hideous, live, flabby mass of octopus. Yet this revulsion was absurd, for did not people order these *polipi* in restaurants and consider them a delicacy? We had often enjoyed a dish of them ourselves, but this day we were glad that Dominica had provided us with

a luncheon hamper, although we did not want to hurt
Cesare's feelings by telling him so.

When Cesare had completed his haul, the boat landed us
on the beach and we set out for the mysterious ravine of the
Cava Scura – the Dark Cavern – where the hot springs
whose lavender-coloured waters were so highly valued by
the islanders took their source.

A high wall of cliffs ran the whole length of this magnificent beach. They were bright yellow sandstone and matched
it perfectly. The entrance to the ravine was a mere fissure
in the wall of rock, and we would certainly have missed it
had it not been for Cesare. A trickle of water, making a deep
groove in the sand, was all that was left of the spring by the
time it reached the sea. We followed this trail barefooted;
the sand was beautifully soft, the water pleasantly cool, and
it was amusing to give oneself up to the guidance of the thin
lavender-coloured thread as it wound its way between the
high cliffs, knowing that it could not lead us astray.

Zigzagging upwards, the ravine changed into a gorge;
the cliffs closed in upon us, higher and more precipitous,
shutting out the fierce heat of the day, casting deep shadows
that were filled with silence and were just a little eerie.
Nowhere was a soul to be seen. From cold, the water
around our ankles became tepid, then warm, then decidedly
too warm, and it had increased to a stream. We had to
abandon hurriedly its smooth sandy bed and make our way
over the rocks that bordered it.

Our path had twisted so often that we had lost all sense of
direction, and with each bend Nature had become more
austere and secretive. At last, at the end of a long deep
chasm, we came upon the spring.

To a pagan mind it must have appeared like the approach
to the innermost temple of a strange god, for, on the wall

of the rock that blocked all further passage, Nature had sculptured a grotesquely sinister face such as might have inspired an artist of the Barocco. Under a mighty beak-like nose, a great wide mouth curved upwards into an obscene leer, while a mossy beard added a startling reality to this weird face. The most uncanny touch of all was added by the little puffs of steam which silently issued from the parted lips, as though the monstrous deity were actually breathing. From the black pool at its feet the boiling spring bubbled up.

Here was one of those mysterious natural phenomena which fired the imagination of the ancient world, causing men and women to make long pilgrimages to consult an oracle, to burn incense, offer sacrifices, search for auguries in the entrails of birds or beasts, be initiated by secret rites into divine mysteries, be cured of spiritual and bodily ills. They were the retreats of strange and powerful gods, to be approached even by the mightiest with awe.

To-day, in spite of all the saints of the island, I am not sure that some of this awe does not still linger in the minds of the peasants. In any case, the miraculous power of the water – the power to cure women of their sterility – is still firmly believed in, and, if what they say is true, this belief extends far beyond the island's boundaries.

At the base of the steep cliffs on either side of the spring we saw a row of black holes hewn out of the rock in a regular formation that showed evidence of human workmanship. They were, Cesare told us, the baths of the establishment! They were certainly the strangest baths in the world.

The interior of these cubicles was pitch-black, but, peering inside, we could just see a rudimentary bath-tub chiselled out of the floor, with a narrow ledge for the bather to undress and leave her clothes. The plumbing was as ingenious as it

Sant' Angelo - Ischia -
RM

Ahead of us . . . was the little village of Sant' Angelo, nestling by the water

p. 188

was primitive. Two holes had been drilled under each compartment. To fill the bath, any handy rock from the profusion of them that littered the chasm was placed in the middle of the stream, thereby directing its course into the upper hole, the other having been previously plugged. When the bath was full, the boiling water was left to cool to the desired temperature. The emptying process was even simpler; one merely kicked the stopper out of the lower hole. As a final touch of luxury, a piece of sacking was hung at the entrance of each cubicle to ensure perfect privacy.

Owing to the unique properties of the water, these baths were said to have been taken by a number of high-born ladies, including a large percentage of royalty. How little did their faithful subjects, reading in the Court chronicle the glad tidings of the birth of a royal heir or heiress (the waters did not guarantee a male issue), dream that it was all due to a furtive visit to the Cava Scura! Did these great ladies make the ascent of this lonely valley behind the closed curtains of a litter, wearing their robes of State, attended by their maids of honour, preceded by a guard with trumpets and a page bearing their crown on a velvet cushion, or . . . did they pick their way barefooted over the uneven rocks, stubbing their toes and swearing roundly as we had done?

The Ischians scratched their heads and puzzled over the question when I put it to them. They liked the former idea better, but on the whole they thought that 'the poor things' would prefer to keep it dark by coming incognito. Owing to the decline in crowned heads since the war, attendance at these baths had fallen off sadly. The Ischians themselves, never being at a loss for offspring, had no use for them, so, as we could plainly see, the miraculous waters were going to waste.

By the time we had returned to the beach it was almost lunch-time. Knowing that the heat would be too fierce to picnic there, a friend of Cesare had generously placed the loggia of his house at Sant' Angelo at our disposal. Before going there we wanted to see the *fumerola*, the smoking sands at the far end of this curious beach. By shading our eyes we could see the slender column of sulphurous smoke rising in the distance.

On the way, we passed another crevasse in the rocks leading into another valley, and with another stream running down it. This came from a cold spring known as the Olmitello, cold but fiery in its effect. It was much looked down upon by the chemists of the island, because its excellent purgative qualities robbed them of an important branch of their trade.

The islanders, like most Italians, believe implicitly in the wisdom of frequent and regular interior spring-cleanings, and treat this subject with the natural simplicity it deserves. For them it is no dark, unfortunate occurrence, to be mentioned only in whispers, and, if its tyrannical effects keep one indoors, the fact does not have to be hypocritically disguised as the result of a headache, or the urgent need of catching the last post. On the contrary, it provides an excellent topic of conversation, and is often a suitable excuse for declining, without fear of giving offence, an invitation, a business trip, a glass of wine, or a dish of peaches. '*Grazie, ma mi sono purgato*,' is a statement sufficient unto itself.

If the waters of the Cava Scura are in very little local demand, the Olmitello enjoys universal favour. As it is a long way to go to fetch a glassful, anybody making a trip to that side of the island is usually entrusted by a friend with a *damigiano* – a large, wicker-covered green glass bottle generally used for the transportation of wine, and holding about twenty-five litres. This, when filled, is stored away in the medicine-chest along with the red quinine powder which the family sprinkles on its *risotto* when it has a cold, and it will last a long time. A generous supply of Olmitello water also enables the owner to show less fortunate neighbours a little hospitality. It is an everyday occurrence, as we saw when we lived at the Albergo del Porto, where there was always a bottle on hand, for an urchin to come drifting in with an empty glass and a request to 'Please fill it up for mama!'

What an island! With hot springs on tap at Porto d'Ischia, mud baths there and at Casamicciola, the iron springs at Sant' Anna, and, on this side of the island, the Cava Scura and the Olmitello, one cannot say that Nature does not provide the inhabitants with every means of curing their ills and enabling them to enjoy the other bounties which she hands out with such a liberal gesture: fish, fruit, and excellent wine, warm sun, blue sky, and a happy, lazy disposition.

In the middle of these reflections we were startled to see before us the head of a man lying on the sand. It was the sort of sight which, had we been travelling in Manchuria, would have given us a nasty turn. But this head was well cared for. An umbrella was propped up beside it to keep off the glare of the sun, and at a respectful distance two youths in bathing-shorts, black as niggers, kept watch over it. The head was old, tired, and very sick-looking, but it was not severed from the rest of its owner. Most of us have been buried in the sand at some time or other, but the job is usually a crude one. This man was so magnificently interred that not even the faintest hump or ripple on the sand showed where the rest of him was.

Kit, who says that men never dare to ask the simplest questions, bent down and asked him with her sweetest smile what was the matter with him. He explained that he was a sufferer from severe stomach trouble, and had chosen this particular spot because it lay on the outer fringe of the *fumerola* and was impregnated with sulphur. I asked gravely if I might photograph him, and with equal gravity he acquiesced.

At some distance from where the yellow smoke was rising, it was noticeably hotter underfoot, and just below the surface the sand was burning. A strata of volcanic fire ran from the cliff wall to the sea and to an unknown distance beneath it, but, curiously enough, only in certain veins. Owing to this we were able to find a path through the centre of it and up to the miniature crater. There the sand was bright green, it shifted ceaselessly with a dry, crackling sound; the heat was like the blast from a furnace, and the odour . . . well, everybody knows what sulphur smells like. Here eggs could be baked by merely pushing them into the sand, and a complete meal, in fact, could be cooked by placing the pots and pans on the surface.

The beach did not run as far as Sant' Angelo. To reach it on foot would have meant climbing over steep cliffs, but, as the boats had followed our progress, we clambered aboard and with a few swift strokes of the oars were transported to our destination. If Sant' Angelo looked charming from the sea or from up at Barano, it was even more lovely at close quarters. It owed none of its enchantment to distance. The dirt and dilapidation which at Procida contributed so generously to Latin picturesqueness played no part here. Houses and alleys were scrupulously clean, as though the wind had swept them. Broad arches and loggias and outdoor stairways leading to flat terraced roofs were the predominant features of its architecture, while pink, blue, and beige alternated with white in its colour-scheme.

Sant' Angelo had no need of the Spaggia dei Maronti, for it had two magnificent beaches of its own, formed by the causeway that joined it to its isolated rock. The main part of the village clung to the coast, but a few adventurous houses had wandered off and established their independence in the shadow of the rock, and between the two settlements boats were drawn up, nets were being dried and mended, and bathers idled. The rock so strikingly similar in shape and size to the castle at Ischia was devoid of habitation. It was entirely planted with vineyards, and was owned by the gentleman whose bright blue house was placed at our disposal for lunch.

Cesare's friend was a discreet and amiable host. His loggia overlooked a sparkling expanse of blue water and was as cool as an oasis. One corner of it was occupied by a long table decked with a white cloth, plates, silver, and glasses. A picnic it might be, but he would have failed to keep the Ischian traditions of hospitality had he not allowed himself the pleasure of supplying the wine and the bread. He also supplied, as we soon discovered, a generous assortment of *antipasti*, and insisted on cooking Cesare's baby octopi. We did not turn with a shudder from this dish when it appeared in a rich sauce of tomatoes, herbs, and spices, for it was delicious.

By the time we had done justice to these contributions, Dominica's lunch-basket, which was to have been the main-stay of the party, lost its rosy significance. By the time we had partaken of our host's cheese and fruit, we wondered what to do about it. We could not possibly hurt Dominica's feelings by returning with her delicacies untouched, so we urged the four boatmen, Cesare's and our own, to eat them. This they did very politely, although I have a suspicion that they would have preferred their own slices of bread and garlic to this sumptuous fare.

It was fortunate that we accomplished before lunch everything that required any effort, for the contrast between the heat outside and the delightful shade of the loggia, and the effect of our copious lunch had reduced us to a state of passive contentment. We would have liked to linger on, and so would Peter, for whom the sea trip ahead held no joys, but it was a long way back to the Villa Buonocuore, and, if our boatmen were to get any sleep before setting out on their night's fishing, we had to make an early start.

With reluctance we took leave of our host and also of Cesare, who had no pressing business to drag him out into the afternoon heat. He was staying behind to indulge in a little siesta before undertaking the steep climb up to Barano. At the thought of this long ordeal ahead of him, we pitied him profoundly. However, at the last moment he would probably think better of it and confide his weary limbs to the care of an *asinello*. Donkeys were constantly covering the trail between Sant' Angelo and the hill-towns, laden with barrels of wine. It would be an honour for one of them to carry up the mountain the owner of the vineyards which produced most of it.

CHAPTER XVII

FROM KIT'S DIARY

I

I LIKE LIVING in this colony of fishermen and their families. They are simple and wise; what they do, they do heartily; they love, they laugh, they sorrow, and – from what we have heard of the *vendetta* – they hate, all whole-heartedly. Birth and death are deeply reverenced. The years between hold arduous work and much privation; but they also hold quick laughter and the undemanding, delighted enjoyment of little things, which is the greatest gift life can offer.

I have never seen a life so hard and bare in outline, yet so gay and happy in accompaniment.

Their homes typify this. Living conditions are, I suppose, appalling. It is only the sun that could save these houses, many of them centuries old, from squalor. They are divided into many *appartamenti*, and families of eight or ten live in a room or two, sleeping heaven knows how many to a bed.

Yet, as we walk through the little alleys and look through the big, low windows into these family rooms, there are none that are not scrupulously clean and orderly. Moreover, in spite of their poverty there is always an attempt at decoration in the Ischian style: gaudy chromos of sacred subjects on the walls, wax flowers and holy dolls under shining glass globes. In one corner there is sure to be an image of the Virgin, and before it a saucer of oil in which floats a little wick, perpetually alight.

In size and importance the matrimonial bed holds the centre of the scene. It is the first possession every would-be bridegroom acquires, and, though it may now accommodate father, mother, and many children, its early glories are still undimmed. Robust brass cupids rear themselves on coils of brass tubing and gaze fatly down on the family they have hallowed, waving a true lovers' knot in benediction. The linen is immaculate, and turned back to show the wealth of filet, embroideries, and the heavily embossed '*Buon Riposo*' on which the wife worked for so many hours of her girlhood.

Outside, the houses are equally well cared for. Most of them are freshly colour-washed each year, the owners choosing the charming pastel shades according to their taste, and doing the work on the feast-day of the village's patron saint, when it may be done without payment of the usual iniquitous tax which is levied on all whitewashing, interior or exterior.

The thresholds of these houses stand on the sand of the beach, and it is on the beach, where the vivid colours of the boats make a bright fringe to the tranquil water at the shore, that family life is lived; and here there is always gaiety and talk. First, there are the children – numberless children – running on the sand, around the boats, in and out of the water. They are dark and wiry, nearly naked. Their mothers, sticklers for decency, put little cotton breech-cloths on the boys, and on the girls tattered old pinafores that fly up as they duck into the water, showing the slim little brown bodies underneath.

Then there are the men, busy about their boats; and the women always, it seems, in their doorways, talking, laughing, shouting with their neighbours. Some of these have toddlers attached to their skirts; some nurse a baby at the breast as they stand talking; some have new babies on the way; and still others have all three. None seem to resent the pain, care, and expense of their many children, and the philosophy with which they accept the expectation of each new arrival turns to passionate love, shared by the father, on its birth.

'*Buona sera, signore, signora!*' They know us well now. We pause to watch four men heaving their boat into the water, and they stop their work and, breathing hard, show us the powerful lamps in the stern of the craft, now lit and hissing under the pressure of the oil.

A flock of children run up, shouting 'Goo-goo! Goo-goo!' to irritate Peter, and when he flies furiously in pursuit of them, barking shrilly, they race light and swift into the shallow water, where he will not follow, shrieking with delight. The women laugh too, and hold up the smaller members to see the fun; one baby whimpers at the deafening noise of shouting and barking; his mother shakes him and screams in his ear to be quiet and look. The men stop their work at the boats for a minute to laugh and call, 'Hurry thyself, Peppi!', 'Faster, Mari!', '*Caspita!* The little dog almost had thee that time!'

Then the boats slide into the water, one by one, and slip away through the clear evening light; Peter quiets his barking as we walk slowly along the beach that bears the name, lovely as itself, of La Mandra. Our day is nearly done; soon it will be time to go back to the quiet darkness of our garden, to wash in the clear cold water from our well, to cross to the little white house where the yellow light of candles is like a jewel set in the warm night, and Giovangiuseppe is waiting with a smile to wish us '*Buon appetito.*'

But the fisherman's day is only beginning. All through the night he is in his boat, his lights shining fathoms deep into the water, spreading his nets over and over again, pulling in their weight slowly, knot by knot. With the first light he comes back to the island, and before he rests he must pack his catch in little flat baskets, one sort of fish in each: blue fish, scarlet fish, green and golden fish, fish with horns and snouts like devils, eels neatly coiled, and octopi, so disgusting to see, so good to eat.

In the late afternoon we often go down to our little private beach. There the fishermen, refreshed by three or four hours' sleep, are laying their nets again off the rocks by the old prison. We watch while they are pulled in; two men are at each end of the net; their muscles stand out as they work.

We wait until the catch, pitifully small, lies flippering on the shore. Sometimes I choose our evening meal from it, and send one of the men up to settle the price with Dominica. We have a beautiful supper; a vast platter of whitebait, for which I have paid three halfpence. I would like to give more – I am sorry for the fishermen – but Dominica says no, we must set no precedents. She bargains down to the last soldo.

II

These people are so generous. Whatever their faults – and certainly by common standards they are far from perfect – they are genuinely eager to give pleasure.

ISLAND IN THE SUN

Among people whose only possessions are the fruit of continuous hard labour, whether in the cultivation of their land or in the drawing of a meagre living in nets from the sea, generosity of any sort has a doubled value.

There is Giovangiuseppe's mother. She comes down from the hills once a week to trade at the Port. She is an old woman, nearly seventy; Giovangiuseppe is the youngest of her eleven children. But her age does not release her from any of her duties; neither does it seem to distress her. She rubs the sweat from her forehead and neck after her long walk, but everybody does that; it is very hot now, even in the little shady cobbled lanes that criss-cross the island through the vineyards. She dismounts a large basket from her head, and accepts a cup of black coffee from Dominica.

Then, if I am not already there, I am called, and we exchange friendly greetings, especially friendly because we communicate mostly in smiles. She has a dialect with which I shall never come to terms; occasionally Dominica, smiling tolerantly, translates some salient remark, but otherwise I am left groping for the light; and that what I say is completely incomprehensible to her she shows by polite shrugs and little amused shakes of her head.

She points to her basket, covered with a clean blue cotton handkerchief, and says, 'Signo', ho portato qualchecus' per Vui.' Or so it sounds. In the basket are packed some fine tomatoes, and a shining purple eggplant from her garden, cherries and nespoli from her trees, perhaps two or three eggs, a bunch of flowers, and a bottle of wine from her husband's vineyard. All that she brings is the produce of their property, and to give it to us must mean a sacrifice for them.

So far I have been able to make no return for all her gifts, but she expects none; it is she who is grateful to us because we give her boy work, feed him well, and treat him kindly.

She takes her leave quite easily: *'Signo'*, *me ne vad'*, *statevi be'.'* She does not suffer the excruciating difficulties that many in the so-called higher classes endure before they can bring themselves to go away.

She walks through our gate, swinging gracefully with the perfect carriage of one who has carried burdens on her head all her life, a charming figure of an old woman, her face thin and brown, inquisitive and kindly, her faded skirt full, and gathered in at the waist to a tight bodice, the hem almost touching the ground around her bare feet.

III

Then there is Antonio and his family. Antonio is a fisherman, not very young any more; he lives in the Via Rougemont and owns the *barca blu* that we see drawn up on the long beach outside our garden gate. He has small twinkling blue eyes, rare here, and he pads around quite silently on hard bare feet.

He has four grown sons who are fishermen like himself and go every year to Morocco with a fishing-fleet from Genoa. There is a small son too, a dark brown wiry wisp, who is already nimble with the nets and very quick at sorting his father's catches.

Antonio's wife is big and deep-breasted, and still lovely with her white hair and brown skin and fine white teeth. She has such a wealth of natural wisdom that the least thing she says, if it is only about the seasons when her hens lay, appears to issue forth in form of a proverb. As she talks she spins rough flax into thread with a skill that demands no attention, the spindle whirling unceasingly on the ground at her feet.

The family of seven live in three rooms, one of which is

the kitchen. Even this is used for housing: two rabbits, man and wife, live on a shelf high above the stove. Lately they have had a family – nine yellow balls who peer down with tiny shining eyes at the kitchen below, never doubting, I suppose, that they belong to an aerial race.

Yesterday morning Antonio came to our gate and issued an invitation. They were going to fish at the beach called Carta Romana in the afternoon; it would be *una bella passeggiata*, and they would be honoured if we would come. They would show us how the nets were laid and drawn in, and we could also visit the famous springs of Sant' Anna which bubbled up at one end of the same beach.

When we went down to the shore at two o'clock it was immediately clear that this was to be no ordinary boat ride. Everything was being done in the grand manner. The boat was already lying in the shallow water; I pulled up my skirt to wade out to it, but before I could do so a stream of dialect burst from Antonio and at once one of the sons picked me up and, too embarrassed to offer any explanation, carried me to the boat.

The *barca blu* had been especially fitted for our comfort. Two kitchen chairs stood stiffly in the bow; there was a blanket folded on them and an overturned wooden tub for a footstool. We would have rather sat on the deck, but Antonio's pride in his arrangements put this out of the question.

So, sitting erect and proper, we set out, the four sons bending to their oars, their mother waving excitedly from the shore and adding a fine air of importance to our departure. We slid at a good pace past our garden wall, past the old prison, and along the length of the fishermen's beach and La Mandra.

Antonio, meanwhile, stood by us and entertained us with

a spate of conversation and information. There, where the *pineta* now grew close by our house, the one-time town of Ischia had stood. In the eruption of the Epomeo in 1301 it had been completely destroyed; the inhabitants had fled to the castle for refuge from the river of molten lava.

Did we know that there was a giant, Tifeo, imprisoned beneath the island? So the legend said, anyway. *'Guardate!'* We could see the outline of his colossal body if we followed the direction of Antonio's pointing finger. There, under the sharply peaked mass of the volcano, the monstrous head lay. Now that the giant had ceased to struggle against the load that bound him, the mountain was quiet. But in the old days – *'Mama mia!'* – how angrily he had belched fire and smoke from the crater over his face! And the mineral springs that gushed up in all parts of the island were, they said, his tears transformed by kindly Venus into healing waters. His chest had pushed up the hill above San Dominico; the knees, still flexed from the monster's struggle, were humped under Monte Campagnano, there where the pink houses clung to the side of the steep green hill. Antonio indicated this small village, perhaps six houses in all, with pride. He said, 'That, *signori*, is Campagnana, the city of my wife's birth!' Finally the giant's toes had pushed up the castle rock from the very bed of the sea. *'Speriamo che mo si trova content',* said Antonio.

Now we had passed under the causeway and were nearing the shadowed water under Monte Campagnano. Antonio pointed out the openings of many caves that pocked the rounded contour of the hill. They were hollowed out of the soft rock by farmers and were used as storehouses for tools. But – and here his voice grew sibilant – in some of the caves *munielli* had come to live, and these caves were ill-omened and the farmers had no choice but to close them up and never use them again.

For these *munielli* were wicked and dangerous; it was enough that a man set eyes on one that he must follow wherever the spirit might lead. Impotent, powerless to reason or resist, unconscious save for the mad activity of his limbs, he would fly swift and blind across the sleeping countryside in pursuit of the tossing, malevolent *muniello*, that would end the chase perhaps with its victim's leap over some tall cliff, or his disappearance fathoms deep in the cold night water.

Incredibly, we could see on the hillside certain of the caves closed and barred with stout logs. Giovangiuseppe's precautions on the night of our footpad were explained.

We drew in close to the Carta Romana, a lovely long crescent of white sand, hemmed in on three sides by steeply rising ground and the rich green of summer vines. The sons nosed the boat in carefully to the shore, steering between four long-legged mules, three horses, and several dogs that were standing tranquilly in the water cooling themselves.

We left Antonio and his sons to lay the nets, and set off along the beach. Where the sands ended we clambered over great boulders, and came to the springs.

There were three of them, bubbling up nearly at boiling-point from the sandy sea bottom into the salt water above. Around the spots where they rise, generations of bathers have made loose circles of stones, which keep out part of the cold sea-water whilst letting in enough to temper the fierce heat within. The stones were reddened and crusted with mineral deposits.

According to Jasolino, an Ischian doctor quoted as an authority in our little local guide-book, 'This clear ferruginous water is excellent for the "false phlegm," and for the blood; it dries tears and cures sore eyes, restoring and comforting them; causes women's functions to become normal; aids weak hearts, chests, and lungs; disperses coughs; stops hair from falling; relieves colic, aching legs, and piles; etc., etc.'

And again: 'The spring water sharpens the vision; reinforces broken bones; steadies loose teeth; is good for dizziness and the gums; completely removes blemishes from the face; most happily amends sterility; breaks gallstones; and renders the voice clear and melodious for those who sing.'

In one of the improvised baths a thin man and several women half floated, half reclined on the warm sandy bottom. They were all wrapped in cotton sheets which seemed determined to expose their wearers either by floating away, or by clinging more closely than the most extreme bathing-suit to mountainous thighs and tumultuous bosoms. On the dry rocks near by were piles of discarded clothing – cotton dresses, wooden clogs, and sturdy pantaloons and petticoats.

The atmosphere in the bath was one of the greatest friendliness; talk and laughter were hilarious. Had their feet been touching under a bridge-table instead of floating together in mineral water they could not have been more completely social.

Our appearance disturbed them not one whit. '*Venite, signori!*' they cried. 'Take your clothes off!' They clutched an escaping sheet and screamed with laughter. They grew serious. They expounded the miracles of the baths of the holy Sant' Anna. One woman was barren; one was losing her hair; one had a *dolore* in her kidney. All confidently awaited a complete cure. Even the man, who looked grey and ill, said the waters had brought him back from death's door.

In the late afternoon we often go down to our little private beach

p. 202

ISLAND IN THE SUN

In this dramatic country, one is continually missing death by a hair's breadth. Dominica, who had a boil on her face, was told by the chemist that had she not been so strong she would be dead; I suppose I had a narrow escape during my attack of too much Flit!

As the bathers talked, including us in their friendly group, a young girl, slim and russet brown and lovely, ran lightly down the long flight of steps on the steep flank of Monte Campagnano. She carried a big green bottle on her head. She jumped easily from stone to stone until she reached the first of the springs where the people lay. There she bent down and held her bottle under the water, among the legs and sheets, until the bubbles ceased to rise from its neck. She swung it to her head, jumped as lightly as before over the rocks, and was off up the side of the hill.

Our friends told us that the girl's mother suffered much from her stomach. What? Oh, no, she would not bathe in the water her daughter brought; she would drink it!

'*Buona sera, buon bagno!*' we called hastily, and escaped, promising to come back another day and (perhaps) have a bath – but certainly not a drink!

Now the hill had stolen the sun; the beach was cool as water; the sea stretched out flat and white from the hot calm of the day.

Soon Antonio and his sons had drawn their net to the sands, and a tangle of fish was quivering in its meshes. One son went to the boat which lay, a splash of colour, linking sand and sea. He brought out the wooden tub and filled it with water. Into it, one by one, he gravely dropped wriggling little fishes, taking always those of the brightest colours, or the most luminous scales, scarlet, blue, and silver.

Were they to be kept alive until they were sold? we asked.

Oh, no, answered Antonio with fine pride, that was not the reason at all. The *vasca* of living fish was to be placed at my feet lest I should be bored; throughout the homeward ride I could amuse myself with the swimming of the little fish.

This truly gracious act was the climax of the carefully planned afternoon's entertainment.

All the way home, through the castle's rose-coloured reflection, past the old town to our beach, I watched the bright, flickering things swim in their tub, while the four sons, silent with us to the last, smiled on us benevolently, mightily pleased with the pleasure they had given.

CHAPTER XVIII

EVERY TUESDAY, at the stroke of midday, Giovangiuseppe came running across the garden to the loggia where I sat writing, to announce '*Signore*, Sant' Antonio is at the gate!' With equal haste at the thought of keeping a saint waiting, I collected my modest offering and hurried down to meet him.

He was dressed in the coarse brown habit of his order, and around his waist was knotted the double thickness of rope which served as a scourge. His cowl was neatly folded at the back of his head and his feet were shod with sandals. In his hand was a little wooden box on which was pasted a coloured reproduction of the miraculous image of Sant' Antonio in the Ischian church, and he had come to collect offerings for the poor.

Although by my express orders our boy, who at first used to leave him standing outside the closed gate, now invited him into the garden, he never ventured further than a step across the threshold. Greeting me with a quiet '*Buon

211

giorno,' he would extend his box and, as I slipped a coin inside, would gravely raise his skull-cap in acknowledgment, then glide away as noiselessly as he had come, not to be seen again until the following Tuesday.

His face was fine, kind, and holy, and although he was not, as Giovangiuseppe seemed to imply, a vision of Sant' Antonio, but a frail flesh and blood Franciscan monk collecting in his name, I have little doubt that he was one of the many obscure and humble saints who followed his example.

Leaving to their more exalted brethren, the Dominicans, the rôle of teachers, preachers, collectors and preservers of priceless sacred manuscripts; leaving the Trappists, with their vow of silence, to save humanity by their prayers – these humble, self-effacing monks devote their lives to feeding the poor, nursing and caring for the sick and aged, helping wherever human kindness is needed.

Although a few bring considerable sums to the Order when they join, none of them possesses anything, for they take the vow of poverty. No case is too desperate, no disease too dreaded, no upheaval too great, to prevent them from carrying out their mission of charity. In the great cholera epidemics, which until forty years ago were the scourge of Naples; in the violent earthquakes and appalling eruptions of Vesuvius, which between them have repeatedly laid waste both the fertile countryside and the populated regions of the Gulf, they have always been the first on the scene. More than fire, molten lava, disease, death, and destruction is required to keep them from their work.

On this peaceful island, far removed from the turgid misery of the great city across the water, they still had their hands full, and, if there were no desperate cases among the poor, no starving or homeless people, it was again because of them. Every day at noon and in the evening, seated on the stone benches in the courtyard of the little Chiesa di Sant' Antonio at Ischia, could be seen the seventeen destitute old men and women of the commune, waiting to be fed. Presently the monks would appear with steaming bowls of macaroni covered with an appetising sauce, which they would ladle out in generous helpings, together with a large chunk of bread, to each one.

Their good work was recognised by the poor. They were loved and respected because of their voluntary poverty, their hard and frugal lives, their tireless work on behalf of others, because they gave everything and kept nothing, because they were the trusted friends of all who were in need. Every Ischian, no matter how hard up, peasant or fisherman, gave with a willing smile when the monk with his little wooden box passed from door to door on his weekly rounds, not omitting the Villa Buonocuore. When we came face to face, Sant' Antonio and I, we did not carry on the usual bright Ischian conversation, although we were on the friendliest terms. We hardly spoke; yet, for some reason I could not have explained, I always found myself thanking him for his visit.

This Order of Franciscans is very powerful, probably because no accusing finger can be lifted against it. Collections are taken up in every city, town, and village in Italy; on board trains and boats, in restaurants and in cafés. Because the monks have no money of their own, and on account of the nature of their work, the steamship companies which control the services between Naples and the islands, the State railways, and the owners of most of the local means of conveyance, grant them free transportation, and I believe that this is the case throughout the country.

In connection with this, I was told an amusing and true

story by young Dr. Palermo, who, although an Italian of the modern school, on the whole anti-clerical, was a fervent admirer of the *Frati*.

The director of a certain local train service on the mainland had consistently refused to allow the Brothers free travel on his line, and the Abbot of the Order, an able man renowned for his wit as well as for his saintliness, had remonstrated with him repeatedly, but in vain. One day the latter came to his office when the director was very busy, and, without waiting to be announced, entered his private office and walked slowly up to his desk in silence. Inserting his hand in the ample folds of his habit, he drew out a little wooden statue of great age and beauty, and gravely set it down before him.

'*Ecco*,' he said, 'Sant' Antonio has come to see you! You have refused me many a time. Will you now dare to refuse *him*? For long you have stood in the way of his good work. What must he think of you?' Lifting up the statue, he banged it down again with a determination which made all the other objects on the desk jump. 'Sant' Antonio will stay with you until to-morrow,' he continued, 'when I shall return and, in his name, ask for an answer.' Before the director could recover from his surprise, the Abbot had walked out of the room.

The director was sorely perplexed. It was one thing to defy the Abbot – in his mind an overbearing man who wanted to get something for nothing – but it was quite another matter to defy Sant' Antonio. He cursed the Abbot under his breath – for even blasphemy is forbidden by law nowadays – but he did not dare to remove the statue from his desk. In its poor brown habit, the little figure looked down at him with gentle reproach; perhaps there was something more than reproach in his gaze, something of the fiery domination of the old Abbot. What, indeed, would Sant' Antonio think of him, and what might he not do to him if he continued to hinder the good work of the *Frati*? Every time he raised his eyes from the papers on his desk, the director caught sight of the statue, and it quite spoilt his day's work.

The idea would not leave him in peace. It pursued him home, destroyed his appetite for dinner, and interrupted his sleep with horrible nightmares in which he burned in eternal fires.

The next morning he returned to his office in a bad temper but with a shaken will. Blast the Abbot; blast the entire Brotherhood! It would cost him a lot of money to allow the monks free travel on his line, but not nearly so much as all the Masses which would be required to get his soul out of Purgatory if he didn't. When the Abbot arrived, his face was wreathed in smiles. He received the director's consent without showing the least surprise. He knew his little plan would work, he said, for he had tried it often before! It was, he remarked good-humouredly, just another miracle of Sant' Antonio!

CASTELLO
d'Ischia
R·M

CHAPTER XIX

THE *vendemmia* was at hand, and the entire island was in a
turmoil of excitement. The grapes that had been turning
deep purple and deep golden in their opulent bunches were
ready to be picked, and on the southern side of the island,
where the Giusto vineyards were situated, the fiercer sun
had ripened them earlier and the *raccolta* had already been
made and the new wine pressed.

We had taken many strolls through the vineyards since
our return from Sant' Angelo and had got lost in them more
than once. Unlike the French vines, that are kept low, the
Ischian vines are allowed to grow eight and ten feet high,
so that the vineyards become little forests criss-crossed by
paths like a labyrinth.

From the peasants we learned a good deal of the hard-
ships that attend the cultivation of the vines, and of their
hopes and disappointments. While the fishermen reap, in
the night's haul, the immediate result of their labour, the
entire year's livelihood of the peasants depends on the success

of the *vendemmia*. It is a great gamble, for the grapes are not safe from the multitude of things that can go wrong with them until the actual moment arrives when they are finally picked and carried away in great wooden tubs on the heads of the womenfolk.

Constantly, the year round, the vines have to be cared for, the soil around them hoed and fertilised, the leaves sprayed with sulphate of copper to protect them against that dreaded blight with the charming name, the phyloxera, until the vineyards and the paths through them gleam with the metallic blue-green of verdigris. Even when the grapes have matured and hang in magnificent bunches, beautiful as a picture, they are not safe. Often in the last weeks, sometimes on the eve of the day on which they are to be picked, great black clouds will pile high into the blue sky, the air becomes chilled, and hail comes pelting down. In half an hour it is all over; the sky resumes its serenity and . . . every opulent bunch in the vineyards is withered and worthless. One cannot be surprised that, when the day of the *vendemmia* is actually reached without disaster, general relief finds vent in singing and dancing.

A good deal of ancient tradition handed down from father to son through the centuries attends the picking and, above all, the pressing of the grapes, and, knowing that we were interested, all our friends on the island asked us to assist. Giovangiuseppe, however, was the first with his invitation, having assured us early in the summer with his habitual optimism that the weather would be beautiful and the sight well worth seeing, both of which predictions turned out to be true.

It was our first visit to his family and to his native village, a tiny hamlet clinging to the hillside on the way to Barano. We drove up in the afternoon, as, in addition to seeing the *vendemmia*, we had been invited to stay to supper. Leaving the carriage at a certain point on the road, we followed Giovangiuseppe through the vineyards to his father's house. There his six brothers and four sisters were busy gathering grapes, and we realised how useful it was at certain times of the year to have a large family.

We were most cordially received, and while they showed us around the property the father outlined the afternoon's programme. Painstakingly he had planned what he thought would most interest us. First, Giovangiuseppe was to conduct us to his godfather's property, where the wine-making was in full swing. He apologised for not being able to accompany us, but he would meet us for supper at his son-in-law's house, which had a fine view and was more comfortable, he said, than his own humble *casetta*. We knew that this invitation entailed a lot of extra work; we knew also that they would have been deeply hurt had we refused.

The owner of the house to which we were escorted had evidently been chosen as godfather on account of his social status in the little community. He was the chief landowner, and resided in a large red house devoid of all native character, surrounded by a hideous garden ornamented with cement statues. This was to impress neighbours with the fact that, unlike them, he was a *signore*, a man who did not have to work and who could afford to hire labourers to do it for him. After we had solemnly admired the garden, we were taken to the back of the house, where the real life of the family went on. Here were the cellars, the olive and wine presses, and the kitchen, all opening on to a courtyard, with the vineyards beyond. Here also the godfather laid aside temporarily his rôle of 'gentleman' and took an active interest in what was going on. Everywhere there was a feverish activity, as our boy's father had predicted.

He took us into the vineyards, where women and children were gathering the heavy purple and golden bunches and piling them high into big wooden buckets on the ground. Everybody was laughing and singing and carrying on animated conversations. As soon as one *tino* was full, it was hoisted on to the head of a sturdy young peasant girl who, barefooted, carried it to the courtyard. Most of these girls were pretty, and some were beautiful, with classical features bronzed by the sun, full red lips, and dark eyes veiled by magnificent lashes. They had flowers in their hair, and when they smiled their white teeth flashed. Walking with arms upraised to support their heavy load, they had the grace and poise of ancient Greek statues.

The courtyard was the real centre of activity. It was the meeting-place of all the workers and the temporary store-house for the grapes. Neatly lined up in the shade, the big tubs, filled to the brim, were waiting to be taken to the vats, while others were constantly being lifted down from the heads of the women and added to the row. From distant parts of the vineyards, mules were led in, their flanks saddled with enormous wicker baskets overflowing with more grapes. From the cellars, men strolled out for a cigarette, their bare legs stained with the purple juice. Children fought, played, and chased each other around the barrels and tubs, filling the air with their shouting, while under the pergola men and women sat talking and laughing before going back to work.

Our host took us to see the wine being made. In a large, high-ceilinged, whitewashed room, a corner had been squared off to form a gigantic vat. Its sides reached up to the shoulders of a tall man, and it was filled with a high mound of grapes. Leaning against it was a ladder. When it was filled to its utmost capacity, three men with naked feet climbed up on to the mound and began to trample it down. This they did very evenly, one man at either end and the third in the middle. Their steady rhythmic pace was like a dance, and they kept time by singing.

Their song had innumerable verses and a refrain, and it could be continued almost indefinitely. It was the old traditional wine-song reserved exclusively for the trampling of the grapes, just as there was a song for the picking of the olives and another for beating the mortar on the domed roofs of the native houses. This wine-song gave the exact *tempo*, the peasants said, to obtain the maximum juice from the fruit. When one set of workers was tired, another took its place, and the song continued from where it was left off.

As they trampled, the level in the great vat sank, while from a narrow opening at its base the juice flowed in a swift, steady stream along a cemented canal into an adjoining room. This other chamber was built on a lower level, and contained another tank of still vaster proportions, which gradually filled with the newly made wine. When the grapes had been crushed dry they were shovelled out of the vat and carted away. Water was added to them and they were pressed again, this time in a steel press worked by a vertical screw. The juice obtained from this mixture fermented rapidly. It was sold for very little to those who could not afford even the cheapest wine, and it was known as 'poor man's beer.'

Again the girls entered with their wooden buckets, the vat was replenished, and the entire process was repeated. It took many vats full to produce an equal quantity of wine, and the trampling of the grapes continued for days, until the last bunch had been picked from the vines and the last drop of juice expelled from it.

This was the ancient method of wine-making, handed

down from time immemorial throughout all the civilisations of the world. In this manner was made the wine drunk by our Lord in Galilee, by the Pharaohs in Egypt, and by the Cæsars in Rome. To-day many wine-growers will tell you that it is the best and the only true way to make good wine; that the labour-saving and money-saving machines bruise the grapes, and in some subtle way impair the quality of the juice.

Our boy's godfather was delighted that we had admired his *vendemmia*, and was anxious to show us also the interior of his *palazzo*. This prospect did not afford us the slightest pleasure, but, as it was Giovangiuseppe's show as much as his godfather's, we saw no way of getting out of it. We followed him up a pretentious staircase into the drawing-room. From its musty odour we judged that it was only used on special occasions and remained closed for the rest of the year. As our host threw open the windows and shutters, a flood of light illuminated red papered walls, a grand piano buried beneath a pseudo-tapestry and potted palms, and some particularly hideous Neapolitan furniture. The most important feature of decoration was the collection of pictures on the walls.

In heavy gilt frames hung portraits of all the family; his grandparents, both paternal and maternal, his father and mother, his uncles and aunts, his cousins, his first wife, and one little baby in its crib. All these people, with the exception of the baby, were stiffly seated on straight-back chairs, dressed in their best clothes, and all of them stared vacantly at the camera. The men were bearded and moustached and wore frock coats, high collars, and black ties; the women were in black silk. Everyone was in deep mourning.

There was something peculiar and unwholesome about them; a fixed stare and a sinister pallor. Their rigidity suggested that they had been photographed against their will. We approached to examine them more closely and recoiled with horror. These were all photographs of dead people!

Watching eagerly for our reaction, our host told us with great pride that this was his own idea. As soon as a relative passed away, he dressed him or her up in the frock coat or black silk gown kept especially for this occasion as an ultimate proof of their gentility, and, propping them up on a chair, he had them photographed. It was not an easy matter, he said, and it was often necessary to strap them to a board at the back to prevent them from slumping, but the photographer was *molto bravo*, so that it did not show. The photographer had certainly excelled himself. A more gruesome exhibit could not have been imagined.

'*Una bella idea, non é vero?*' our host asked. 'Something at the same time reverent and original?'

His next comment was less reverent and in no way original, for we now discovered that he had brought us to this chamber of horrors in the hope of renting it to us. 'I have been told' – he smirked in the direction of his godson, who was standing in the background looking very uncomfortable – 'that you find your villa very hot. Here, on the contrary, the air is famous for its insuperable salubrity.' He walked to the door and flung it open. 'This is a nice room with a matrimonial bed, and you can have the exclusive use of this beautiful *salotto*. If you wish we can make *una piccola combinazione*.'

With great firmness we declined, and hurried down the stairs into the sunlight. Oh, that dreadful room, and that dreadful expression: *una piccola combinazione*! The owner must surely have been of Neapolitan origin, for the Neapolitans are the greatest exponents of that shady business, 'the little arrangement.'

Innocent as it may sound while you are being talked into it, you soon discover that you have been 'done.' To the astute Neapolitan, life is nothing but a series of *piccole combinazioni* to get the better of strangers, of friends or enemies, of the Government – although that is more difficult – and even of the Almighty if He does not keep a sharp look-out. Many are the saints who have been promised fine, tall, pure tallow candles before their images if they did what was required of them in the way of miracles, and, once the bargain was concluded, received miserable little ones made of inferior grease! One cannot be surprised if even they occasionally turn a deaf ear to their flock.

We wondered if our boy was also in league with his god-father in this diabolical scheme to make us abandon our beloved Villa Buonocuore in favour of this dreadful apartment. One glance at his frightened face convinced us happily that we were wrong.

'It is getting late, Giovangiuseppe,' we said. 'Your parents will be expecting us.'

'*Davvero, signore,*' he replied manfully, 'we must leave at once.' After this display of loyalty, poor boy, I do not think that his godfather had much further use for him.

The sun was sinking on the horizon, its mellow light casting long shadows, as we took leave of our host and followed Giovangiuseppe once more through the vineyards, this time to his brother-in-law's house.

This charming little *casa contadina*, with its low thick walls crowned by white cupolas, was situated on the edge of the hill; the vineyards extended to the back of it, while in front stretched a wonderful panorama over our side of the island and embracing the whole Bay of Naples.

While supper was being prepared, the family led us to a terrace, where there were three chairs, and then retired,

This charming little *casa contadina*, with its low thick walls crowned by white cupolas

leaving only our boy's father to sit with us. We did not know if this arrangement was due to a dearth of chairs, or to the urgent need of help in the kitchen, or because, in his rôle of head of the clan, only the father had the right to be spokesman.

What a difference between the wealthy godfather and this simple, hard-working peasant, aged beyond his years by unceasing toil under the hot Mediterranean sun! His face and neck were deeply furrowed and his hands were calloused. He wore a clean, white, much patched shirt neatly closed with a stud but virgin of collar, and over it his best jacket. He possessed a dignity and peace completely lacking in our recent host, and it seemed as if his long association with the soil, far from breeding discontent, had given him a deep, tranquil satisfaction. He was proud of the soil, proud of what it produced in return for his sweat. Our interest in the *vendemmia* gave him a real satisfaction, for we were on common ground, and he told us about many interesting old customs that were fast dying out with the older generation.

It was almost dusk, and the lights had begun to twinkle in the windows of the little houses all over the hillside, and in the streets of Ischia at our feet, while out at sea and on the mainland could be seen the periodic flashes of the coastal lights. 'It is beautiful and it is ever changing,' the old man said, and he was right. We who feasted our eyes on a similar panorama every day had never seen what we saw from this little peasant house nestling in the vineyards.

'Ready at table,' the married sister announced, and led us indoors. There Giovangiuseppe, immaculate in the white duck house suit which he had chosen to wear on this visit to his parents, stood beside a table neatly laid for *two*. He was waiting to serve us.

225

'What about your family?' we asked in consternation. 'Are they not going to eat with us?'

'We have already eaten, *signore*,' he replied. 'But, with your permission, my father and mother and my married sister will sit with you when you have finished.'

This was indeed a novel situation. To be waited on by the son of our host, even if he was at other times our own servant, was something for which we were unprepared. The honours were all on his side; if there was any embarrassment, it fell to us to bear it. He was perfectly at ease as he served us an excellent meal cooked by his mother and his sister, and poured out his father's best Malvasia, a fine, mellow, sweet wine. We tried to entice him into conversation, but, although his eyes sparkled with excitement and pleasure, he remained as respectful and attentive as though we were in our own home.

Giovangiuseppe's family had evidently a singular appreciation of beauty, because in the corner of the room where we sat was the biggest and most magnificent gardenia tree that we had ever set eyes upon. It stood in a great terra-cotta pot on the floor, and, judging by its twisted, knotted trunk, it must have been very old. So great was the mass of flowers that the leaves were almost hidden from view. The tree would have been worth a fortune in a Bond Street or Fifth Avenue florist's shop; here it was appreciated because it was sweet smelling and a pleasure to the eye. There were over four hundred blossoms on it, the sister told us when we had admired it.

At the end of the meal the family joined us, sitting at a certain distance from the table. While we talked, the sound of singing was wafted in from the terrace, accompanied by a curious rhythmic clapping, as though hundreds of hands were beating time. There were also mysterious gruntings on a deep bass note. We recognised the song as the one we had heard in the afternoon while the grapes were being pressed, but the accompaniment was new.

From our hosts' faces it was evident that they were eager to join in the fun, and, when we asked them if they would take us with them to wherever it was, they jumped to their feet with alacrity.

Although the vineyards were now pitch dark, they knew every inch of them by heart. The sound of the music became louder; we saw the lights of Chinese lanterns shining through the leaves, and in a moment we had stepped from the blackness into the centre of animation.

We were in a little courtyard filled with peasants seated on the ground in a wide circle. The middle space was taken up by the performers, the singer and his orchestra. The latter consisted of five youths dressed in white duck trousers with bright red sashes around their waists, and white shirts. On their heads were the gaily striped bonnets that used to be worn by the old Sorrento fishermen, very similar in shape, if not in colour, to the night-caps worn by our ancestors, the ends and tassels hanging down over their ears.

They were seated on old wine-barrels and upturned wooden tubs, and held curious instruments between their knees. One of these was a drum that lay flat on the ground, with a tall bamboo stick projecting upwards from the centre of it. The youth spat on his hands and, gripping the pole, made a succession of rapid downward strokes, each stroke producing the deep grunt we had heard. Another instrument was the 'clapper.' It looked like a huge pair of wooden scissors and was manipulated in the same way. The centre was immovable, resembling an inverted croquet mallet, while on either side were two little hammers which at each movement of the player came up and struck it.

We noticed that most of the audience, especially the women, held these 'clappers,' and used them to supplement the band. Each instrument produced a resounding slap, and the movement could be kept up indefinitely, with very little effort and no damage whatever to the hands. It was the only labour-saving device we ever saw on the island.

The singer was the centre of attention; an old man with a beard, who not only sang, but danced, the innumerable verses of the wine-song, each cadence being accompanied by a frenzied orchestration of grunts and clappings. It did not need the multi-coloured lanterns strung up around the court to give the scene a festive touch. Everybody was enjoying himself enormously. Singer, orchestra, and audience were indefatigable, and, although we could not understand a word, for the song was entirely in dialect, it must have been spicy, judging from the way the listeners rocked with laughter. The new wine in big jugs circulated freely. One lady turned to tell us with a hoarse whisper of amusement that the performers had drunk one hundred litres between them since morning. *'Se non é vero, é ben trovato!'* as the old Italian proverb says.

We thought the show was over, when a little boy and girl about eight years old forced their way through their elders into the circle. They were dressed in the old peasant costumes which were once always worn, but were now only kept for fancy dress. They did not look like children, but like a miniature man and woman. The boy had the same white trousers and red sash as the musicians, and, in addition to this, a short embroidered velvet jacket, and around his head a bandana to match his sash. The girl had a long full skirt of velvet and silk, a velvet bodice with lace and silver ornaments, and a soft white scarf around her neck.

They received as much applause as the old man; the band set up a spirited tune, and the little couple solemnly began the opening steps of the tarantella. It was quite a different performance from the one provided by the hotels in Naples for the entertainment of their guests. It was as complicated as a minuet, and they danced it with consummate grace and skill, knowing each step by heart and never faltering. They held each other at arm's length; they waltzed round and round; he knelt and she curtsied, and the dance came to an end amid deafening applause. We had never seen children dance so gracefully and who were so little self-conscious.

Many legends surround the birth of the tarantella. Some say that in the old days this dance was the only cure for anyone who had been bitten by the venomous tarantula. Others hold that it was an imitation of the St. Vitus-like convulsions produced by the spider's virulent poison. Both versions are implicitly believed, although, as far as Ischia is concerned, we had never heard of the existence of the tarantula.

When the children had finished, everybody got up to dance. Kit and I waltzed until we were dizzy, because one can waltz to the tarantella very well if one cannot do any of its steps. No explanations were asked as to how we had suddenly found our way into the party; our host, who turned out to be a youth from the band, brought us glasses and wine, and we were accepted with the same sunny cordiality as the others.

Although these people would be up at dawn to begin another day's hard work, the entertainment showed no sign of coming to an end, and another singer had started his song when we whispered to Giovangiuseppe to guide us back to our carriage. Our coachman was among the audience, and had evidently not spent a boring evening, so we had no compunction in having kept him waiting.

Again the family escorted us through the vineyards, and we parted with many handshakes, our boy once more on his high seat beside the driver.

Only when we were well on our way back to Ischia did we discover a little basket on the floor of the carriage. It was filled with gardenias from the old tree we had admired so much.

CHAPTER XX

FROM KIT'S DIARY

I

A FORTNIGHT AGO I had a letter from Aunt Tess saying that Cousin Sophie was in Rome, travelling alone, and would soon be coming down to Naples to take ship for home; would G. and I meet her and do what we could to help her get safely aboard. This suggested to us a way of getting a wife for Peter, which we have been wanting to do for some time. Cousin Sophie could buy her in Rome and bring her down to Naples, we thought.

This is the first time I have ever seen Cousin Sophie, and I should think it would be the last. I had heard that she was elderly, and lived a very secluded life with two splendid Persian cats, Agrippa and Agrippina, for company. The cats were her passion. She had trained them to sit each on a newel post at the foot of her staircase, and she had had her hall entirely redecorated to provide a harmonious background

231

for them. A vet was in constant attendance, and at regular intervals her own dentist came to the house, examined the cats' teeth, and put in what fillings were necessary, probably in the best gold.

What Aunt Tess did not tell me in her letter was the reason for Cousin Sophie's trip abroad. One of the cats had escaped from the property for the first time in its sheltered life, and, upon seeing a motor-car, a tram, and a plebeian cat, became hysterical from shock, had a fit, and died. The remaining cat pined away and expired in spite of much love and care, and poor Cousin Sophie was so broken up that her doctor told her she must get away.

Knowing her love of animals encouraged me to write her about Peter's prospective wife. I gave her the address of the shop in Via delle Botteghe Osscure, with full instructions about what the dog should look like and how much to pay for her, and after a few days I had a pleasant answer in very thin handwriting, saying that she would bring us the 'wee doggie,' but that she would not buy it until the day of her departure from Rome, as she thought that *perhaps* the kind Italian proprietor of her hotel might not *quite* like to have a *canine* guest.

A few days ago we had another letter, saying that she had been to the shop and chosen the little dog, 'a small *yellow* creature, very *exuberant*,' and telling us the time of their arrival in Naples. 'Of course you will not recognise me, dear child, but I shall wear a *red carnation*, and with the help of that and my *travelling companion* I feel sure you cannot miss me,' she wrote.

They were due to arrive yesterday at three o'clock. We left the island at seven in the morning, on the old *Regina Elena*. It is still hot even so early; the sun was high and brilliant. The ship anchored in deep water a couple of hundred yards off the shore, and we and the other passengers were rowed out to her in a small boat. There were a few women with big baskets of fruit, and a Franciscan brother in a thick brown woollen habit, and the grizzled old ticket-seller from the office on the quay who collected thirty *centesimi* from each passenger in the boat and brought his grizzled little dog along with him.

Naples was steaming under a hot blanket of sirocco when we docked at the Molo Beverello two hours later. It was noisy and dirty after the green quiet of our island, but the time passed quickly and at three we were at the Centrale ready to meet Cousin Sophie and Peter's wife. We bought platform tickets and waited for the Roma-Napoli train to come.

As it slid in, a flock of porters ran along beside it, craning their necks up to the windows of the carriages through which the luggage would be handed out to them, and talking with their hands. Quite a knot of them gathered outside a first-class compartment, where we could see a very agitated elderly lady grappling with a recalcitrant window. Her hat was on one side, and in her struggles it assumed a violently rakish angle. As she paused helplessly, a stern-faced train official, very distinguished in loops and festoons of gold braid, stepped up beside her and opened the window. He eyed the poor lady very coldly. She, in relief, leaned far out, beckoning to all the porters at once, and as she did so we saw a much crumpled red carnation hanging limply from her shoulder.

Was it a coincidence? No, for the very first piece of luggage she passed out to the waiting hands of a dozen porters was a whimpering, half-grown yellow dog!

'Cousin Sophie!' we shouted, and ran forward.

'Oh, my dears!' she gasped, and kept on throwing hatboxes and handbags and parcels out of the window. The official stood just behind her with folded arms, doing nothing but look at her coldly. Cousin Sophie was in a great hurry with her luggage; she only paused once or twice to say to him, 'Just a moment. *Un moment*, please.' In a minute G. was in the compartment, putting out the heavy bags, while Cousin Sophie fluttered agitatedly about, opening her purse from time to time, peeping helplessly into it, and repeating to the unresponsive official, '*Un moment*, please.'

We trailed her porters by the dog's anguished wails, and as we bumped through the crowd we heard the tale of the disastrous journey from Rome in breathless snatches from Cousin Sophie. Before her departure she had taken the wildly excited puppy to a restaurant, where they had both eaten. The dog gobbled up everything that the amused waiters gave her – spaghetti, omelette, duck – and when they were in the train she repented of her rash appetite and deposited all she had eaten on the carpet of the first-class compartment. Alas that they should have been travelling in such luxury! Before Cousin Sophie had time to hide the traces of the crime, steps sounded along the corridor and an official, imposing in gold braid, filled the doorway.

His looks were black and threatening; they implied that she was liable for the whole carriage, if not for the entire Rome-Naples express. In sinister tones he asked if she had had a *disgrazia*. The fact that she had was already so appallingly evident that his words could only have been intended to rub in the enormity of the dog's offence. Then, allowing his face to lighten slightly and suggestively, he said he would fetch a cloth and *try* to repair the damage. The shadow of an outstretched palm was strongly present.

Cousin Sophie grasped that palm with relief, and encouraged the official to get his rag and begin work at once. He did so, and knelt solemnly on the desecrated carpet, dignified and out of place.

Meanwhile, the little dog had been stuffed under the seat to avoid the possibility of further incidents. What she did under there Cousin Sophie didn't know; when the train was rocketing along under way she heard strange sounds, and looked apprehensively at the kneeling official to see if he had heard them too, but he continued his majestic scrubbing and she did not enquire more closely into the state of her companion's health.

When he had cleaned the carpet with, she felt sure, many lire worth of stately labour, the palm was advanced as she had expected. Few Italians are too dignified or exalted for this simple manual exercise. She searched her pocket-book, and placed all the silver she could find in the palm, looking apprehensively at the face above for its reaction. The reaction was plain; the official's face was stonily displeased. The tip was evidently insufficient. The palm remained extended.

As best she could Cousin Sophie explained that she had no more silver, only notes. She would change one when she got to Naples and come back to give him more money. The official withdrew for a time, but when they were near their destination he came back and stayed close beside her.

'He *looked* at me so!' wailed Cousin Sophie. She was much the worse for wear.

'Well, and how much did you give him, finally?' G. asked.

'Dear me!' said Cousin Sophie, 'I really couldn't say. These *foreign* coins all look alike to me. I think I gave him four or five of those large silver ones.'

'It's extortion!' said G., and took hold of Cousin Sophie and me and hurried us through the crowd. 'Come on, we've just got time for a drink before we put you on the boat.'

'But that man . . .' panted Cousin Sophie.

'D . . . No matter about the man,' said G.

It was an exhausted but gay Cousin Sophie whom we finally put aboard her ship. She had had a little cry when she told us about the death of her cats, but another drink – 'strictly non-alcoholic,' G. assured her – made her feel better, and when we left her she had made up her mind to get two new kittens. 'This *experience* with a dog has made me feel I cannot live without them, though I thought I should never bring myself to fill Agrippa's and Agrippina's places,' she said.

At last we reached the blessed peace and quiet of the homely little Ischia boat, where men and dogs and cattle and goats travel together, and can be, and are, sick and never have to pay for it. The little dog lay trembling on G.'s knee; he stroked her soft thick fur gently and for a minute she stopped darting frightened glances around and looked gratefully up at him. Her eyes were very dark against the golden fur, wide-set and expressive. Her pointed ears quivered at each sound. She had been born in that Roman shop and had never left it before; all this busy world was new and strange to her. We named her Silky.

By and by, as G. continued stroking her, she fell asleep. We sat quiet and breathed deeply the good salt air and watched the lovely coast and the blue waves slip past.

It was dusk when we got home. Peter heard us coming down the alley and ran out through the garden gate to meet us and 'make a *festa*' for us, as they say here. G. was carrying Silky, and at first, in the half-light, Peter didn't see her. Then his nose told him there was a stranger, and he stopped jumping and barking and grew very stiff-legged.

'Perhaps you'd better not put the pup down yet,' I said, 'She's had enough scares for one day.'

But G. was already setting Silky gently on the ground.

At the sight of Peter she gave an excited squeal and ran toward him. He was the first familiar object she had seen all day, and, with the easy friendliness of a young one raised in a large family, she launched herself on him and began a scrambling sham fight with him. Peter, taken unawares and deprived of going through the usual formal preliminaries of sniffings and investigations, gave one or two stiff, suspicious leaps backwards. The puppy was not daunted. She continued to tumble about, batting him with her paws, nipping his fur, and in a minute Peter gave a howl of joy, laid his ears back, and led a wild chase round and round the garden, doubled up like a hare and with Silky in mad pursuit.

At supper-time we went across to the little house, whistling to the two dogs to follow. Peter ran after us, then, missing Silky, ran back. She was standing at the top of the stair leading down to the loggia, whining piteously. Peter took the steps in two leaps, stood beside her a moment, then scampered down again, and stood looking up at her. Silky stayed at the top, whimpering desolately and darting from side to side. Sometimes she put a paw gingerly downwards toward the next step, like a bather poking his toe into cold water before a plunge, but she didn't know how to go down. She had never been out of the dog-shop until that day, and never seen a stairway.

Peter ran up again, eager and worried. He jumped from the top step down to the next, and turned around to see if she had watched how it was done. He tried it again, and stood waiting one step below her until, with many a cry, she had overcome the first obstacle and was down beside him. He encouraged her down each step, and at the bottom they had a wild scamper to celebrate.

At bedtime they curled up close together on the clothes

hamper in the bathroom, very weary but very pleased to be together.

II

Rain fell a few days after we had been to Naples. It was the first since some time in May, and it came down in cool sheets and closed up the long fissures in our garden where the earth had cracked open with the heat.

It gave us a chance to see how seaworthy the Villa Buono-cuore is going to be through the long winter rains, and on the whole the house showed up well enough. The ceilings are water-tight; these domed roofs shed the rain well; but we had an impressive river flowing from under the french window in our bedroom, where the rain was beating hard, and across the floor and down the stairs to the bathroom in a fine cascade. The dining-room became more marine than ever, and, like a ship that hasn't had its hatches properly battened down, let in a quantity of water through the ceiling. Its roof is not domed and has sagged with the years till it is as swaybacked as an old horse, and it holds all the rain that falls on it in the hollow place until it filters through the plaster into the room below. We pushed all the furniture out of the way around the walls and told Giovangiuseppe to bring us our meals in the *salotto*. He ran through the garden with a tray of food twirling on one hand and an umbrella in the other.

The day after the rain it was fine again, but the air felt different. It wasn't summer air any more. It was washed and clean, and everything in the garden looked cheered up too, the geraniums and the dusty tired leaves in our little vineyard. The empty vegetable gardens had stopped feeling like rock underfoot. Giovangiuseppe said now was the time to plant. He is not always accurate, but this time he was right; not more than a couple of days went by before the whole place was green with new weeds. It was a second spring. The rose-bush put out new buds and the morning-glory, that I had given up for dead since Giovangiuseppe had ravaged it for our anniversary decorations, covered the old garden wall with sudden shoots of green and bursts of blue flowers.

We bought a lot of seed – spinach and lettuce and carrots and radishes and some others – and set to work. G. got a *zappa*, a sort of mattock, and turned the soil. It was heavy work, but his blisters have all turned into fine callouses now. I made little furrows and put seeds into them, knowing nothing about the job but hoping the earth was fertile enough to discount any mistakes I made. Giovangiuseppe said it was not very good; we were too near the water and the salt from the winter spray would be too strong in the soil for things to grow well. He couldn't get used to our working; I suppose *signori* don't do it here. He hovered near us very distressed, and was always trying to take the *zappa* away from G. and saying in the good island dialect, '*Faraggio io, signore.*' He has got more reconciled to it now, and tolerates it with fewer efforts to do the work himself; we feel he looks on it as an incomprehensible, back-to-nature foible of the very rich, rather like the ex-Kaiser chopping wood at Doorn. We have had to make only one concession to him; he does all the hard work of drawing water from the well and carry-ing the heavy watering-cans to us, then watches indulgently while we actually administer it to the soil.

The dogs do not understand the importance of the vegetable garden. There are smacks and cries when they play where before they were free to go. Silky has settled into the family with feminine adaptability, and with feminine guile has captured first place in everyone's attentions. Peter is his wife's slave, though because of her minority the love which he lavishes on her is only fatherly, and shows his affection by scratching her fleas for her, munching and clicking his teeth under her thick yellow fur. She receives the delicate attention graciously, letting her pink tongue lie between her lips and half closing her eyes in ecstasy. Peter has already the thin, anxious expression of the henpecked husband. Silky is called 'Frilka' by Giovangiuseppe and 'Secca' by Dominica. These are their efforts to say Silky, and both have rejected the simpler translation of the word, 'Setacea.'

There has been an epic upheaval in the kitchen to-day. We were sitting in the loggia having tea, and even there the shouts of battle reached us. I looked a question at G. He shook his head. 'Let them fight it out alone,' he said.

After a while Dominica came across the garden in the dark; we could hear her blowing hard, and when she came into the light her face was scarlet from anger and the wine she had taken to cool it. In this country there's no sulking; you never have to prompt and prime them to tell you what is wrong; it comes out in billows of turbulent words, and a little wine helps the recital along too. Giovangiuseppe had accused her of stealing food and money from the shopping account, and had told her that in the future he was going to do the marketing himself. At this point I had only two thoughts: that Giovangiuseppe was a cheeky little pipsqueak, and that Dominica ought to set herself up against the champion lightning calculator of the world if she could commit to memory the dozens of minute items on her day's shopping-list, arrange to steal from the money allowed her, dictate the many false sums to me, and still make her change come out right. I don't believe it, anyway.

Dominica was nearly crying. We said it was all right, we

didn't believe she had stolen anything. She collapsed back
into good humour and said in a resigned voice that Giovangiuseppe was *special*. She thought this a good description,
and repeated it – '*Lui é speciale!*' she said. Her honour
vindicated, she didn't really care whether Giovangiuseppe
did the shopping or not. Let him try; he would soon see
that the bills didn't go down just because he did the buying.
We parted the best of friends; nothing but crime could
persuade us to forfeit Dominica's friendship. Who else could
make such 'eggs in shirts,' such chowders of *zucchini* cooked
with their yellow blossoms, such potato pie laced with
salame and anchovies?

Giovangiuseppe came along later, seething with the
righteous indignation that I find irritating. He and
Dominica mix no better than oil and water, and he would
like, I am sure, to dislodge her from the household. His
narrative style runs to hyperbole, and to-day he excelled
himself. There were long, difficult passages about the theft
of an egg, a loaf of bread, some coffee. The next was easier
to follow because the opening words were arresting, and we
made an effort to understand. *Piatti*. She had for a long
time been stealing plates. We could ask the neighbours.
She carried them away in her bosom.

I wonder frogs do not jump out of Giovangiuseppe's mouth
when he talks. I have never known such a liar, nor one so
smug and so inept. We sent him to bed. To-morrow he will
begin shopping, and, flinging economy to the winds, I hope
the accounts will go up.

III

Life on our beautiful, happy-go-lucky island has made us
forget that time exists, except in the lovely rhythm of the
maturing and passing of the seasons. We have lived in the

present and have forgotten that a day must come when we shall have to leave all this beauty and peace and *dolce far niente*. To-day comes the first faint warning that our Ischian life cannot go on for ever. G. has heard that he must be back by the end of April, and we will have to leave soon after Easter, which falls on the 5th. It is frightening to have the date fixed, but at least it is comfortingly far away. I now understand why, in almost every lovely, out-of-the-way place, one finds a few happy, indolent expatriates. I should like to stay on here for always, and raise a big family of brown fisher-boys, and learn everything about the sea and the soil and the people and all the things that seem to matter and which figure too little in our complicated life at home.

This afternoon I have been on a shopping expedition to the old town. Shopping is more amusing here than in a city, because you have all the fun of turning the shop inside out to find what you want without any of the temptation to buy more than you ought, and you have a very social time too.

I went to old Collina's to buy some wool to knit myself a jersey. His shop is five feet wide and perhaps eight feet deep but it is called an emporium. Old Collina is generally sitting in his chair on the paving of the street just outside. Sometimes he entertains a friend, an old man with fierce white moustachios on a tiny brown wrinkled face. They can talk with all their acquaintances who pass, and they can see all that goes on of interest in the cathedral just across the narrow street; they can stretch out their legs, which would be impossible in the little shop, only pulling them in when the carriages clatter past at a gallop.

Collina brought out yarn of unhealthy brilliance. I said I would take white instead. 'If you truly want it, *signora*, I will give it to you, but,' he declared, 'these colours are absolutely the smartest.' He held out skeins of scarlet and

242

mustard wool. These are the shades that fond mothers crochet into dresses and little hats for their children to wear on *festa* days. Everyone is delighted with the effect, so why not?

I bought white.

With the package old Collina delivered an oration. He is a great talker, and his breath is more heavily laden with garlic than ever was human breath before, and in a five by eight shop there is no escaping it. His greatest oratory contains a note of complaint. 'Ah, *signora*, the misery, the misery. You do not know, you cannot know, the poverty, the difficulties. You see, *signora*, here in Ischia we have a depression, a slump. That means that nothing has any more its proper value. See, I must sell my stock for less than it cost me; you can have this for . . .' and he names a price that is probably double what we should pay in Naples.

Without surprise or annoyance he allows himself to be bargained down to a sensible figure; he will never hold it against us, because it is what he expects, and he would think us a pair of inexperienced fools if we paid him what he asked.

One day in his emporium G. looked for a jersey and did not find just what he wanted. 'I would like a fisherman's jersey, but with a lower neck' he said.

Old Collina held up his hand. 'Say no more, *signore*, no, not even one word. I understand perfectly, and I will write to Genova where they are made and get the very jersey that you desire. Measure you? Tcha! There is no need. Be tranquil, *signore*; it will be quite perfect.'

A week later he sent word that the jersey of the *signore* had arrived. We walked to Ischia Ponte and edged our way into the crowded, garlic-scented little shop. On the counter in a place of honour, and very noticeable, lay a jersey, so mammoth that it was positively rambling, ugly brown in colour picked out in a natty design in red artificial silk.

'*Buon giorno*,' said G. 'And where is my jersey?'

Old Collina beamed. '*Ah, signore, ecco!* Look how it is beautiful, and just the thing for an illustrious *signore*!' And with that he picked up the giant jersey and held it out proudly to G.

G.'s face was funny. 'But . . . but . . .' he stammered, 'this isn't what I want at all. I told you I wanted a blue fisherman's jersey, and see, this thing is far too big for me, too. It will never do.'

Collina's smile disappeared, and he looked very puzzled. 'But, *signore*,' he said, scratching his head, 'there must be some mistake. I do not understand. I wrote to the director of the factory himself and I said to him, "I want a jersey for an Englishman who is spending the winter at Ischia." He sent this. And now you say that you do not like it and it won't fit you. No, I cannot understand it!'

CHAPTER XXI

I

NOW THAT THE AUTUMN SUN had become a friend whose company was to be sought, instead of a treacherous enemy, and the sea so calm and inviting, it entered our minds how nice it would be to rent a boat and potter lazily about exploring nooks and caves accessible only from the sea.

We walked down to the Port to interview old Pasqualuccio, who kept a few dilapidated boats which he rented to Neapolitans during the six weeks' 'season' when they flocked to the island for the bathing. At this time of the year we had the whole flotilla to choose from, a sorry collection of cumbersome, much battered craft, equipped with oars of unequal length and mighty weight. Had they been the pick of river-boats, light and graceful, he could not have been prouder of them nor have asked a higher rate.

We picked out one, anchored a little distance from the others, which looked less of a wreck. As we pointed to it his old eyes sparkled with pride and cupidity. '*Ah, signore, che*

245

barca! What beauty, what lightness! A real dream!' **He**
scrambled into the nearest boat, and over the side into the
next, and over the side of that into another with the agility of
an old ape, until he had reached the coveted prize and
towed her back for our inspection. Except for an extremely
damaged, much patched-up bow, she looked fairly sound,
and showed actual traces of former paint.

Renting this beauty by the hour was out of the question;
we should have been ruined by the end of the afternoon.
Furthermore, we wanted a boat to keep on our private beach,
ready for an outing when we felt inclined. After a great deal
of bargaining, during which Pasqualuccio told us his life-
story, a long recital of woes, financial disasters, doctor's bills
and hospital bills, a bedridden wife and starving children,
we finally agreed upon a figure which Kit and I subsequently
discovered to be the double of what he had expected. We
also discovered that he was reasonably well off, that his wife
was a massive able-bodied woman with a prosperous little
shop of her own where she sold cheese and *salame* to that
quarter of the fishing settlement, and that they had no
children.

Having assisted Kit into the boat, I paid a deposit and
rowed off. Well, perhaps not exactly that. I grasped the
unwieldy oars and, after a hitch or two, managed to get
them overboard without releasing my hold on them. With
a ponderous splash which drenched Kit, the contact with the
elements was established, but that was about all.

She must have been made of lead under her timber, for
progress was slow and the coast seemed to remain stationary.
With the aid of bits of orange-peel floating past, we had the
satisfaction of knowing that we *were* moving, but I never
realised until then what a long way it was from one end of
the beach to the other and around the point to our little

landing-place. Like the shipwrecked mariner, I had few clothes on by that time, having during the ordeal removed one garment after another, with only a scant concession to decency. Kit was very encouraging and said that I rowed beautifully, but I knew that she knew that this was not true.

Dominica and Giovangiuseppe helped to pull the boat up on to the dry sand. *'É molto pesante!'* they both exclaimed, vindicating my efforts.

On our private beach the boat stayed until our lease or charter, or whatever our privilege of temporary ownership was called, had expired. After that we returned her to Pasqualuccio without regret. When he had greeted us affably, he glanced at her and threw up his hands in horror. *'Mia povera barca!'* he lamented. 'What have you done to her beautiful bow, *signore*? She is ruined.'

We looked with amazement from one to the other. The boat was no beauty, certainly, but she was no worse than when we had rented her. Her bow was still patched up with scraps of iron, rusty nails and bits of wire, but, with anguish in his voice, Pasqualuccio poured forth a long story about the accident she must have had. This, however, subsided, not so much in the face of our flat denials as at the sight of a couple of lire tip, and we parted the best of friends.

We thought we had heard the last of our boating incident until, a week later, Giovangiuseppe came to me in the middle of my gardening and, with a mysterious look on his face, asked if he might say 'two words' to me confidentially. He said there was a plot afoot to extract much money from us for damages to the boat, and that we must be very careful, as a certain lawyer with an unsavoury reputation was at the bottom of the affair. This lawyer, who spent most of his time in a café near the Port in the hope of picking up clients, had overheard Pasqualuccio telling his fellow boatmen about his unsuccessful attempt with us, and, entering into the conversation, he had proposed *una piccola combinazione*. This could not possibly fail, and would bring in a considerable sum if Pasqualuccio would consent to a fifty-fifty split with him. The old boatman, who, according to Giovangiuseppe, was not really a bad man, being vaguely connected with his own family, had allowed himself to be talked into it. It was probably through these family connections that our boy had come to hear of it.

It was high time to take the bull by the horns, so, asking an Italian friend to act as witness, I went down the same afternoon to see the boatman. Confronted with this story, he grew embarrassed, protested in a superb display of oratory against having anything to do with the lawyer in question, and ended up magnanimously by warning *me* not to have anything to do with him either!

Still, there lingered in his mind the hope of damages. How much did he want? Twenty-five lire he thought would be fair. That was exorbitant, my Italian friend said. Let us make it five lire. The boatman thought for a moment. All right, five lire then. Penmanship was not his strong point – he was a *marinaio*, he said – but if one of us would make out a receipt for this amount in full payment of damages, he would sign it just to prove his goodwill. I returned home triumphantly, and not a day too soon.

We had just finished breakfast the following morning when Giovangiuseppe, looking very black, ushered in a smooth, greasy, pompous individual, who advanced with an ingratiating smile and the offer of a flabby, moist hand to shake. Unmistakably the lawyer. Accompanying him was the son of an old hag who acted as caretaker of a villa near by, and was a well-known bad character. Together they formed a charming pair.

Although furious at being double-crossed, I realised that this type of game had to be played with smiles and an excessive display of courtesy, so I bowed them into the drawing-room.

'*Bel palazzo*,' the lawyer said, gazing around him. 'And arranged with such exquisite taste. And what lovely weather we are having; such a calm sea; really ideal for boating, *non é vero?*' As he rubbed his hands with satisfaction at this smooth approach to the vital topic, it suddenly dawned upon me that he knew nothing about my private arrangement with Pasqualuccio, having in all probability not seen him since their interview in the café.

'Ah, that poor Pasqualuccio,' the lawyer exclaimed heavily. 'A much misguided man. Three hundred lire for that little accident to the boat! Too much, too much! I said to him, *va bene* that these are rich foreigners, but let us not exaggerate.' He raised his hand as though to ward off such an iniquitous thought. 'This is no matter for the law courts,' he continued, 'but one to be settled between gentlemen; that is why, *signore*, I have consented to act as intermediary.'

At that moment he put his hand to his breast pocket and deftly drew out an official document typed on blue paper and handed it to me. It was a claim for two hundred lire.

I was delighted, I told him, to have encountered such an eminent lawyer, one who had possibly studied law in Naples, but regretted that in this instance his services were no longer required. I produced with a flourish Pasqualuccio's receipt.

The caretaker's son sniggered and the lawyer adjusted his glasses. He cursed himself no doubt for having brought a witness to his defeat. We walked to the gate in silence. 'Pasqualuccio is a fool,' he exclaimed at last savagely.

'No, *signore*,' I replied, 'merely a much misguided man.' We parted company with smiles in which there was very little cordiality.

Giovangiuseppe, who had probably overheard our conversation from the loggia, was delighted but apprehensive. 'Perhaps for a few days,' he warned me, 'it would be wiser not to go out after dark.' Evidently we had scored our first Ischian enemy and Giovangiuseppe did not want any *vendetta* to deprive him of his employer.

II

Inducing things to grow in our garden was a strenuous job. By things, I mean vegetables, not weeds, although some of the latter, like the morning-glory that ran riot over our walls, were beautiful. Owing to the Italian rural habit of watering and manuring vegetables from one's personal cesspool, we wished to grow as many of our own as possible. Probably they would not thrive so thoroughly, nor attain such magnificent proportions, as those of the local gardeners which were fed on the abominable *pozzo nero*, or black well, as it was sinisterly called. The saying may be true that what you don't know does not hurt you, but we did know. In our garden all help from the *pozzo nero* was rigidly forbidden. The vegetables must grow of their own accord or not at all. As it turned out, they chose the latter course.

This was not entirely their fault, nor ours. The garden of the Villa Buonocuore was not the place to grow anything so prosaic as vegetables. The soil was poor, the proximity to the sea, with the spray in windy weather blowing over the wall, disastrous, and we had, in addition, to contend with the malignancy of innumerable rats and the good-natured destructiveness of Peter and Silky. The rats dug up our peas

as fast as we planted them. The first row they neatly dis-
embodied, leaving only the husks; the second row they did
not care about, but waited until the new shoots, like little
green shepherd's crooks, appeared above ground, then
nipped them off and left them scattered where they fell. This
was real sabotage, and our blood, which had been hot
enough when we had planted them, boiled with despondent
fury.

We baited traps, but, as Dominica said, the rats were
molto furbo and not so easily caught. Cesare recommended
poison, a black powder which had to be inserted into bits of
rotten fish and strewn about the garden. For a long time we
shied at such forcible measures, but, after the pea episode, I
sent up to Barano for a trial packet. We had to use extreme
caution, because Peter and Silky were also fond of rotten
fish and this baiting had to be done at night after they had
been locked in the house. The powder could not be entrusted
to Giovangiuseppe, for at the best of times he was a reckless
youth, and, in the perpetual state of feud existing between
him and Dominica, we did not want to run the risk of losing
our cook from an overdose of arsenic.

So after dark, every night for a week, a greasy newspaper
packet, from which issued nauseating odours, was laid upon
my desk, and with the aid of a penknife I doctored half a
dozen putrid fish. Accompanied by Giovangiuseppe, sheltering a lighted candle under his coat, I deposited them in the
garden. In the morning what remained of the fish was
removed by Dominica, who was always the first about, and
burned.

Was gardening worth this? We decided in the negative,
and after that our efforts were confined to vegetables which
the rats did not care for. As far as I can remember, these
consisted only of beans.

'What on earth do you do all day long on your island?' an English friend in Naples asked us. As if our days were ever idle! They were much too short, and we were always reluctant to put an end to them by going to bed.

It was often past midnight before we thought seriously about it. The actual hour depended on how long it took to get Silky indoors again once we had let her out for her evening airing, this being after we had finished experimenting with the rat poison. Silky was the most innocent-looking and the most aggravating dog in the world. Like many pretty women, she was scatter-brained and self-willed. Common sense held no place in her small, attractive head, and as to obedience, that most endearing virtue in dogs, she understood well enough what the word meant, but she had no use for it. When caught and menaced with a whipping, she rolled on her back and howled in anticipation.

To this must be added that she had low tastes, possessed an endless appetite for the uneatable, and a remarkable faculty for rejecting later, usually at our feet, what was beyond her powers of digestion.

As soon as the front door was opened, both dogs would dash past and run riot in the garden. After ten minutes, during which we tried not to think of our seedlings, we stood on the loggia and called: 'Peter, Peter! Silky, Silky!' Out of the darkness came the patter of paws, and Peter arrived wagging his tail, but of Silky there was no sign. The hunt was on. Down to our private beach, up on to the ramparts – our feudal name for the garden wall – and over every inch of ground between them, we searched, calling at first affectionately, then, as time passed, less affectionately, and at last with something akin to murder in our hearts. In despair we would lock her out, intending to give her a serious lecture in the morning. Long before that, however, she would return, and, sitting smugly on the loggia, howl us out of bed to let her in.

We wondered where she went, what distant journeys she took, until one night, during the search hour, the light of my electric torch happened to flash upon the *mondezza* heap at the bottom of our lane. This was the refuse dump of our particular neighbourhood, where advanced comestibles, tin cans, remains of fish, rabbits, and rats, and other less readily distinguishable things, were piled, waiting to be carted away by the municipal authorities. On the summit was Silky, wolfing in great hungry mouthfuls whatever was highest if not topmost, her soft brown eyes gleaming in the torchlight with diabolical avidity. Of course she had heard us, but she trusted to the cover of the night not to be discovered. No wonder she was so popular with the fishermen around us, for she did the work of the refuse cleaners promptly, efficiently, and free of charge. On this occasion there was not a particle of dust left in her fur after I had spanked her.

Another of Silky's aggravating traits was self-pity. When her fine pointed ears itched, she scratched them, but, as her paw was heavy, this hurt her. She was not one to suffer in silence, nor had she the sense to stop scratching once she had got well started. From a gentle soul-rending whine, her wails rose in crescendo to a shrill plaintive note, which she kept up until her paw grew tired. As she slept in a basket on the floor of the so-called bathroom, and as she scratched herself repeatedly throughout the night, her degree of popularity by morning was hardly worth mentioning. We ended where we should have begun, by locking her up in the dining-room down by the sea. All said and done, these were only human frailties. She and Peter were a devoted couple, and that alone was sufficient to secure a place in our affections, even if at times we did rebel.

III

By the time December had arrived our thoughts turned toward the heating problem. The Villa Buonocuore had come up to all our expectations as an ideal summer home. While the sun was broiling outside, and coming indoors meant delicious freshness, a subdued light filtering through the green shutters and as few garments as possible, all was well and good. Now it was different. During the day the sun was still sufficiently strong for us to welcome the protection of our big native straw hats, but the nights were distinctly chilly. Like La Fontaine's improvident *cigale* who danced and sang throughout the fine season without a thought for the future, it had never occurred to us that there would be a winter season, and, judging by the total lack of heating arrangements, it had never occurred to the builders either.

This was in keeping with the Great Mediterranean Myth. For centuries the populations of southern Europe and northern Africa, Christians and Mussulmans alike, have refused to admit the existence of winter. It is not that they are immune from cold. On the contrary, they suffer acutely, huddled in layers of old clothes, the majority of which are not removed until the first almond-blossoms are out. Yet with spring comes forgetfulness, and no preparations are made to alleviate their misery when winter comes round again.

The ancient Romans were wiser. The mosaic floors of their exquisite villas were heated by an elaborate hot-air system, which for comfort has never been bettered, since it is one's feet that get cold first and what could be more delightful than resting them on a heated floor? No wonder the Roman historians were long-winded; one could write indefinitely with warm feet.

An Italian villa could not be transformed into a cosy cottage, but at least one could build a fireplace. 'But why?' the Ischians asked. 'In Italy it is never cold.'

We went so far as to be willing to endow the Villa Buono-cuore with one at our expense, and wrote to the old colonel in Naples, waiting for his enthusiastic consent. By return of post he sent us a most courteous reply. He had heard of fireplaces, but he did not want one in his house. When we left, he wrote, it would be difficult and expensive to remove! If we found the place chilly, which was amazing in such a mild climate as Ischia, why not try a *braciere*? Its warmth was delightful.

Why not, indeed? It was the native method of heating, if the fumes it gave out could be mistaken for warmth, and was still widely used throughout Spain and Italy. It looked nice, resembling a vast copper ash-tray, which it really was, and one filled the centre of it with charcoal embers smothered with ashes to prevent them from burning too quickly. It was not intended to remove the chill from lofty rooms, but, if you crouched over it, your breath would not form icicles, although in your eagerness to get warm you might well be asphyxiated.

With great kindness Dominica brought us a brazier from her house, and lit it for us from the kitchen fire. We watched her with interest though with no confidence whatever. Removing three minute sticks of burning charcoal, she placed them tenderly in the centre bowl and added a couple of unburnt pieces on top as a reserve supply of fuel. With her fat cheeks distended to their utmost capacity, she blew mightily upon them until they glowed, then she shovelled ashes generously on top until all sign of fire and all trace of heat were securely buried. The *braciere* was then carried into the drawing-room and placed on the stone floor to work its miracle. If we did not touch it, Dominica said, the embers would remain ardent until morning.

I am afraid we did not play the game. We sat over it, using the broad brim as a footstool, waiting for something to happen, but after a long time we decided recklessly that it would be better to have a swift hot fire than this lingering buried spark, so we disinterred the embers with a stick and, getting down on our knees, repeated Dominica's tactics. We blew so hard that everything in the room, including our-selves, was covered in a layer of fine grey ash, and when we stopped for want of breath, *we* were glowing beautifully. The brazier did not look pleased; it probably resented our getting warm even through our own efforts.

How fortunate it was that Giovangiuseppe took it all as a huge joke, since it fell to him to clean up the mess we had made!

There was nothing left for us to do but to invest in an oil stove, and the following morning we went to Ischia to look over the various models and choose one likely to give the maximum of heat with the minimum of smell. At the unique emporium our request was met with a blank stare. A lamp of such vast dimensions that it was capable of heat-ing an entire room? No. They did not have such a thing in their shop. If we said that such a thing existed, then of course it existed, but it had never been heard of before. Perhaps in Naples, where there were many, many things for sale, especially foreign things, this might be among them. The owner of the emporium was going there himself after the New Year. Did we wish him to make enquiries? His eagerness implied that he would gladly comb the city, spending several days there if necessary, in search of this gigantic lamp; we had only to say the word.

Remembering the fisherman's jersey that had been ordered from Genoa specially 'to fit an Englishman living on an island,' we dared not plunge headlong into this scheme. There was no telling what the fertile imagination of the owner of the emporium, backed by the prospect of foreign capital, might produce. Furthermore, we did not want to wait until after the New Year to get warm.

What about going to Naples ourselves? Since our marriage we had been there only once. Often at night we had watched the reflection cast in the sky by the lights of this third biggest city in Italy without any desire to see it again, but now we suddenly felt its lure. Our baser instincts craved for orgies, the most desired being to wallow in a hot bath in a full-sized bathtub. Then there were all our preparations for Christmas to be made, but it was the oil stove that decided us.

Our minds made up on the spur of the moment, we were tremendously elated. Flying to Timbuctoo would not have been half as much fun as this prospect of a return to civilisation after the proud disdain with which we had turned our backs on it. Going home, we frantically ransacked our wardrobe, loading down Dominica and Giovangiuseppe with discarded city clothes to be brushed and pressed. I had almost forgotten what a dinner-jacket looked like, and wondered also how my neck, which for so many months had enjoyed the freedom of open shirts, would like being squeezed into a boiled shirt and a stiff collar.

Looking from these to Kit's veritable fashion parade of a trousseau, laid out over the backs of chairs and over tables – tailor-mades and afternoon dresses and evening gowns – we

257

laughed to think how little use they had been, and how little either of us had realised the life we really wanted to lead. It was like Cinderella getting ready for the ball.

We were going with an open mind. No date was fixed for our return, which would take place when we had had enough of city life or when our funds had given out. Giovan-giuseppe was to remain in the house during our absence, and a telegram would inform him when to expect us. Our bags were packed and breakfast ordered for six in the morning.

Leaving for Naples meant early to bed and early to rise, for the *postale*, as the mail steamer was called, dropped anchor beneath the castle rock at seven. Had we wished, we could have started the same journey at three in the morning, without getting to Naples any sooner, for the *postale*, which berthed at night in the Port, set out at that hour to pick up her first passengers at Forio at the other end of the island, and had to come all the way back to her starting-point before setting out on her real voyage across the bay.

Who said the Italians were lazy, just because they took a siesta every now and then?

CHAPTER XXII

IT WAS WINTER ALL RIGHT, once the ship had left the lee of the island, plunging headlong into the teeth of a sharp north-east wind and a choppy sea. We were the only passengers on deck, the others being huddled into the cabin below, and we were glad of our heavy coats as we paced up and down, lurching with each plunge and roll of the ship.

But the weather was fine, the sky blue, the air clean and good to breathe. The bay was a seascape of fast-moving green hills and valleys flecked with white where the wind swept off the crest of the waves in flying spray. After Procida, in the clear winter light, the coast was visible on both sides to a great distance. From the summit of Vesuvius a long trail of white smoke, tinged with yellow, swept across the sky toward Sorrento.

The two hours' crossing seemed short to us, but to the majority of the passengers aboard it must have been an eternity. Kit and I were congratulating ourselves that we were immune from sea-sickness until, in order to escape the cold wind on deck, we went below. Many times our Ischian friends had told us with pride that the Italians were the most intrepid sailors in the world. If you wish to believe it, you must not visit the lower deck of the Naples boat, or indeed any other Italian boat, in rough weather.

Scenes of desolation and utter collapse met our eyes everywhere. Representatives of this hale race of island fishermen clung limply to every available projection of the ship's structure in attitudes of despair and abandon, completely indifferent to the world and to the fate of their best black suits. Sturdy members of the crew, looking none too cheerful, passed by with pails and mops, removing spaghetti and tomatoes as they went. We made the remarkable discovery, which has since been frequently confirmed, that, no matter what an Italian eats, it is always spaghetti and tomatoes which he renders to Cæsar when the sea is rough. In this he shows a striking similarity to Peter.

To escape this scene of torture, we darted into the cabin, but retreated almost immediately. It was a floating hospital for the lady passengers. Not only the benches, but the tables and the floor, were strewn with their bulky forms, and from this confused mass of humanity arose groans and prayers and other frequent and more distressing noises. Those who were not already beyond help were alternately sucking lemons and smearing them over their faces and hands, this cooling massage being considered a remedy against *il mal di mare.*

In a little cubby-hole off the saloon, with no ventilation except from it, a steward, some officers, and one or two passengers with iron constitutions were calmly playing cards in a cloud of black smoke. If it is the exception which proves the rule, I take back what I said about Italians being bad sailors. To sit in that atmosphere in a rolling ship to the accompaniment of the scenes taking place before their eyes; to smoke a black cigar and be happy about it – that was indeed the crucial test.

It put us to shame. We might be good sailors on the upper deck; we would certainly not have been if we had stayed below. Happily our journey was almost at an end; we were already entering the harbour of Naples and the captain had manœuvred his ship round in order to back her into the berth reserved for her between the Capri and Amalfi boats. This manœuvre was not to be carried out, for the dock was in confusion.

Ships' sirens were blowing, motor-launches were tearing back and forth across the harbour; in row-boats gesticulating individuals stood up waving their arms and screaming at the top of their voices, and even passengers were giving un-solicited advice on how to manage everything. Only gun-powder and fireworks were lacking to complete the illusion of a *festa*.

The trouble centred around the Amalfi boat, which was vainly trying to disentangle herself from her moorings and sail for her destination. Every time she managed to get a few yards out, the other ships rushed headlong at her and blocked the way, with every promise of a grand collision. All the anchors, including that of a near-by gunboat and a submarine, were securely fouled at the bottom of the harbour.

Meanwhile, the captain of our ship, which with a great rattling of chains had dumped her anchor on top of the others, was pacing the bridge, rubbing his hands in glee, or maybe in despair – it was difficult to tell which in the excitement – and shouting directions through a megaphone to his colleagues on board other ships, who were too busy doing the same thing to hear what he said.

As far as we could see, two simple manœuvres were being tried out alternately. One consisted in releasing the winch of the Amalfi boat, when all the ships relaxed gracefully and glided back to their former positions. The other was to start all over again in the hope of better luck, when the ships once more took on their tense, preoccupied look and dived into concentrated action.

A passenger who had watched the proceedings with perfect gravity said that they would soon have to send down a diver to disentangle the anchors. Owing to the carefree habit with which the captains of this local service dropped them, regardless of where they might come to rest, this was, he said, an almost daily occurrence. The business of sailing, it was plain to see, was not so simple as it looked on the company's time-tables.

How long it took the Amalfi boat to get free we did not discover, because, when the bloom of the excitement had blown off, the captain of our ship turned his attention to his own passengers and we were allowed to land via a small boat.

On the wharf we took a taxi, but at the gate of the docks we were held up by the usual armed guards whose business it was to see that no Italian goods were smuggled from one part of Italy to another without the payment of a few centesimi tax. These guards in grey-green uniforms, black shirts, and black gloves were more privileged in the matter of hats than any of the other innumerable armed forces which watched over the welfare of the population. On our previous visit to Naples, they had been wearing Boy Scout hats with a chin-strap; at the time of our marriage the hats were of green felt lifted at one side and ornamented with a feather; both had now made way for steel helmets of the latest field type.

ISLAND IN THE SUN

The manager of our hotel was surpassingly affable. He considered us his *protégés*, even after we had discarded his advice and gone to live in Ischia instead of staying on in Capri. He had not forgotten our wedding breakfast, attended by certain high official personages, and he remembered that on this occasion he had received something rare in these days – *carte blanche* in the matter of floral decorations, food, and wines. Sending for the head reception clerk, a dapper little man in an immaculate morning coat, he ordered him to show us to one of the best suites.

'Zi gentlemen ladies vill go to zi opera?' the reception clerk, politely airing his English, asked us as the lift ascended. 'Ze giva zi French opera *Louise*.' We said we would rather go another night when they were giving an Italian opera. He was delighted. 'Many gentlemen ladies preferre not zi French musiks,' he informed us. A little dig at the French was always a pleasure.

At the end of a spacious thick-carpeted marble corridor we were bowed into our apartment. It was truly regal, but the bathroom was one step better. Every detail of plumbing was incorporated in it, and the bath looked to our unaccustomed eyes like a miniature swimming-pool. Throughout the place, central heating radiated a delicious warmth. At the moment Naples was the most charming city in the world.

Our first two hours were spent in bathing and changing into fresh clothes, and the next two hours, Kit said, were going to be spent with her hairdresser.

Nobody could have enjoyed more than we did this re-acquaintance with the city we both knew so well and which held for us only the pleasantest memories. We lingered before shop windows, sat at cafés, lunched and dined at

263

restaurants. We did not go to the opera, but we went to see a famous Italian actor in the rôle of Hamlet.

I have heard Shakespeare in several languages, but one must hear *Hamlet* in Italian to appreciate fully the unfathomable chasm which separates the Anglo-Saxon from the Latin temperament. The difference in language alone makes translation without loss of dignity and meaning impossible. When 'To be or not to be . . .' is rendered with a superb display of hands, an eloquent shrug of the shoulders and a witty gleam in flashing eyes, as '*Essere o non essere, questo é il problema*,' you realise that, as Mussolini said of Fascism, Shakespeare is not an article for exportation.

This Hamlet's vivacity of gestures made us realise also how vitally important gesticulation is to the Italian, especially the southern Italian. In heated arguments, when words fail, the hands can always be relied upon to express with eloquent precision what the tongue is no longer capable of uttering.

These gestures are infectious. In spite of our upbringing, with its horror of superfluous demonstration, we found ourselves instinctively resorting to this convenient way of expressing ourselves. We waved hands and shrugged shoulders when talking Italian, and with alarming ease I found myself raising my hat with a flourish every time I exchanged greetings with another man in the street. On these occasions we would often stand bareheaded on the sidewalk until we had effusively begged each other to 'be covered.'

We worked hard at our enjoyments and returned to our hotel late every night, exhausted and ready for the peaceful sleep which we did not get. Of all Italian cities, Naples is easily the noisiest. The Neapolitans love noise; it stimulates them. The Fascist regulations toward silent traffic, which have worked miracles in Rome, seem powerless to deprive them of this pleasure. The streets by night as well as by day are a pandemonium of screeching horns, cracking whips, and the explosive exhaust of motor-cycle taxis.

This latter means of conveyance is peculiar to Naples. The motor-cycles are equipped with sidecars capable of holding two passengers, and their fare is half that of an ordinary taxi. They are able to get through tight spaces prohibited to larger vehicles, and their drivers, sinister-looking bandits, are the most reckless in the world. They are apparently unhampered by speed regulations, traffic jams, or prudence, and to ride with them is to experience an unforgettable sensation.

In my bachelor days, when in Naples, I used sometimes to hail one of these fellows, preferably the most daring-looking, and, climbing into the sidecar, tell him to get me to the central station in two minutes, this being the maximum time available to catch a mythical train. It was an acrobatic performance of the first order coupled with a unique thrill. The scenery viewed during those two minutes looked like a movie when the chase is on. Trams, motors, street corners, shop windows, and pedestrians loomed up, dashed headlong at us, missed collision by a hair's breadth and disappeared in the distance as we tore through the most congested part of the city. When the station had been reached and the driver paid off with an extra large tip for speed, I would return to my hotel on foot, feeling that it was good to be alive. It is needless to add that since our marriage this pastime is no longer permitted.

Naples does not sleep. Although officially there are few entertainments after midnight, the city is loath to abandon the illusion of gaiety. For a couple of hours before dawn it dozes fitfully, awakening again to a full pitch of clamour with the first ray of daylight.

Yet, with the exception of noise, Naples is probably the city which has most changed and most benefited by the Fascist régime. My acquaintance with it is a long one, for I was ten years old when with my parents I first spent a winter there, and in the following twenty-five years I have revisited the city many times. In this quarter of a century its face and character have unbelievably altered, especially since the advent of Fascism, and if it has lost some of its old atmosphere it has also lost the squalor and stench for which it was noted.

In those days most of the big hotels did not exist, and the broad waterfront and the thoroughfares immediately back of it were a thin crust of veneer that coated a city ridden by vice and ruled by the Camorra. As long as you confined your exploration of the city to those modern districts you were safe except from beggars and pickpockets. It was, however, as much as your life was worth – and that in the eyes of the Camorra was very little – to adventure into the old quarters unaccompanied.

With the exception of the Mafia, which governed Sicily, the Camorra was the greatest and most powerful secret society in the world. Order was not in the hands of the law; it was in the hands of this 'Mother of all Rackets.' Highly organised, this society controlled many branches of the city's life. Not only beggars, pickpockets, and cab-drivers belonged to it, but a host of unsuspected people in higher stations as well. The headquarters of the Camorra were hidden away in the old quarters where no one uninitiated, least of all the police, could penetrate with impunity.

One of the best known and least harmful of its many activities was pickpocketing, and I have been told by Neapolitans who know their city well that there were regular schools where nimble-fingered recruits were trained in the art. As in all work requiring great skill, it was necessary to begin young in order to become efficient. Usually disguised as beggars, they were the bane of a foreigner's existence. From the moment you left your hotel for a walk along the front, until your return, you were accosted by ragamuffins turning somersaults and Catherine-wheels in your path, holding out their hands for *soldi*, and what they did not get out of you one way they succeeded in getting in another, as you discovered the next time you wanted to consult your watch.

Other branches of the racket were dog-stealing for ransom and burglary on an imposing scale. In this game it was not every man for himself; all the booty was turned over to the heads of the society, who apportioned the rewards according to the scale of merit. The organisation was so efficient that if mistakes occurred, and friends of the society were dispossessed of their valuables, these were returned to them usually within twenty-four hours. A friend in the Camorra was a friend indeed!

This venerable institution, like the Mafia, has been stamped out by the iron hand of Mussolini. Its members have fled chiefly to America, where, from all accounts, they are doing even better than they did in their early days back home.

Between Fascism and earthquakes the infamous and dangerous slums of Naples have been demolished. New quarters have been vastly added to, tourist traffic has been made easy and pleasant, and, miracle of miracles, there are no longer any beggars. My hat off to Mussolini!

However, in its zeal for cleansing, the new régime has done away with many picturesque old customs. One of the most familiar of these was the habit of turning the street into a living-room by bringing out from one's house tables and chairs, of cooking and eating one's meals there, exchanging visits with neighbours similarly established, and generally spending pleasant hours of leisure al fresco. The fact that indoor living conditions among the poor were appalling made this expansion into the street even more desirable. The methods employed by the Fascists in doing away with this obstruction to traffic had the drastic simplicity characteristic of all their measures. Street monopoly was strictly forbidden, and families were warned. A first offence brought a fine; the second brought a police van which removed and confiscated whatever furniture had been brought out of doors. It worked well, for nowhere in Naples to-day can one see these street parties that lent so much colour to the life of the old city.

Funerals are about the only pageantry of old Naples not to be engulfed in the new order. They continue to be the same magnificent affairs; the post-mortem extravagance of the populace. No matter how poor the deceased may have been in life, no matter how miserably he may have been obliged to eke out his existence, once dead his last journey will be a splendid affair. Three times – at birth, at marriage, and at death – a fuss has been made of him, but the last is the greatest. Sometimes it is the Neapolitan's only chance to cut a figure – *fare figura*, as the Italians say. His survivors, including even distant relatives, will, if necessary, club together to meet the expense of a showy burial, which in this case means not only honouring the deceased's memory but upholding the family's social status.

Neighbours, friends, enemies, and even strangers, seeing the expensive and splendid cortège passing through the streets, will be impressed and perhaps a little envious. The southerner's love of pomp and public attention will be fully satisfied.

ISLAND IN THE SUN

The hearse is almost entirely glass, so that the coffin and the wreaths, which are entwined with broad ribbons bearing in large letters the name of the deceased, may be fully visible, and it is drawn by black horses with imposing black plumes on their heads. Preceded by the clergy, with acolytes, incense, and lighted candles, it is followed by the relatives in closed carriages and by a more insignificant though sometimes more numerous attendance on foot, the latter being mostly idlers on the look-out for free entertainment and perhaps a share of the funeral breakfast. If there is money enough, there will be music. As the procession slowly advances through the crowded streets, traffic stops, men take off their hats, and women cross themselves, and the deceased, insignificant in life, receives a brief universal recognition before sinking into oblivion. No day passes in Naples without this spectacle.

Our stay in Naples was not idle. With only three weeks to go before Christmas, we had much shopping to do. Having such a variety of native crafts to choose from, we knew at least where to look in order to be safe from duplicating the habitual Christmas gifts for people at home. There was the choice of exquisite hand-embroidered linen made chiefly by Sicilian women, inlaid woodwork carved by the inhabitants of Sorrento and the neighbouring villages, beautiful leather-work peculiar to no particular place but typical of all Italy, the hand-painted pottery of Vetri.

Then there was our own shopping to be done; our Christmas presents for each other to be bought. This was most exciting, and for the first time in our married life we reluctantly agreed to separate for a few hours at a time. The plan originally chosen, by which one of us should stand on the pavement at a discreet distance, eyes carefully averted, while the other furtively slipped into a shop, was not a success. With the most honourable intentions it was impossible to avoid seeing the nature of the shop and imagining things! But, to secure her modicum of liberty, Kit had to promise not to cross streets, to go everywhere in a taxi, and to meet me at frequent intervals for rest and refreshment. Paradoxically, we looked for our mutual gifts among the things that were not Italian; imported goods from England and France, which had the lure of being different.

Our Christmas shopping included a plum pudding, mince pies, champagne from the best Rheims cellars, excellent cognac, a Christmas tree and all the paraphernalia for trimming it, crackers and many other things that took our fancy. In a country where import duties were so high that tea cost approximately fifteen shillings a pound, these 'foreign' extravagances for the celebration of a normal Christmas told heavily on the exchequer. And, of course, we bought our stove – a German one big enough to warm all the Villa Buonocuore.

It took us five days to appease our craving for city life, but after that we could hardly wait to get home. Ischia, with its peace and beauty, its absence of trams, buses, motorcycles, noise, and bustle, seemed like the promise of a better world. We missed the Villa Buonocuore; we missed Peter and Silky; we missed Giovangiuseppe's enthusiastic grin and Dominica's delicious cooking. We longed to discard our city finery and get back into comfortable, shabby country clothes. We were, in fact, craving for our natural element.

As usual, we made up our minds at the last moment and telegraphed Giovangiuseppe that we would be returning by the afternoon boat, instructing him to inform Dominica so that supper should be ready. We sent the telegram *urgentissimo* – very urgent – at three times the normal rate, to be sure that it reached its destination before we did.

The Italian postal authorities apparently regarded telegrams more as an ingenious method of transmitting words by electricity than as a means of rapid communication. An ordinary telegram might or might not be delivered before a letter. If you were particular, you could send it *urgente* at double the tariff, in which case it was more or less guaranteed to get there sooner, although how much sooner was not specified. As a letter might take four days, and in one instance did take eleven days, to go from Naples to Ischia, this allowed ample time for the urgent telegram to get there first.

If you were fussy, and for some incomprehensible reason wanted your message to reach its destination the same day, you could send it, as we did, *urgentissimo*, at treble the cost. But that was not all! There was still a fourth way of sending telegrams, and that was by 'lightning'! This *lampo* service, as it was actually called, guaranteed delivery within half an hour of any message sent from one town to another in Italy. Such a disturbingly energetic service was naturally so costly that few ordinary mortals could afford to use it, and, furthermore, it did not extend to the islands. One cannot say that the Italian Telegraph Company did not offer the public the spice of variety.

We had never sent a 'very urgent' telegram before, so that it was doubly gratifying not only to have been able to hand it in at the post office in Naples, but to have been personally present at the gate of the Villa Buonocuore when it was delivered an hour after our arrival on the island. In this manner we benefited twice by the marked respect which is shown to both the sender and the recipient of one of these rapid and costly communications.

Had it arrived earlier in the day we might have been spared some shattered illusions. Except for the enthusiastic welcome of Peter and Silky, our home-coming was disastrous. Beds were unmade, rooms unswept, and in the same whirlwind of disorder as we had left them, while of Giovangiuseppe there was not a trace. It was the grape-vine telegraph, infinitely more rapid than the Government one, which finally summoned him from wherever he had been gallivanting, and brought him tearing down to the house in time to receive the full blast of our wrath. His habitually large stock of plausible excuses failed him this time, and it was a much chastened Giovangiuseppe with a bad reputation to live down who sped through the accumulated dust of five days with unaccustomed thoroughness. During this time Dominica placidly cooked us an excellent supper. She was well aware that, in the old feud with our boy as to who was the better servant, she had scored a major victory.

To make matters worse, Kit discovered that in our absence a jumper she had been knitting had been chewed and unravelled by the dogs; strands of wool were found for days after, planted in various parts of the garden in lieu of the tender shoots which had been dug up in the process.

All the same, our home had never been so welcome to us. No place in the world seemed to possess such repose, such mellow charm, such sweet fragrance, as this little walled-in garden by the sea, with its orange-trees and its wrought-iron gates and its quiet deep loggia; no house so inviting in its gentle simplicity as the Villa Buonocuore. It was indeed good to be back.

No place in the world seemed to possess such repose,
such mellow charm

p. 272

CHAPTER XXIII

I

WITH CHRISTMAS so near at hand, the Villa Buonocuore was in a turmoil of excitement. This was our first Christmas on the island and the first one of our married life.

Although official Italy leaves *Natale* to the Church, and reserves its celebrations for the New Year, Ischia, with its love of religious feasts, makes much of it. Christmas is indeed the one great *festa* until the coming of Easter. So to Dominica and Giovangiuseppe our preparations did not seem strange as did so many of our habits, and, knowing how much this particular Christmas meant to us, they were determined to act their part in a way we should always remember.

In the kitchen mysterious things were going on; there was much surreptitious whispering and exchanging of knowing glances, and, united by this common and kindly cause, there was for once complete harmony between our cook and our boy.

This excitement was not confined to the kitchen. For

weeks, packages adorned with special Christmas labels had been arriving from the family at home, their condition somewhat battered from examination and repacking by the customs, and all heavily taxed regardless of their contents. A startling percentage of the latter, we later discovered, had disappeared on the way, having possibly been appropriated by some fatherly official to take home to his family. It was an easy way to do one's Christmas or New Year's shopping without expense, and a unique opportunity for selecting a variety of presents not to be found in Neapolitan shops. Although these packages were so hastily tied up after examination that we could easily have looked inside without undoing them, we refused to spoil the fun and stored them away in a cupboard to await Christmas morning.

Kit and I had for once our own secrets, too. Certain drawers in certain pieces of furniture were by mutual agreement not to be opened, or even approached, except by the lawful owners, and there was much crinkling of tissue paper to be heard behind closed doors. Although most of my purchases for Kit had been made in Naples and brought back with me, a few things had required time to complete, such as the embroidery of Kit's initials on some handkerchiefs, and here Enrico was to prove invaluable.

Enrico was Ischia's most important courier, the brightest, smartest, and most useful lad on the island. Taking the place of his father, who had retired from business, he went every day at dawn, and at this time of the year considerably before dawn, on the first boat to Naples, returning in the evening. All his time ashore was spent in doing errands for the islanders for a small fee, and these errands covered an amazing range of human needs.

One client required a pat of fresh butter, another a small terrine of clotted pig's blood sweetened with sugar, a special delicacy for the coming *festa*. The postman's new boots were too small and had to be changed for a larger size, preferably with pointed patent leather tips to them, while the wife of the ironmonger wished to match two pieces of scarlet ribbon for her underwear. Then there were letters which their writers were in a hurry to have delivered and therefore did not dream of sending by post, and to these he was expected to bring back an answer in the evening.

As he charged for his services only a small percentage on the cost of each purchase, it did not look like a very lucrative business. Yet he not only worked hard for his living, he seemed to enjoy it, for he was always unfailingly cheerful even at the end of the busiest day.

We had employed Enrico many times during the summer. When we needed money we made out a cheque in his name on our bank in Naples and he brought back the cash in the evening, for he was honesty personified. As the Ischians are loquacious, I think he found us refreshing after the habitual discussions over the size of two cabbages, the cost of a bottle of castor oil, or whatever it might be, which regularly greeted the delivery of his goods.

Enrico had other qualities besides being an excellent shopper; he was a born diplomat, and my delayed gifts provided an excellent opportunity for displaying this talent. The handkerchiefs, and other little surprises which Kit was to know nothing about, were smuggled in without her being any the wiser. If she was in the room when he made his evening appearance at the Villa Buonocuore, he would engage her attention with a sprightly account of his adventures in Naples, choosing the moment when her head was turned away to slip the package in question on to my knees as I sat at my desk. How much the diplomat he really was, I never suspected until after Christmas, when I discovered that his secret services were likewise being employed by Kit for her own ends! No wonder there was always such a broad smile on his face at each visit.

Christmas, even in Ischia, would not have been complete for us without a turkey, and this was certainly the most voluminous of Enrico's commissions. As no turkeys were raised on the island, we had instructed him to bring one back from Naples. Perhaps he mistrusted the shops where such things were to be found, so he ordered one from a farm outside the city. It was a splendid bird, weighing eighteen pounds, and he brought it back alive! We had said we wanted a fat one, and the farmer had advised delivery ten days ahead of time so that we might fatten it to our own satisfaction.

This was our first close acquaintance with a live turkey, and appearances were not in its favour. I do not know what we thought a live turkey ought to look like, but it was certainly not as Nature had fashioned it. The loose, flabby, scarlet trimmings that draped its reptilian head like the remnants of an unfinished surgical operation, were particularly unattractive. Another gory strip dangled from its nose as it strutted around, and at every step the creature was seized with some sort of fit, its head jerking forward convulsively, while a horrible grating sound emerged from its scraggy neck. 'Awacka gobbela gobbel! Awacka gobbela gobbel!' Turning its back upon us, it hissed and strutted, exhibiting an aggressive fan-shaped tail.

Poor thing, I do not suppose that it felt any more at home with us than we did with it. At least we felt that we should never become attached to the bird, nor feel any compunction in eating it when Christmas arrived. In this we were mistaken. All too soon the creature became acclimatised, and exhibited an alarming friendliness, even posing for its photograph. If it was to play a star rôle in our dinner, this would never do. On the callous principle of 'Out of sight, out of mind,' we handed the bird over to the care of Giovangiuseppe, with orders to keep it in the background.

Three days before Christmas the weather, which had been cold and gloomy, changed overnight into the perfect example of what a Mediterranean winter ought to be. From a blue and cloudless sky the sun shone down magnificently warm on land and sea. There was not a breath of wind to dispel the illusion that spring had come. Orange- and mandarin-trees, laden down with fruit ready to be picked and packed off to various parts of the world, filled the air with their fragrance. We were conscious of our good fortune to be living in such a beautiful corner of the earth.

That evening, as I sat at my desk trying to write, while Kit, curled up on the sofa, was busy knitting, Giovangiuseppe blew in with another of his startling announcements. The Baby Jesus had come to see us, and evidently was not to be kept waiting. It was the custom, he explained, for the *Bambino* to visit every house before *Natale* to collect offerings for His coming feast. Thinking that, like Sant' Antonio, the Holy Child would be represented by some worthy monk, I asked him in. To our amazement, four muscular fishermen, much too large for their best suits, entered, carrying between them a cradle. It was a typical peasant cradle lavishly ornate, with muslin draperies suspended from a hook at one end, to protect the baby's face from the sun and flies. With clumsy fingers one of the men parted the curtains and revealed a large, florid wax doll in a little white dress and a lace cap with pink ribbons: the Infant Jesus. With loving care and an eye for effect, its arms had been stretched up in a gesture of appeal and welcome.

Taking the cradle in his arms, the fisherman held it out to

me. It was a trying moment until my eye fell on a pile of small notes and coins reposing at the feet of the Holy Child, and with an inward sigh of relief I realised that, if I could not purchase my way into heaven, I could at least buy an exit from this embarrassing situation. Hastily I added our modest contribution, but nothing happened! True enough, the fisherman looked pleased, but he continued to hold out the cradle. What was wrong? Had I not given enough? No, it could not be that; these were Ischian fishermen, not Neapolitan porters. Something more was expected of me, and expected quick. What could it be?

Perhaps I had not made enough fuss over the *Bambino*, and I hastily cast around for something appropriate to say.

'*Bello, bello,*' I exclaimed in despair. '*Molto, molto carino!*'

But still there was silence. The fisherman advanced the cradle nearer and nearer, looking as though he would prefer to be buried alive, while his companions in the background were twisting their caps and getting restless. Their embarrassment was nothing to what I felt; the cradle was now only a few inches from my face and the air was electric with suspense. I do not know what would have happened if Kit with her woman's intuition had not come to the rescue. 'Kiss the Baby,' she whispered, 'and have done with it.'

No man likes to kiss a baby in public, especially when it's a wax one. However, taking a deep breath and blushing profusely, I leaned over the mass of lace and ribbons and made the required noise, being careful to avoid actual contact with the wax cheeks, as these showed signs of having already been well kissed by the inhabitants of the old town. Immediately the tension relaxed; the fishermen unfroze and smilingly bore off the Holy Child to the kitchen to be kissed by Dominica and Giovangiuseppe, and perhaps to rest a time on the table while they refreshed themselves with a few glasses of wine.

When they had departed, I sent for the boy and gave orders that no further surprises were to be sprung on us. 'I venerate and admire these ancient customs,' I told him severely, 'but in the future I first want to know what is expected of me.'

By Christmas Eve there was not a room in the house from which one of us was not barred. The dining-room and kitchen had been smilingly but firmly denied both of us, while Kit and I were on terms of defensive secrecy. When the evening meal had been cleared away, I had the living-room to myself, while she took exclusive possession of the bedroom, the door between being closed and locked. This could not muffle the sound of crackling paper, of drawers being opened and closed, of the soft scratching of a pen over paper. But when, about midnight, our preparations were finished, not even a detective could have found anything out of the ordinary in the immaculately tidied rooms except, perhaps, for a faint smell of sealing-wax.

II

I had intended to wake up at dawn and play Santa Claus to Kit. It was well past dawn, but she was still fast asleep. I had just finished arranging my packages on a little table beside her when I discovered a similar table beside my own bed which was groaning under the weight of neatly tied-up parcels. On the top was a little note in my darling's hand-writing. No wonder she was sleeping so peacefully, for, having stolen a march on me, she had no longer any reason to keep a vigil.

'*Buon Natale!* Most happy wishes! A hundred years of life!' Giovangiuseppe brought us breakfast, smiling and wriggling with excitement, and dashed out, to reappear dragging behind him a huge wicker basket. 'From my home,' he said, and, unable to contain his impatience, threw back the lid. On top, neatly arrayed in little rush trays, were samples of all the products of his family's farm: clusters of oranges and mandarins, ripe and heavy, with little twigs of glistening green leaves still clinging to them, and giving out a delicious fragrance; new potatoes, lettuces, carrots, beetroots, and *finocchi* – fennel – which the Italians eat raw as a fruit; a great bunch of flowers and three bottles of the best home-grown Malvasia.

'Also Dominica wants to wish you *Buon Natale!*' the boy admitted generously, and a moment later the cook appeared in the doorway dressed in her best clothes, her feet wedged in the high-heeled black patent leather shoes reserved for special occasions, and her face heavily powdered. In her arms was a load of magnificent red and white camellias, and she beamed with friendliness. Heaven knows how or where she obtained them, for we had never seen any on the island, and in southern Italy they are a rarity. Camellias are Nature's retort to wax flowers. They don't last quite so long, but, then, they don't melt. Prim and spotless, yet romantic, they have a strange fascination. We filled what vases there were in the house with them, and, as there were others left over, we placed them in the big tub reserved for washing the dogs.

The morning passed rapidly in eager examination of our own gifts and of the packages from home. The prize of the day was a set of beautiful ivory brushes with my initials in gold, a present from Kit. It was an extravagant gift, and one for a lifetime. Ivory is extremely difficult to obtain in Italy, but what there is of it is exceptionally fine.

In the shower of gifts that rained upon the Villa Buono-cuore, Peter and Silky were not forgotten. It is difficult to know what to give dogs to make them really happy and not merely to please the donor. As they were both badly in need of new collars, the original ones having been thoroughly chewed up and digested, we chose for Peter a manly brown one and another for Silky of a becoming shade of green. To our delight they were highly gratified. Long ago we had discovered how quick they were to distinguish between mock and real praise. When we teased them, which we were not above doing occasionally, by crowning them with paper hats and telling them how smart they looked, they knew that thay were being made fun of and hung back dejectedly. On Christmas morning, when we strapped on the new collars and told them the same thing, they pranced around as proudly as prize-winners at a dog show. From America they each received an artificial bone, genuinely imported from England, which had travelled a good way around the world before reaching its destination. We hoped these bones would prove an acceptable substitute for Kit's knitting. No doubt delicious in taste, they were guaranteed to be inde-structible. For all we knew they might well have been, but as, within two minutes of receiving them, the dogs had securely buried them in the garden, we could not vouch for it. They never reappeared, for, in spite of repeated diggings, the dogs were unable to find them again. Perhaps they were triumphantly carried off by the rats under the impression that they were chicken bones.

That was a memorable morning. Not only our household, but all our friends on the island, contributed to make it so.

Our garden gate bell rang continuously, and little urchins, acting as messengers, brought us basket upon basket of fruit, flowers, and wine, The lady who had lent us Penelope's husbands sent us live rabbits; the Giusto family sent us a cake made by the old lady, some embroidery for Kit from the sisters, and a few bottles of Cesare's choicest vintage for me.

As each messenger asked for the return of his basket, we heaped the contents on to the stone-flagged terrace. Against the background of this old Italian garden, with the warm southern sun streaming through the jasmine-trees, this growing mound of rich, ripe, bright-coloured fruit was a picture. We felt that never again should we need to buy oranges, mandarins, or lemons, that the vegetables would see us through the winter, while the flowers put to shame the entire year's output of the Villa Buonocuore. As for wine, even taking into account Dominica's special talents in this direction, there was enough to last us all a long time.

So that the household might have the afternoon and evening free, we had arranged to have our dinner at midday. Except for their brief appearance at breakfast-time, Dominica and Giovangiuseppe had both been in the kitchen since dawn, and the dining-room doors were locked. At their special request, Kit had left the entire preparations to them, stipulating only that the turkey should be the main-stay of the meal.

At last, when dinner was announced and the doors were opened, we did not recognise the room. As on the celebration of the first two months of our married life, it had been trans-formed into a garden. But this time it was somebody else's garden and not ours that had been stripped to decorate it, and with what flights of imagination! Garlands of vines trailed from the four corners of the ceiling to a central motif, and precariously entwined in them were masses of roses, carnations, periwinkles, and mimosa. The table was decorated with camellias, and at each of our places lay a bouquet. Talk about the old Roman banquets, where guests dined beneath a shower of rose-leaves; here one incautious movement would have been sufficient to bury us beneath the whole complicated arrangement!

Although only two places were laid, four chairs were drawn up to the table, as usual. Of late, Peter and Silky had been in the habit of sitting beside us at meals, a habit we encouraged because it kept them out of mischief, and above all out of the kitchen, where they often drove Dominica to despair. Peter sat next to Kit and Silky on my right, for, like children, they had to be separated to make them behave. With this precaution their manners were irreproachable; they never begged, and always extended a paw politely before receiving a tit-bit. They never fidgeted except when we paid too much attention to one another and not enough to them.

When the turkey made its appearance, they had to exert rigid self-control, and no wonder, for a more appetising dish had never come their way. It had been our intention to make pigs of ourselves over the turkey, but we were prevented from doing so by the profusion of other dishes which Dominica had previously given us, and by the thought of the plum pudding to follow. Kit said, with a sigh of regret, that this was all the better, as there would be plenty left for the morrow, and what could be better than cold turkey? It was one of those questions to which there is no answer.

That afternoon the Villa Buonocuore, usually so alive with echoes from the kitchen, was silent, and we had the place to ourselves. The Ischians were busy merrymaking in their homes and the island was somnolent. We went for a walk through the vineyards with the dogs, and climbed down to a little hidden cove where the rocks and the sea were enclosed on three sides by tall umbrella pines. Side by side we stretched ourselves out on the warm sand until the blue sea changed slowly to lavender as the winter sun crept towards the horizon, and a chill came into the air.

By candlelight – for the electricity had not yet come on – and in the warmth of our new stove, we had a late high tea, with a wonderful cake which Dominica had secretly made and laid out in readiness for us. No doubt this sounds a dull ending for Christmas Day; for us it was not. We were completely happy and at peace with the world.

IV

'We can have it cold,' said Kit, whose appetite had been refreshed by a long night's sleep, 'and to-morrow we can have it hashed. Even then there will be enough left over to think of some other way of eating it the next day. You don't mind having turkey four days in succession, do you, darling? It's *so* good!'

'*O signora, signora!*' Dominica came running across the garden as fast as her short fat legs would carry her. 'A terrible disaster. The turkey! The dog! Come quickly!'

The door to the corner cupboard in the dining-room was ajar. On the second shelf, resting on our biggest platter, lay the turkey, and beside it, on his haunches, sat Peter, licking its roasted brown flanks with tender solicitude. He had been too occupied to hear our approach, and as we stood in the doorway, horrified and fascinated, we could see his little pink tongue sliding back and forth with rhythmic delight over the smooth surface.

'Ruined!' said Kit, at first doubtfully, then with resigned finality. 'Go on.' She turned to me. 'You're the master of the house; scold him.' Peter was really her dog, as she often proudly asserted when he was good; only if he misbehaved did I become automatically the master of the house. But I could not bring myself to chastise him for such a human failing.

With a gesture of despair, Kit gave the turkey to Dominica to throw away. But Dominica knew better. Perhaps she merely cut off the outer slices which had actually come in contact with Peter's tongue; perhaps she did not even do that. What Peter lost in popularity with us, he regained in the kitchen, where Dominica and Giovangiuseppe had the meal of their lives.

As Kit herself had asked, 'What could be better than cold turkey?'

CHAPTER XXIV

FROM KIT'S DIARY

I

ONE MORNING, about a week ago, before I was awake, G.
brought me a present. When I opened my eyes, I was
looking straight into another pair of eyes, clear yellow, wide,
and as wild as Pan's. It was a tiny goat, curled up comfortably on top of me.

She was only a week old, and her shaggy coat was golden
brown, with white maps spread out over the soft fur. Her
forehead was round and childish, and on her head we could
already see two hard little bumps where one day the horns
would cut through. Her tail flick-flicked most of the time;
she had long legs that looked too big for the rest of her
because the fur was so thick, and big round knee-joints and
tiny clean hoofs.

We named her Hester. When we took her into the garden
she gave a nasal '*Ma-a-a*,' suddenly, as though you had

287

pressed a button, twisted her head to one side, and leapt straight into the air.

When we went into the house she hurried after us, and jumped gracefully into a Victorian chintz-covered chair, looking quite at home there and scattering neat little indiscretions with an unmoved face.

Dominica and Giovangiuseppe exclaimed admiringly, though probably they thought us mad to allow a goat in the house; for them a goat, however young, belongs with the flocks that are driven through the streets and down to the houses at the water's edge for milking.

After a while the 'ma-a-a's' grew more frequent and insistent. The little goat seemed unhappy. 'What is the matter with her?' we asked Giovangiuseppe.

'She wants to eat,' he said.

'Then get her some milk,' we replied.

Giovangiuseppe hesitated. He is very prudish for a young man raised on the island, and he was approaching a delicate subject. Swallowing hard he said, 'Please, the *capretto* can only drink the milk of her mama.'

This was a problem. We looked at the kid, who was bleating piteously now and didn't seem able to enjoy her gymnastics any more. We thought sadly that we would have to sell her back to the *capraro* – the goatherd – because we couldn't think of any substitute for her mama. I didn't want to lose my present so soon, and G. was annoyed, too, because he hadn't considered this practical point before buying the goat. He said we wouldn't have thought it would be so hard to feed a young animal that would grow up to eat tin cans.

Meanwhile Giovangiuseppe had had an idea. 'Please,' he said, 'if you wish it, *signori*, I myself will carry the little goat back to the stable of the *capraro*. There she can suck from her mother and I will bring her back again.'

In the summer her fishing industry keeps her busy

p. 301

'Yes,' we said, 'that's all right for this time, but the goat must eat every day, perhaps several times a day. What of that?'

Giovangiuseppe's face was beaming with eagerness. He really does like to be useful, especially in a way that is spectacular. Sweeping under beds is not spectacular.

'*Signori*, I will carry the little one to her mother each morning; if I go at six I shall be back in time to do my morning work before breakfast. Then I shall take her again after the *signori's* tea, that she may be with her mother before the *capraro* takes the herd through the village for milking.'

'It's a long way to the *capraro*, Giovangiuseppe,' we said warningly.

'Oh, *signori*, that doesn't matter.'

So he picked up the goat and carried her off, immaculate in his uniform. Hester wasn't accustomed to move except on her own stocky legs; she bawled deafeningly and must have kept it up for the whole mile and a half to the Port. We could hear the bawling *diminuendo* for a long time after they were out of sight.

That night, after a second successful trip from which she returned well rounded and playful, the little goat slept in one of the rabbit-houses.

She is gay and mischievous. She likes to balance, all four hoofs together like a circus pony, on top of one of the crumbling old columns around the garden beds. From this vantage-point, though she is supposed to be able to digest nothing but her mother's milk, she succeeded in eating most of a pair of my satin trousseau pyjamas that Dominica had hung out to dry.

Our friends all think we are keeping her to fatten and eat. When we tell them that she is a pet they do not understand at all, but they are indulgent and laugh and do not like us any the less. In Italy, kid takes the place of lamb on the menu. Roast kid is good; *capretto di latte* – suckling kid – is supposed to be especially delicate, though there never is much to it.

In the old days it was always thought that the best way to kill them was to skin them alive. It was unbelievably brutal. The kid was strung up in the butcher's shop and the butcher, after slitting the skin in various places, pulled it off the miserable animal. One doesn't like to believe it of such nice people, but they say that the skinning of a kid was always the signal for a crowd to gather; the show was especially exciting for children.

About ten years ago the new Fascist régime made a law putting an end to the practice. The old butchers rebelled against this law; they thought the meat inferior when the slaughtering had been painless, and, though there were no more public shows, kids were still skinned alive in back rooms and dark corners. The butchers were running no great risks here; Ischia is very far from the 'continent,' farther in feeling than in actual distance. There were few *Carabinieri* and *Guardie*, and they were busy patrolling the coast for smuggling.

But it happened that the new head of the local Fascist Party, a certain colonel, was a lover of animals, and was determined to enforce the new law. One day he heard a piteous crying coming from the open front of a butcher's shop. He was a man of fiery temper, and he was never so easily roused as by the sight of an animal in pain. He ran through the butcher's empty shop and in a back room found the man with his knife in his hand. On a hook was hung a little kid. The butcher had already made the first incisions and was beginning to strip off the fluffy hide.

In one bound the colonel was on him, tore the knife from

his hand and put an end to the animal's life. Then he turned on the frightened butcher and, brandishing the knife in his hand, told him what he thought of him.

'How would you like to be skinned alive, eh?' The butcher quaked; the knife was very near; the colonel was roaring furiously. 'How do you start? Here at the wrist, eh?' The butcher's eyes were closed; he was only waiting for the end. '*Madonna, O Madonna*,' he prayed rapidly. His only hope was that he would be finished off as quickly as the kid and not be skinned alive.

The colonel had given the man such a scare, threatening him with the law if he was caught again, that no more kids were skinned alive on the island.

That, anyway, is the story they tell.

The same colonel was a champion of the *carrozza* horses, and always interfered when he saw one being ill-treated. Once he found a man thrashing his horse because it could not pull its overloaded carriage up a steep hill.

'If I catch you beating your horse again I'll put *you* between the shafts and see how you like it,' he said.

Eventually the man was caught at it again.

'Unhitch your horse!' roared the colonel. His position with the Fascist Party was powerful; the man obeyed.

'Stable him!' commanded the colonel. This was done.

'Now,' said the colonel, 'get between the shafts!' He climbed into the carriage and said, 'I want to go to Barano.' And they say he did go, flicking the man with the whip whenever he lagged.

Giovangiuseppe has just gone out of the garden gate bearing Hester off to her evening meal. She has got used to riding and bawls no more. Her childish face bobs complacently on his shoulder as he carries her away.

Poor Giovangiuseppe has had about enough of the job;

it is no longer spectacular in our eyes, and he is beginning to resent the way his friends laugh when he plays nursemaid through the streets of the Port. Soon I think he will produce from that ingenious head of his some new plan for the nourishment of Hester.

II

I was right. After a few days he came to us, eyes shining with enthusiasm.

'*Signori!*' he exclaimed. 'The *capraro* is willing to sell the kid's mother!'

'Sell the mother?' we repeated in a way that must have seemed very stupid to Giovangiuseppe. 'But who wants to buy her? And how will the little goat be fed?'

'But no, *signori*, you do not understand. The *capraro* is willing to sell her to *you*! He will make a very good price; I myself have arranged with him; it will be a bargain. She is a marvellous goat; she gives milk of the richest quality, two litres in the morning and another two at night. You would no longer have to buy cow's milk from the dairy.'

We looked at each other, amazed at the boy's good sense. It seems to take us a long time to learn that his ideas are fine but that they almost never work out as promised. In this case we saw that the crucial point was: would the goat give as much milk as her owner said?

A trip to the stables decided us. The mother was a fine creature, brown and white like Hester and with a massive ridgepole running along the top of her. It was her horns that really reassured us. They were long and curving, and if you had mounted them anyone would have been proud to hang them up as a trophy. We thought that a goat with

292

such a decoration on her head must know all the secrets of the successful production of milk.

She had a wooden collar round her neck, and to this the goatherd tied a bit of rope and Giovangiuseppe led the goat home to the Villa Buonocuore, while we followed, full of pride.

When we reached the garden, Hester threw herself on her mother and, kneeling down with her front legs, sucked noisily, flicking her tail in high excitement and giving vicious nudges with her nose. We watched, enchanted, until it occurred to us that, at the rate she was going, there would be no milk for tea and supper. We were right. When Giovangiuseppe milked her there was just enough to cover the bottom of a glass.

After that we separated the mother and daughter. We put Bridget, as we named the antlered beauty, into a pen at the foot of the garden, and let Hester play about. She was allowed to visit her mother twice a day for a limited time, but this, like every phase of the goat arrangements, failed to work out as we had planned. Bridget continued to give from a quarter to a half a cup of milk morning and evening, and Hester, who is a fine acrobat, was discovered several times in her mother's pen when she had no business to be there.

Giovangiuseppe's next move was picturesque but practical. He bought a piece of red and white striped mattress ticking – it cost four *soldi* – and he sewed it into the shape of a bag with two streamers attached to the opening. This he slipped over the goat's udders and pulled the streamers up around her waist and tied them in a big red and white bow on top of her backbone. Hester could nuzzle all she pleased; the ticking was too thick to let the milk through.

We did get about half a glassful morning and evening after

that. Something was wrong, though. I thought perhaps it was Bridget's diet; she never ate anything but sacks of dry leaves and cut-up branches of cactus, spines and all. Giovan-giuseppe said it might be that she was not drinking enough; he knew what they did in Fiaiano in a case like that. He filled a litre bottle with the water our macaroni had been boiled in, held Bridget's head hard between his knees, forced her teeth open with the neck of the bottle, and let the macaroni water flow uninterrupted down her throat. He did this several times a day, and after a few struggles the goat seemed to get used to it. The milk didn't increase, though.

The boy's next theory was that Bridget didn't get enough exercise, and above all didn't choose her own food. 'She needs to be taken out walking, *signore*,' he said earnestly to G. 'That is good for the milk. *Ecco* – that is why the *capraro* walks his whole herd around the village twice a day. As she walks she will choose from among the grasses and herbs those which she needs to eat.'

'Well,' said G., 'take her walking then.' We were getting tired of Bridget, who was neither friendly nor useful.

Giovangiuseppe took Bridget out walking twice that day, leading her by a rope tied to her wooden collar. Hester bounced along foolishly after them, leaping into the air with piercing bleats. Bridget looked disdainfully at the poor selection of weeds that grew along the path near the water's edge; once in a while she lowered her spreading antlers and cropped a bit of green. Hester didn't; she can only eat satin pyjamas and her mama's milk. She flung herself frequently at the red and white striped bag.

The second day that they went out walking they met the *capraro* out with his flock for the evening milking. He was in front of Antonio's house, squirting the dead-white liquid into a glass for Antonio's wife. Apparently all his goats recognised their old friend Bridget and she recognised them too. She broke away from Giovangiuseppe and, amid a great chorus of 'ma-a-a's,' she ran toward them and was absorbed in the herd. Hester stayed on the outskirts, bounding about and calling for her mother like a mad thing.

Everyone in Via Rougemont enjoyed the sight of Giovangiuseppe, in his neat uniform, grasping Hester under one arm and wading into the sea of goats after Bridget, who had made up her mind not to be recaptured and went for him with her horns.

The day after, he came to us with news of a little boy from Fiaiano whose family was very poor and who would like to have work. His name was Pierluigi.

'We don't need anyone else,' said G.

'Oh, *signore*, this *ragazzo* knows all about goats. He could take our two out walking, because really' – he wriggled – 'my work does not leave me time for it. You need pay him almost nothing. He will be glad to work for his meals.'

Giovangiuseppe with his usual guile had the boy waiting outside the garden gate, and when he came in neither of us could say no.

He was eleven years old, but such a small little fellow. His face was pinched and pale; only his nose had some colour. He had on a little peaked cap and someone's old suit, cut down and fitting him badly, and big leather boots with thick wooden soles. He saluted smartly and said, '*Signore, signora*, good day!'

He has been with us nearly a month now, and the thin cheeks are gone. He has fattened up like a little suckling pig; I think Dominica must stuff him with good macaroni and the favourite haricot beans. She has a maternal weakness for him, and says he is a *buon ragazzo*.

He is always busy with the goats, giving Bridget her macaroni water, brushing Hester, walking along the shore with them, hardly bigger than they. His wooden boots and Hester's little hoofs play a tattoo together on the paving of our garden terrace. Once I saw him, through our bedroom window, skipping around with her when she was doing some of her gay, silly bouncing. When I went out, though, he drew himself up to attention and saluted stiffly, very much the little man.

He lives at home, comes five kilometres down from the hills each morning to be at his work by seven, and trudges home again when Dominica has given him his supper at five and he has put the goats to bed. Quite often he brings down with him a little basket with a few vegetables in it, or a bottle of wine. These presents are not so abundant as the ones Giovangiuseppe's mother brings; Pierluigi's family is very poor and the mother must be grateful indeed to spare even these few things.

Well, I am grateful too; grateful to Bridget for bringing little Pierluigi to our gate. With all the care he gives her, she can't yet squeeze out more than two glasses of milk a day, and that pint must cost us a good deal. Another goatherd has told us that she is much too old to give milk at all; he was surprised that she had managed to have Hester, the child of her old age. He pointed to her horns as a sign of her antiquity.

But Pierluigi is fat and happy and very proud of his job. He is the one worth-while outcome of our goat venture.

CASTELLO
d'Ischia

R.M

CHAPTER XXV

AT THE TOBACCONIST'S there was a great commotion. The shop was crowded with fishermen, an unusual sight for the morning, and a heated argument was in full swing between them and the owner of the shop, a kindly but disreputable-looking individual. Sprawling over the counter, with a greasy forelock emerging from beneath his soiled cap, a collarless shirt and finger-nails that were evidently in deep mourning for someone, he was expounding facts which they openly disbelieved.

As I approached, he stopped short and, pointing dramatically at me as though I were the subject under discussion, shouted, 'The *signore* will know. He is a foreigner and has crossed the ocean in a big ship.'

'*É vero,*' someone muttered, and there was a silence as the crowd parted and engulfed me in its midst. Sprawling still further over the counter, the tobacconist paused to get the last ounce of drama from the situation, and then launched the vital question.

'Is it or is it not true that a first-class passenger can have soup *and* spaghetti *and* fish at the same meal? These *imbecilli*' – waving at the audience – 'they say you must choose one or the other. I say you can have all three. Speak, *signore*, speak!'

'Why, yes,' I stammered. 'In first class you can have anything you want. They give you a list as long as this' – here I made an imaginary measurement–'and you can have the whole lot if you are hungry enough.'

The tobacconist glowed with triumph as he faced his audience. 'There now, what did I tell you? Idiots! Imbeciles! Country louts! Uneducated peasants! Hear what the *signore* says.' He turned to me. 'You must excuse them, *signore*; they are only islanders' – this with a shrug of profound and pitying contempt. 'They know nothing about life!'

The crowd did not seem to mind this deluge of uncomplimentary remarks; perhaps it was only friendly banter, for the men nudged one another and burst out laughing. 'He's going to America,' they exclaimed hilariously, 'and he'll be sick the whole time, so it doesn't matter how much he eats.'

Ignoring the uproar, the tobacconist launched into a detailed explanation of the whole matter for my special benefit.

'It is like this,' he said. 'My brother, who is now in New York, grows very rich in the last two years. He is now a gentleman like yourself. We are, in fact, all gentlemen in the family. He sends me a thousand dollars and a first-class passage on the S.S. —— to join him. The captain of the ship is my brother's best friend, so I shall sit at his table. It is time,' he added with a good-natured grin, 'that I left this island of savages.'

I looked at his ragged, dirty clothes, at his face covered with bristly stubble – for it was Friday and there was still another day to go before the weekly shave. I thought of the famous, ultra-fashionable new liner he had mentioned. Oh, so, I thought to myself, the fellow has probably these periodic attacks of the *folie des grandeurs*, although it was unkind of the fishermen, who must have known it, to make fun of him.

My face must have been easy to read, or else he had rightly presumed that I should not believe a word of his story, for, without further words, he removed the toothpick which had been wobbling up and down in his mouth during the entire discussion, discarded it with a lordly gesture, and, opening a drawer, handed me an envelope.

Inside was his passage, first class, to New York on the ship he had said. The ticket had lost its pristine freshness, having been sprinkled lightly with tomato juice, and in places it was a little transparent with grease stains, but its validity was not impaired. He offered to show me the cheque for the thousand dollars, which was locked away somewhere, but I begged him not to trouble. This was evidence enough!

Although the fishermen must have seen and handled this precious document many times, they gathered around for another glimpse. In spite of their scoffing, it held for them an element of magic, and a dreamy look came into their eyes, as though they had already visualised their friend as the most important passenger aboard, strolling at ease through gilded rooms and seated on the captain's right hand. It was more than I could do.

Only after I had heartily congratulated the tobacconist, accepted a glass of vermouth, purchased my cigarettes, shaken hands all round, and started home, did the explanation of this amazing story dawn upon me. 'My brother grows very rich in the last two years.' Eh? The Ischians

299

might be innocent of the ways of the world as long as they remained on their island, but when they got to America they were, no doubt, as quick to use their wits as the rest of their compatriots. What better opportunity was there for getting rich in a hurry than bootlegging in prohibition days ? It was a flourishing industry and almost exclusively in the hands of southern Italians.

It took some time to persuade Kit, when I got home, that I had not made up the story, but, when she finally believed it, she readily agreed with the bootlegging theory.

In spite of his good luck, his fine black clothes, and the flashing diamond ring which he would surely buy out of his liberal allowance, we wondered if he would be entirely happy in his new rôle of *signore*. We wondered also what subtle diplomacy the captain would resort to in order to honour the brother of such an important friend and yet evade the necessity of having him at his table. Perhaps the tobacconist would be offered an unoccupied suite where he could devour his spaghetti in solitary splendour. We never knew, for shortly afterwards, leaving the shop in the care of his sister, he had a great send-off, and that was the last we ever heard of him.

Such incidents only faintly ruffled Ischia's winter slumber. Even in the matter of seasons the island was a paradox, having everything her own way, which was not at all the established Mediterranean way.

Although in recent years foreigners flock to the Mediterranean at all times of the year, winter remains the trump card. Snow and ice, rain and fog, whatever variety of northern climate it may be, it invariably turns people's thoughts to sunshine and warmth, and this natural human longing is artfully exploited by the travel agencies. Alluring shipping posters showing snow-white vessels ploughing through deep blue seas under cloudless skies, and a flood of equally enticing pamphlets to be had merely for the asking, do the rest. Meanwhile the Mediterranean is equally busy. From hotel proprietors and shopkeepers down to simple fishermen who have a boat for hire, the inhabitants are rubbing their hands in anticipation of the varying sums to be extorted from the unsuspecting foreigner when he arrives. The Bay of Naples indulges largely in this dream, with the exception of Ischia.

Ischia has her own season and her own brand of foreigners. For six weeks in midsummer, her beautiful shores are infested with a horde of noisy Neapolitans who are not rich enough to frequent more fashionable resorts. This doubtful privilege she owes to her superb beaches and shady pine-woods, above all to the fact that they face north and are exquisitely cool when the coast of the mainland is a scorching inferno.

In the summer, also, her fishing industry and her vine-yards keep her busy, to say nothing of her innumerable *feste*.

This is all very exciting, but also fatiguing, so, when the last of the Neapolitans has returned to his city and the *vendemmia* is over, when the autumn sun no longer beats down so fiercely, she prepares herself for a long, lazy sleep, a sleep that shall last until the spring. The feverish activity of the mainland leaves her indifferent. Real foreigners do not interest her; she has nowhere to lodge them and cannot be bothered, anyway. If some of the more ambitious members of the population dream spasmodically of turning the island into a second Monte Carlo, without quite knowing how to set about it, that is their problem. Ischia, serenely beautiful, serenely untroubled, slumbers on.

There is nothing like the knowledge that one is leaving,

perhaps for good, a place one has dearly loved, to bring into sharp, almost painful relief its beauty. We had certainly never been blind to Ischia's loveliness, nor to the open-hearted generosity of its inhabitants, but so far we had enjoyed our good fortune without a pang. Now that only a few brief weeks separated us from our departure our happiness was tinged with melancholy. It was not only Ischia and the Ischians we were saying good-bye to, it was that first unforgettable year of our married life, that gay, insouciant life we had begun such a short time ago with the Bonifacios in the little Albergo del Porto.

Whether we returned to the island, as our friends assured us we would do, or not, there was something in this past that could never be recaptured, just as nothing could alter the memory we should keep of it. Nobody owed Ischia a debt of deeper gratitude than we for the unique happiness she had given us. Who could deny that the peace, the beauty, and the friendliness with which she had surrounded us at the outset of our marriage should in some subtle way make its beneficial influence felt throughout our lives to come?

CHAPTER XXVI

THIS WAS THE LAST LAP. Winter was over, and spring had spread its luxuriant southern mantle over the island. There were flowers everywhere – in the pinewoods, in the orchards, on the hills, and along every path. Breezes came heavily laden with the fragrance of a thousand aromatic shrubs – thyme, verbena, wild rose, bay and myrtle – distilled by the hot Mediterranean sun. The garden of the Villa Buonocuore mocked us for our departure; or perhaps she was decking herself out to bid us farewell. The cycle of our Ischian year was almost completed.

In those last weeks we revisited our favourite haunts as though we wished to impress their images more deeply on our memory. We lay side by side on the soft needles beneath the tall umbrella pines; we sauntered through vineyards and along the great golden beaches; we watched the days grow more splendid, and the sun sink behind the distant purple mountains of Gaeta. And we packed!

We had felt so completely at home at the Villa

Buonocuore that we had almost forgotten that there was an old *colonello* of the same name who happened to be its rightful owner, and, above all, that there was such a thing as an inventory.

We had not played havoc with his furniture, but we had changed it around in a way that must have seemed to him just as bad. Worse still, we had removed from sight the innumerable exhibits of wax flowers beneath their tall glass globes that had decorated every table, together with the saints and madonnas similarly encased, and had stored them in a vast cupboard. We had removed to the same cupboard the gaily coloured steamship and railway posters, depicting the glories of Sicily in spring and of the Eternal City, both at reduced fares, with which he had tremulously and touchingly disfigured the graceful arches of his loggia. Still, these things could be brought out of hiding and rearranged, but as for the breakage in the kitchen, that was beyond calculation.

Between Giovangiuseppe, who, according to his own virtuous estimate, never broke or stole anything, and Dominica, who, according to the same authority, broke liberally and stole the rest, chiefly by removing it in the folds of her ample bosom, there was no telling the extent of our liabilities in the little house by the sea. Neither Kit nor I could remember how plentifully it had been stocked with china, glass, and kitchen utensils, and, as the old colonel had been fussily accurate in making out his inventory, to the length of underlining heavily in red ink such items as 'one corner cupboard in real pitch-pine,' we looked forward to a stormy time when it came to handing the place over to him. It might be as well to add here that we had long ago lost our copy of this inventory.

Not wishing to leave our encounter with our landlord to the very last, we had written to him in Naples to fix a date

In those last weeks we revisited our favourite haunts

p. 303

for his visit, to which he had replied most courteously that this was impossible, owing to the uncertain conditions of the weather, the sea, the temperature, and the state of his health. One day, if these various factors combined favourably to make the journey possible, he would be pleased to arrive and accept our gracious invitation to lunch.

As the days passed without further word, we hoped that the elements would defy him to the last, and that he would be content with an adequate cash payment for breakage. One morning, a week before our departure, when the house had reached its climax of disorder, this hope was shattered. Climbing over packing-cases and half-filled trunks, Giovangiuseppe announced that the *colonello* had arrived, and was at that moment making his way slowly across the garden.

Giovangiuseppe stood in considerable awe of the *colonello*, for the old gentleman had the habit of poking angrily with his black ebony stick at those who did not obey his orders quickly enough. We, also, felt a little panic-stricken as we told the boy to show him into the *salotto* while we rapidly removed the grime from our persons, and Kit gave orders to Dominica to prepare some special delicacy for lunch. It was evident that, as the colonel had not advised us by telegram of his proposed visit, he intended to take us by surprise.

He was seated by the window, dressed entirely in black and looking very depressed, a bad though natural enough sign considering the tumultuous disorder of the room. In his hand was a little bouquet of red carnations, and, as Kit entered, he rose and presented them to her with a charming smile and a courtly gesture. He was sorry if they drooped; it was the heat, he explained, and the fact that they had been so long out of water. He had made a special trip to the market to buy them before taking the boat. This little speech over, the smile faded away and he sat down heavily, his game leg stretched stiffly before him.

We had forgotten what an old gentleman he was, much frailer in appearance than when we had first seen him, and it was evident that the journey over had cost him an effort. Furthermore, he seemed preoccupied by something quite unconnected with the house. In reply to our customary enquiries, he told us that his wife had had a stroke. She was seventy-two, he said, and then surprisingly added, 'What can I do with a wife who can only sit in a chair and say boo-boo-boo?'

It was not an easy question to answer, and we expressed our sympathy as best we could. His black suit, tie, shoes, hat, and gloves looked most lugubrious, almost like a sign of premature mourning, but we remembered that in this part of the world black was the correct attire for ceremonious calls.

After a decent interval, it was a relief to broach the subject of the inventory.

'Inventory!' he exclaimed, as though such a thing had never existed. 'What need is there for that?'

'But you will want to see . . .' I began.

He thumped his rubber-tipped cane impatiently. 'See what? Are we not gentlepeople? What need is there to see anything?'

Kit and I exchanged amazed glances, and again I tried to bring up the subject of the kitchen, of the things that had been broken and the things that were missing. The old colonel grew irritable. 'I will see nothing,' he snapped. 'Of course things have been broken . . . and stolen too. It is always that way with peasants.' He paused, smiled, and shook his head gently.

'Do you think I have come all this way merely to count my

possessions? No, *signore*, I have come to say good-bye to the *signora* and to yourself, to . . . to . . .' – he paused, hesitating – 'to proffer the hope that you will come back some day to this little house.' He leaned back, pleased to have expressed so neatly the words he had wanted to say.

We were dazed. Where, in this busy grasping world to-day, was a similar landlord to be found; one so confident in the integrity of his tenants and so disinterested that he neither wanted to check up on the damages nor receive payment for them? How fortunate it was that we had written asking him to lunch, and were not merely urging him to stay to a meal, for this might have looked suspiciously like a spontaneous gesture of gratitude. What a splendid idea Kit had also had when she told Dominica to prepare some special delicacy. As she had cooked for him in the past, she knew his tastes. Little did we suspect what she had in mind or we would have dissuaded her from putting it into action, and thereby have saved ourselves from a fiasco.

With the word *speciale* ringing in her ears, Dominica had remembered a couple of ancient pigeons whose existence we had almost forgotten. They had been given us when we first came to the island, and, for some good reason of their own, had taken up their living-quarters under the cupboard called pitch-pine in the dining-room.

Pigeon was, it seemed, the *colonello's* favourite dish, but at such short notice, and with the added difficulty of being obliged to lie on her stomach on the floor to catch them, she was unduly rushed. This resulted in the first dish, which was macaroni, and habitually of unsurpassed excellence, being under-cooked. Think of it! Dominica's macaroni under-cooked!

We were dumbfounded and so apparently was the *colonello*. With increasing slowness he munched on, his efforts at polite conversation dwindling with each mouthful, while his dental plate, which resented the tussle as much as its owner did, clicked out and back again with mournful regularity. 'Tough,' he remarked, shaking his head with disapproval. 'Very tough,' he added a little later. By this disarming frankness, he wished to show that the blame was attached solely to Dominica and not to his hosts, but it was meagre comfort.

With the appearance of the pigeons, our hopes, that had soared momentarily, were dashed beyond remedy. If this had not been his favourite dish, he would probably not have been able to diagnose its defects with such alarming clarity. Alas, he knew all there was to know about pigeons, and it did not take him long to discover that these were old birds who had lived a sedentary life far removed from the sun's beneficent rays, that they had been killed much too recently, and that no power on earth could make them tender.

With dreadful fascination our eyes followed his tremulous and repeated onslaughts, and the success with which the late departed resisted them. At last he gave in. Being a naval man, he must have realised the superior strength of the adversary. '*Non mi riesce*. I do not succeed,' he declared plaintively, and laid down the implements of battle. Dessert, excellent coffee, and a glass of French cognac atoned somewhat for this appalling lunch, but we knew that for the rest of his days he would never be able to hear the word pigeon without recounting this dramatic experience.

Badly as we felt as hosts, we were more sorry for Dominica, who could not hope to live it down. After the colonel had left, we consoled her with a piece of news which so far we had kept strictly secret. With our departure only a few days distant, it had been understood that Dominica and Giovangiuseppe, much as we regretted to lose them, would have to find another place. Probably they would return to the bosom of their families to await the summer influx of Neapolitans, unless some foreigners came to settle on the island in the meantime.

Giovangiuseppe had proved a mixed blessing. The scales, that had often been tipped in his favour by his eager enthusiasm, had been brought down of late with a heavy bump on the opposite side. He was by no means indispensable. A cook, however, especially such an excellent cook as Dominica, was quite another matter. We had some time before decided that our return home should not deprive us of her company. As we were breaking our journey in Rome, we planned that she should remain on the island in our service, receiving her wages as usual, until we should send for her to join us.

Crestfallen over lunch, she foresaw in our joint appearance in the kitchen door only a reprimand. At first she could not believe her ears, but, when she did, the torrent of gratitude was overwhelming. 'Everywhere, always, I will serve the *signora* as long as she is satisfied, yes, even to my dying day.'

We stemmed the tide with a note of warning. Giovangiuseppe had been prudently despatched on an errand to the village, and we solemnly told Dominica not to breathe a word of this to anybody. Love had not been wasted between them in the past, and we had no desire, now that everything was so splendidly fixed up, to lose our cook through a *vendetta*. We could not actually imagine the boy sticking a knife into her, but he was not above getting somebody else to do it for him. Anyhow, it made an impression, for *vendetta* is a word that every southern Italian understands perfectly.

During the following days, Dominica's efforts at gloom

ISLAND IN THE SUN

were comical. Nobody could have appeared more dejected, have heaved heavier, more lugubrious sighs, have voiced more pathetic laments over our coming departure, than she did . . . when the boy was around. She was so completely dejected in spirit that Giovangiuseppe almost forgot his own fate through the malicious pleasure he derived from this sight. Certainly he never suspected anything.

Easter was our last *festa*. It was celebrated by roast kid for dinner, which in Ischia replaced the traditional lamb, and by the blessing of our house. This latter seemed rather late in the day to do us any good, as we were leaving on the morrow, unless we could take the blessing with us.

Remembering the visit of the Infant Jesus at Christmas, we were careful to enquire what was expected of us, and learned with relief that our rôle was confined to making an offering. The rite was performed by a young priest, accompanied by an acolyte, in the shortest possible time. Having blessed a great number of houses that morning, and having many more to bless before the day was over, he had no time to waste, but he was thorough. The acolyte carried an embroidered velvet purse and a small bucket of Holy Water; the priest a book and a sprinkler. Having received our offering in the purse, they set about it at a great pace. We caught a brief glimpse of flying surplices and heard a mumble of Latin words as they dashed through the dismantled rooms, into every nook and corner, including the cupboards, and inundating our luggage with Holy Water. In a trice they had finished and were off to the next house.

In the old days, an Ischian friend told us, this used to be different. Nothing happened until the offering had been received, on the basis of no offering, no blessing. The money was supposed to be given while the priest read a short preliminary prayer, with one eye on his book and the other on the purse. He read slowly, to allow plenty of time, but, when he reached the end, if nothing had been received he darted a significant glance at the owner of the house, sighed heavily, and began over again. After a few such repetitions he was apt to show irritation, while the acolyte jingled the coins in the purse in ominous silence. This always produced results.

The priest had not only excellent eyesight but also a sound judgment. If he considered the offering conspicuously small, if he knew that the family could afford more and were merely hoping to get away with less, he blessed one room only and was off. For a generous donation, however, he blessed everything in sight – house, furniture, and occupants – and stayed perhaps for a chat and a glass of wine afterwards.

All this was fair and square. The priest was a good man, doing them a good turn, and he intended that his parishioners should behave equally well. This intimate understanding between Church and people, or rather between the Heavenly Hosts and the Ischians, was the best thing in their lives. It is still clearly manifested in many ways, especially in the celebration of the religious feasts, even if the Easter house blessings are apparently conducted on more up-to-date lines.

CHAPTER XXVII

I

APRIL 6TH. It had come at last. Days, weeks, months, almost a year; how smoothly, serenely, and rapidly the time had passed. Was it possible that the coming of one other day could mean so great a change, and bring with it such an aching sense of melancholy? We would have liked to fool ourselves; to turn over, close our eyes, and refuse to admit that it had come, this sixth of April when we were to say good-bye to Ischia.

It was no use, of course, to make believe, even at four o'clock in the morning, for in the next room we could hear the muffled footsteps of Enrico, the courier, and his assistant removing the heavy cases that contained our books, together with other unwieldy possessions. Although we were leaving only at half past ten, Enrico was to take our heavy luggage with him to Naples on the early morning boat.

After that, there was not much sleep. With early breakfast came a tearful Giovangiuseppe pouring out a tardy confession

313

of sins and ending with the dramatic words: 'I repent, *signore*, I repent bitterly. Not even my mother and my father have I loved as much as I do you.' As the tears poured down his face it looked as if the rascal momentarily believed this abominable string of lies. I felt sorry for him, and tried to find some complimentary words, and was annoyed with myself for doing so.

The sun had risen, touching the island to life with its warm sparkling light, adding another exquisite day to its calendar. We had said *addio* to our friends and to most of those in the old town with whom for nearly a year we had come into daily contact. We had now to say good-bye to Peter and Silky. That was much harder, even though the separation would be short. They were going up to Barano in a *carrozza*. Cesare Giusto had sent down a local one to fetch them, entrusting the coachman with a farewell present for us – two bottles of his oldest and most valued wine. Good Cesare!

But the coachman was waiting, and it was not a pleasant moment. Silky was placidly unsuspicious, but Peter's unerring instinct told him that separation was near at hand. Although he was not in the least timid of strangers, he crept under a chair and I had to drag him out. I gave him to Kit, who held him in her arms with a tight squeeze of affection before reluctantly handing him over.

We heard the coachman's step going across the garden, out of the gate, and up the alley to the little piazza where the carriage waited. Thank heaven they were going to the Giustos, who would take good care of them. We busied ourselves with odds and ends, not trusting ourselves to talk. Suddenly we stopped and listened. That unmistakable patter of feet! At headlong speed Peter came dashing back. He jumped up, looking at us anxiously, seeking in our faces the confirmation that it was all a stupid mistake, then, taking it for granted, lay down between us and rested his head confidently on Kit's foot.

Poor Kit, it was harder still for her. She wanted so much to be able to explain to him what it was all about, to make him understand that she was not breaking trust with him. She got him a drink of water and stroked him gently. The coachman was coming back, and I went to tell him to return to the carriage and wait. After a while Kit picked Peter up and carried him to the little piazza. Perhaps he understood after all, for he was very quiet, and settled down beside Silky in the big country basket which had been prepared for them. We stood watching as the carriage drove away.

The Villa Buonocuore looked empty and lifeless. The goats had been given away; our belongings, all save a few bags, had been removed hours before, and their traces swept clean. Little Pierluigi, the goatherd, had returned to his home in the hills the day before, laden down with a strange assortment of our discarded wearing apparel which his mother would make over into a useful if somewhat quaint wardrobe for him, and with a little present in cash for himself. Giovangiuseppe had been despatched on friendly terms but without regrets. Only Dominica remained to see us off.

She came to tell us that the other *carrozza*, the one we always took, was waiting. It seemed as though we had been up since time immemorial, yet it was only ten o'clock. Our boat did not leave for another half-hour, but it was not too soon to get started, for the carriage was only to transport our bags. We were going to walk to the old town for the last time.

'*Arrivederci*, Dominica.'

'*Arrivederci, signori*.' We shook hands. 'A most happy journey, and for you, *signora*, many, many wishes.' We shook hands again, and this time she produced from behind her large back a little bunch of sweet-smelling flowers. There was nothing mournful about this leave-taking. Alone with us, her face was wreathed in smiles. 'I will be waiting,' she continued, 'waiting till you send for me.'

We walked slowly up the alley, without looking back.

I said we had exhausted our farewells; it was not true. There was one person we would have liked to see, someone for whom we felt a deep respect, although in all the time we had been on the island we had exchanged barely a dozen words with him. Was it by accident that we met him now, on our way to the boat?

He was coming toward us, his sandals clicking on the cobblestones, the long knotted cord swaying and flapping against his coarse brown habit. He was not carrying his little wooden box with its coloured picture of Sant' Antonio pasted on the side, for it was not the day for his collection for the poor.

He stopped, and his weather-beaten face, usually so austere, was smiling. He held out his hands and clasped both of ours between them. We could feel the rough callouses as he gave them an honest squeeze.

'May Sant' Antonio be with you everywhere and watch over you always.' His voice was warm and friendly. 'And may he bring you back to Ischia.'

Before we had time to answer, he had released our hands, raised his skull-cap with an abrupt little gesture of courtesy, and was off at a rapid stride down the street.

'And bring you back to Ischia.' How often and in what a variety of forms – sometimes as a definite statement, sometimes as a kindly wish – had we heard this expressed. This monk was a good man. Perhaps Sant' Antonio would see that what he asked should come true. We could not wish for a better blessing.

II

As the smoke from the ship appeared above the tops of the pine-trees, we took our places in the rowboat. It was the time-honoured signal that everybody knew. The fishermen, standing erect, bent to their oars with a rhythmic stroke; the boat, gently released from the land, glided over the glassy water for a short distance and stopped. Rounding the point, the ship appeared, advancing at a leisurely pace. It was etiquette for the little rowboat with its load of passengers to await her pleasure, and not for her to be kept waiting.

She seemed to be bearing down upon us, proud to be able, by comparison, to show off her size and power. There was a familiar sound of bells, of engines being reversed, the familiar sight of blue water being churned into white foam, the familiar plunge of the anchor followed by a long length of rattling chain.

The fishermen put energy into their long strokes, and our rowboat drew alongside. The *Principessa Mafalda*, disdainful of such an unimportant calling-place, was impatient to be off. Sailors were waiting by the lowered gangway to help up the passengers. They caught hold of Kit and deftly hoisted her on board. The anchor was already coming up, slowly this time, as the chain wound itself around the puffing windlass, and before we reached the upper deck the ship was gliding quietly past the castle on its mighty jagged rock.

We watched the shore recede, with its row of pink and white houses sandwiched between the long golden beach and the green, vine-clad hills, between the sombre castle on one side and the pinewoods on the other. We watched the Monte Epomeo, as yet foreshortened by our proximity, slowly raise its solitary, majestic peak toward the sky. To the right, where the last of the pines dipped their roots into the sea, emerged the roof of the Villa Buonocuore, and on the top of the dining-room terrace someone was waving. That some-one was Dominica.

This was the Ischia we knew and loved so well, but the little slips of paper in my pocket were not return tickets, and our emotions that day were very different from those of our previous journeys to the mainland. I was glad that there was nobody on deck to see those two idiotic foreigners with tears running down their cheeks and not even bothering to wipe them away.

We were called from our thoughts by the clanging of bells in the engine-room, something that was not in the regular routine. Abrupt orders in a hoarse voice hailed from the bridge, followed by a slowing down of the engines. The ship had stopped. There was considerable agitation aboard. Sailors ran to and fro, while the captain paced his bridge in a frenzy of impatience, occasionally unclasping the hands behind his back in order to shake them angrily at the heavens above.

Had we been looking in the right direction we would have realised what the fuss was about. A boat had put out from the shore, manned by two fishermen rowing at a furious pace. They stopped now and then to gesticulate frantically, cupping their hands to their mouths and calling out words which we could not catch but which were plain enough to understand. A passenger had arrived too late and had been left behind; a passenger who had, perhaps, urgent business in Naples. But there did not seem to be anybody in the boat beside the rowers. Possibly there was a sick person lying on a stretcher; an urgent case. We could not imagine the haughty, self-important *Principessa Mafalda* waiting for anything less.

Everyone was on the lower deck, including the crew,

leaning over the side, consumed with curiosity. The ship gave a mighty list. As the boat drew nearer, the gangway was again lowered to receive the late-comer. The rowers were out of breath, but except for them the boat was empty!

A sailor ran up and tugged at my sleeve. '*Signore*, please come below at once. It is for you.' Incredulous, I jumped up, followed by Kit, who thought perhaps that they had come to take me off. The sailor had cleared a way for us through the crowd to the gangway. When the rowers in the boat saw me, they grinned. One of them stooped down and, pulling a package from under the seat, handed it to me. 'You left it at the villa, *signore*,' he shouted. 'The *carrozza* driver brought it and we caught you just in time. *Buon viaggio!*'

The ship was snorting with disgust and already under way. Still mopping the sweat from their faces, the fishermen drifted suddenly away from us. I had just time to shout '*Grazie!*' and throw haphazard a handful of coins, which by a hair's breadth escaped the sea and landed at their feet. The men waved; we waved back. Everybody smiled, vastly amused.

Clutching the parcel, we made our way to a secluded spot. Inside were Cesare's two bottles of old and treasured wine which, in the sorrow of Peter's departure, we had forgotten.

On a slip of paper in his neat handwriting were written in English the words: 'Good friends. A happy journey, a quick return.'

THE END